Deliberation
Representation
Equity

Research Approaches, Tools and Algorithms for Participatory Processes

Love Ekenberg, Karin Hansson, Mats Danielson, Göran Cars *et al.*

https://www.openbookpublishers.com

This book is a documentation of research funded by the Swedish Research Council FORMAS, Strategic funds from the Swedish government within ICT – The Next Generation, and The International Institute for Applied Systems Analysis (IIASA).

Every effort has been made to identify and contact copyright holders and any omission or error will be corrected if notification is made to the publisher.

PHOTOS Åsa Andersson Broms, Love Ekenberg, Anna Hesselgren, Björn Larsson and Rebecca Medici. Photographs not attributed to specified persons have been taken by Love Ekenberg.

COVER IMAGE Love Ekenberg

DESIGN Karin Hansson

ILLUSTRATIONS Gov2u

ISBN Paperback: 9781783743032
ISBN Hardback: 9781783743049
ISBN Digital (PDF): 9781783743056
ISBN Digital ebook (epub): 9781783743063
ISBN Digital ebook (mobi): 9781783742974
DOI: 10.11647/OBP.0108

All paper used by Open Book Publishers is SFI (Sustainable Forestry Initiative), PEFC (Programme for the Endorsement of Forest Certification Schemes) and Forest Stewardship Council(r)(FSC(r) certified.

Printed in the United Kingdom, United States, and Australia by Lightning Source
for Open Book Publishers (Cambridge, UK)

Table of Contents

Contributors

Love Ekenberg is a senior research scholar at the International Institute for Applied Systems Analysis (IIASA) in Laxenburg and full professor of Computer and Systems Sciences at Stockholm University.

Karin Hansson is an artist and a postdoc in Computer and Systems Sciences at Stockholm University.

Mats Danielson is vice president and full professor of Computer and Systems Sciences at Stockholm University, and an affiliate researcher at the International Institute for Applied Systems Analysis (IIASA).

Göran Cars is full professor of Societal Planning and Environment at the Royal Institute of Technology in Stockholm.

Lars In de Betou is a media producer and a musician at Betou media AB and at Stockholm University.

Joost Buurman is assistant director and senior research fellow, Institute of Water Policy, Lee Kuan Yew School of Public Policy at the National University of Singapore.

Manilla Ernst is a lecturer at the Centre for the Studies of Children's Culture at Stockholm University.

Tobias Fasth is a researcher at the Department of Computer and Systems Sciences at Stockholm University.

Rebecca Forsberg is the artistic leader and director of the RATS Theatre in Stockholm.

Johanna Gustafsson Fürst is an artist and senior lecturer at University College of Arts, Crafts and Design in Stockholm.

Karin E. Hansson is assistant professor in Computer and Systems Sciences at Stockholm University.

Petter Karlström is a senior lecturer and program coordinator in interaction design at the Department of Computer and Systems Sciences at Stockholm University.

Florence N. Kivunike is a lecturer in the Department of Information Technology, School of Computing and Information Technology, College of Computing and Information Sciences at Makerere University.

Aron Larsson is associate professor in Computer and Systems Sciences at Stockholm University and Mid-Sweden University.

Thomas Liljenberg is an artist in Stockholm.

Hans Liljenström is full professor at the Division of Biometry and Systems Analysis, Department of Energy and Technology, at the Swedish University of Agricultural Sciences (SLU) and the director of Agora for Biosystems at the Sigtuna Foundation.

Adina Marincea is a researcher at the Median Research Centre (MRC) in Bucharest.

Adriana Mihai is a researcher at the Center of Excellence for the Study of Cultural Identity (CESIC) at the University of Bucharest as well as an affiliated researcher at Median Research Center.

Mona Riabacke is a consultant in risk and decision analysis at Riabacke & Co in Stockholm.

Willmar Sauter is professor emeritus of theatre at Stockholm University.

Uno Svedin is visiting professor at the Department of Computer and Systems Sciences at Stockholm University and senior researcher at the Stockholm Resilience Centre (SRC).

Michael Thompson is senior research scholar at the International Institute for Applied Systems Analysis (IIASA), fellow at the James Marin Institute for Science and Civilization, University of Oxford, and senior researcher at the Stein Rokkan Centre for Social Research, University of Bergen.

F.F. Tusubira is managing partner at Knowledge Consulting Ltd in Kampala. He is also the founding former CEO of the UbuntuNet Alliance.

Harko Verhagen is senior lecturer and researcher at the Department of Computer and Systems Sciences, Stockholm University.

Måns Wrange is an artist, former vice-chancellor of the Royal Institute of Art in Stockholm, and visiting professor of Computer and Systems Sciences at Stockholm University.

Prologue

Participation has become an important part of research and design processes, not least in fields such as art, urban planning and design. At the same time, there is an ever-growing demand for fair participatory processes, supported by IT-based methods such as voting systems, communication platforms, and various crowd-sourcing techniques. However, the success of these has been very variable. Loosely speaking, communications have been tremendously successful in some domains, whereas tools for more analytical support have failed to a significant extent.

The question arises whether this is to do with the specific tools, or whether there are some hidden mechanisms that are more dominant, for instance relating to the conceptualisations involved. We might have ideas of democracy, fairness, and equity that are inadequately represented in the tools available, making them useless for anyone concerned with such notions. Concepts like these are of course social constructs, and there are no final and unifying ideas regarding what participation and deliberation actually mean in relation to them – totally independent of whether the methods involved are IT-supported or not. Nevertheless, the tools must at least mimic the preconceptions, whatever they are. Often there are underlying liberal notions of democracy and equity involved somewhere, where an individual's right to participate is emphasised and assumed, but the idea that the same individual should be provided with at least some reasonable means of doing it on an equal basis is not necessarily present.

In these contexts, there is often a strong tendency to try to reach, or even impose, consensus, ignoring the fact that unequal power relations in a group of participants can actually be both meaningful and motivating, and can enlighten the various conditions, unspoken norms of community and the different

3

interests and diversity found in all societies. It therefore seems a good idea to attempt to specify what we actually mean by the various concepts we have here, and, assuming that we accept these concepts, investigate how we can instrumentalise them when forming fruitful concepts of fairness, equity, participation and democracy in this digital era.

The problems involved are not easy and there are (fortunately) no definite answers, but trying to clarify this seems to be worth the effort. Moreover, if we also can utilise the concepts and provide some accessible tools as structural and analytical support, we can probably better understand the decision structures involved. If we identify and analyse the various components and processes involved, much can be gained. In this book, we discuss various aspects of these problems: our aim is not only to analyse them but to provide solutions and methods, while still keeping in mind the significant conceptual problems involved.

To make this reasoning more concrete, one central question has been to combine a reasonable concept of deliberate democracy with a reasonable notion of equity and representation. And even if we are able to do this, there are several more practical issues to be resolved. If we take participatory democracy seriously and really want to obtain large-scale citizen involvement and transparency in public participatory decision making, then decision making processes become significantly more difficult. The various decision scenarios are usually far from clear, and likewise the process of the decision formation.

Firstly, it is complicated conceptualising participation in relation to representativeness and engagement as well as a multitude of other factors, including the methodology. Secondly, even if we have a clear picture of the participating agents, it is still very difficult to understand what are the true preferences involved. To elicit these involves several complicated tasks. Thirdly, even if we have access to these preferences and attitudes, we want to be able to utilise them, for instance, for more analytical and transparent decision making. However, neither these preferences nor the factual information available can normally be assigned precise values, making the processing and calculation of this complex information also very difficult from an algorithmical viewpoint.

To tackle these problems, we have for some years been working with various aspects of participatory decision making, and have created IT-supported process models for decision making in such settings. By combining a number of fields – such as mathematics, social science, and the arts – we have addressed both the problem of communication, internally within governmental bodies and externally to citizens, and that of modelling and analysis of decision structures and processes. We have, not surprisingly, found that collaborative information sharing and deliberative discussions are important parts of a democratic process which should take place on a multitude of platforms. We have also found that the vast number of specific tools and methods available are seldom used to any significant extent. Surprisingly little in the literature records actual use of decision processes with elaborated tool support, and very little research relates to successful uses of inclusive decision processes. Even if they incorporate peer communication and discussions as a way of reaching consensus, the discussions are seldom combined with any sophisticated means of enabling deliberative democracy, with all the complexities involved, even disregarding the obvious practical factors, such as time, access, and means to participate in the collaborative work.

Despite this rather lugubrious perspective, we nevertheless believe that the potential of more systematised tools would be substantial if these problems were better understood and handled, and here is also where the tool support becomes instrumental. In the work behind this book, we have not only been studying descriptive aspects, but have also aimed to solve problems by developing and using new tools, methods, and working cultures, even in more innovative forms such as artistic performances, as a basis for constructive dialogues and expressions of preferences and analysis. We have tried to find new problem formulations and solutions, with the intention of carrying the decision from agenda-setting and problem awareness to feasible courses of action via formulations of objectives, alternative generation, consequence assessments, and trade-off clarifications. Our ambitions have been to provide applicable and computationally meaningful public decision mechanisms, involving various components such as multiple-criteria, multi-stakeholder points of view, uncertain scenarios, uncertain appraisals of the consequences involved, vague value assessments, and visual formats for presentation of risk information.

The work in this book has been partly funded by the Swedish Research Council FORMAS as well as by strategic funds from the Swedish government (SFO) within 'ICT – the Next Generation'. It has been developed partly within the eGovlab at the Department of Computer and Systems Sciences and partly within the International Institute for Applied Systems Analysis (IIASA) in Austria. The result of all this is that we are now considerably better able to analyse the decision components of the different interests at stake as well as organise the necessary decision making procedures, where, for example, municipalities in constructive modes can handle dialogues and decision making, even in conflicting situations. Furthermore we know much more about the effects of a proposed plan, how conditions for constructive dialogues can be created, how options can be valued, how the decision situations can be organised against the background of perceived values and problems, and how to utilise the potentials of various models and tools when applied from government, public administration, urban planning, and citizen/stakeholder perspectives. We believe that this socio-technical construct is a major step in the use of well-informed decision analysis for evaluation of critical societal issues, and hopefully will have a significant impact of the applicability of decision theory in general and on modernising the field of decision, policy and societal risk analysis.

Love Ekenberg, Karin Hansson, Mats Danielson and Göran Cars
Vienna, New York, Stockholm

Introduction

Tools and methods to support participatory decision making often focus on a specific part of the process, ignoring the wider context. In this project we have started out from a broader picture, situating particular parts of the process in relation to each other and trying to promote a mutual recognition of different levels of information production that play a role in the decision making processes. The research project has looked at participatory decision making processes in the following cases:

RINKEBY-KISTA: URBAN DEVELOPMENT

The suburbs of Husby and Kista are situated next to each other in Rinkeby-Kista in the north of Stockholm, and were built in the 1970s and 1980s. There are huge differences between the two areas. The population of Husby has over 12,000 residents, registers high unemployment rates and has a high proportion of first- and second-generation immigrants. Kista is known as the Silicon Valley of Sweden; it contains several of Sweden's leading companies in new technologies and IT, and over 25,000 people work there. It is an expanding area with many new developments and there are tensions arising from gentrification.

SVARTÅN RIVER: POLLUTION

The river Svartån flows through Örebro, the sixth largest city in Sweden. The river is under intensive agricultural use, and is polluted from nitrate fertilisers, with quite severe social and economic consequences including a decline of cultural and economic value of the land. The aim of the case study was to reach a more sustainable long-term solution with improved water quality in spite of socio-economic constraints.

THE RED RIVER DELTA: FLOODING

The Red River Delta, and more specifically the Bac Hung Hai polder in northern Vietnam, exhibits characteristics of a region in stress: increasing numbers of floods, dense and increasing population, and a lowland terrain. The 225,000 ha of the polder is largely agricultural land, with an elevation ranging from sea level to 10 metres. The case study involved 11,200 persons (out of a total population in the polder of 2.8 million), all of whom are at risk of flooding. The aim of the study was to design, with strong stakeholder involvement, a disaster risk management insurance scheme for the region.

TISZA: FLOOD RISK MANAGEMENT

The Tisza river traverses Hungary from north to south. Repeated floods are severe, especially in the north eastern part of Hungary: financial losses, and costs of compensation to victims and mitigation strategies are increasing. The aim of the case study was the same as for the Red River Delta, above.

ROȘIA MONTANĂ: GOLD EXPLOITATION

Roșia Montană is a commune of Alba County in western Transylvania with rich mineral resources that have been exploited since Roman times. It is also the context for a longstanding conflict around plans to open a new mine. The aim of the study was to clarify the decision components involved and suggest a course of action.

UPPLANDS VÄSBY: URBAN DEVELOPMENT

Upplands Väsby is a municipality in the northern part of the Stockholm region with just over 40,000 inhabitants. It experienced rapid growth in the 1960s and 1970s, becoming a commuter suburb for the labour-force in workplaces in the central region. Rapid growth of the Stockholm region has opened up new possibilities for the future development of Upplands Väsby and the plan is to increase its population, and also the number of workplaces, and to strengthen public and commercial services.

THE STOCKHOLM-MÄLAR REGION: A LOW-CARBON SOCIETY

The Stockholm-Mälar region is home to almost three million inhabitants, with a rapidly expanding population. It is also a region with very high innovation orientation, involving global high-tech, telecom, medical/pharmaceutical specialities and other cutting-edge technologies. The design of policies for the region is highly relevant for future-planning in other areas.

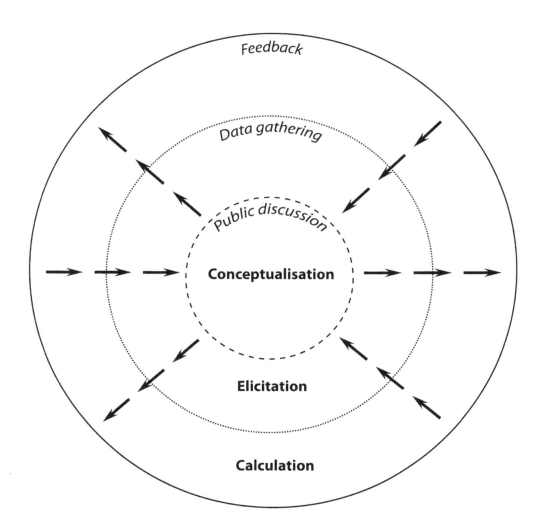

Figure 1. The participatory analytic decision model.

A comparison of our case studies shows how information is developed and structured on different levels. On what can be called a conceptualisation level, various ideas and meanings are expressed and developed in a plurality of forums, from the dominant public sphere in global media resources to the webpages of local organisations, residents' closed social media groups and semi-private e-mail lists, as well as agencies' direct communication with residents in meetings, focus groups and surveys.

On an elicitation level, the municipal, organisations or individuals are using a variety of methods to extract data produced in some of these public sources. On a calculation level, the data is analysed and developed to create meaningful and more informed feedback to the discussions and decision making that takes place on the first conceptualisation level.

The Participatory Analytic Decision Model (Figure 1) on the previous page consists of three interacting layers: the conceptualisation layer where public opinions are developed and surveyed, enabling feedback from inhabitants and stakeholders; the elicitation layer where data is gathered; and the calculation layer where data is modelled and analysed using multi-criteria decision analysis. The challenge here is to acknowledge the inequalities and power asymmetries on the conceptualisation level where problems are acknowledged and developed, but at the same time to use the data produced in these contexts in a meaningful way.

Participants in a decision process are never a homogenous group. Within a neighbourhood, differences in interest due to intersecting factors such as age, sex, professional status, ethnicity or religion may occur. Some people spend their entire lives at the site, while others are in a stage of transfer, and the local commons is intertwined with many parallel social commons. Residents living in a neighbourhood might have very different interests to residents in adjacent areas of the municipality and the region. In order to conceptualise the problem, definitions and interests at stake, the public spheres that create discourse at the site need to be understood. Given the fact that residents have conflicting interests it can be analysed and discussed to what extent these differences can be overcome by reformulations of possible solutions, and how mechanisms for conflict resolution can be incorporated. To identify conflicts and common interests, the interplay between stakeholders has to be addressed. This effort includes a mapping of interests among stakeholders involved.

Before making any decision, the problem has to be clarified, and the stakeholders have to be defined. The democratic problem is that the public sphere – where the issue is most often recognised and defined – is not representative of all but is most often dominated by powerful groups. Digital media strengthens the influence of these already vocal circles. Furthermore, the public sphere is fragmented and one might talk about multiple public spaces rather than one. Therefore it is important to understand how the public opinion is formed in order to identify the communication structures on site. This might help to clarify the representativeness of the so-called public opinion, and thus give elected politicians a better understanding of the opinions expressed in this room. It might also give us insights into how we can design communication systems that support alternative public spheres, in order to strengthen a broader citizen participation in the formulation of the public agenda. Thus, an important part of the research project was to create means for active citizenship and communality, and the development of a diversity of public discourses.

Contemporary participatory methods are also locked into traditional ways of using computer-based text and images that largely restrict the capacity for communicating. Therefore, in the context of public administration in general, and public planning in particular, multimodal communication using a variety of techniques and tools for the mediation of preferences, opinions and values should be encouraged, enabling the enrichment of the content communicated between decision-makers, stakeholders and the general public. It is important, then, to design process models for how such enriched content may be incorporated in public decision making and planning. This calls for a common model encompassing different points of view, multiple objectives and multiple stakeholders using different methods of appraisal.

The book is structured after this model, presenting research that focuses on different levels of the model: conceptualisation, elicitation, calculation. The conceptualisation section introduces methods and projects that focus on the inequalities and conflicts within participatory processes, as well as providing alternative public spheres and modes of communication. The elicitation section describes research that focuses on the quantification of qualitative data, solving problems such as how to extract data in participatory processes where information is derived through user input and the retrieved information is situated in a structure. The calculation section describes studies focusing on finding efficient processes to solve the quite complicated mathematical structures that these types of complex decision making can generate. The final section describes applications that employ tools and procedures from one or more of these different levels.

CONCEPTUALISATION

Communication processes are complex as well as dynamic and therefore it is not possible to understand them using one single method or standpoint. To understand the modalities, communication tools, and processes in public decision making, we therefore use a variety of research methods and approaches as well as different types of researchers; twisting and turning the situation under study to illuminate it in several complementary ways. This way of using a mix of approaches is referred to as triangulation, combining and integrating methods, or mixed methods. This simply means that one mixes different quantitative and/or qualitative approaches.

As the theme is public participation, participatory research methods have also been an important part of our research and the development of our democratic concepts and models. The rationale behind our participatory approach is not only to gather or conceptualise data with the help of research participants, but also to develop models that will enable change by way of participation, since those that are affected by 'problems' have been involved, assuming that the implementation of the outcome of the research will then also be more effective and sustainable. In general, this is the rationale for using participatory approaches, such as participatory urban planning and participatory design. Such methods are used to create a better-informed planning and design process, based on the basic democratic idea that all, regardless of age, gender or level of education, have a right to participate in decisions that claim to generate knowledge about them or that will affect the way they live or work. However, in these interdisciplinarity settings the differences between research paradigms are sometimes significant. That is why there is a need for tools and models clarifying the relations and conflicts between different researchers and methods.

In *Chapter 1* we therefore describe what it means to work with participatory methods in an interdisciplinary research project, and how to deal with differences in ontologies and epistemologies. As a way of communicating different researchers' positions, we draw a map of different positions for researchers and participants. Furthermore, we introduce the concept of gameplay as a useful model for understanding conflicts in the interdisciplinary research setting.

We know that participatory methods have become an important part of the research and design processes in the field of information and communication technology (ICT), and in fields such as art and urban planning and design. But there are no unifying ideas on what participation actually entails and there is often an underlying liberal notion of democracy, where the individual's right to participate is emphasised and unequal power relations in the participatory situation are ignored. Unspoken norms of community and ignorance of the different interests and diversity found in most groups become problematic when translated from one cultural context to another. There is also a tendency to ignore the fact that unequal power relations in a group of participants can actually be meaningful and motivating. Therefore it is important to clarify what we actually mean by democracy in these contexts and in *Chapter 2* we describe how we look at democracy and present a model for evaluating democracy based on these observations and the results of *Chapter 1*.

There is an excessive focus on the method in participatory approaches, while the role of the artist/designer/researcher is overshadowed. As participatory methods depend on the person enacting them, the researcher using the method should be an equally important object of study. However, as participatory methods have become more mainstream, issues of technology have been emphasised at the expense of concerns about relationships between people. Within the arts there is also a criticism that the concept of participation has been reduced to an aesthetic that acts more in an excluding than an including way. In *Chapter 3* we therefore describe and analyse the more artistic parts of the undertakings in the book, focusing on the role of the artist/researcher within research and exploring art as a participatory methodology in the case of Husby. *Chapter 4* explains the plural rationality approach and then lays out the various methods by which it has been applied and discusses the differences between this approach and the more conventional ones.

1

Interdisciplinarity and Mixed Methods

The researchers in this project have worked in diverse fields, including e-government, e-participation, decision support and analysis, design research, urban planning, and art. Interdisciplinarity has been a core value of the project, while using various methodologies from various fields, not the least qualitative and mixed methods. As we also engage with research participants in various ways, sometimes as informants, sometimes as co-researchers, a diverse group of people has been involved. This diversity, regarding both contexts for the research and the demographic of the participants, added even more complexity to the project. In this chapter we focus on what interdisciplinarity means in this context and what combining different fields and different groups of people entails in practice. We also introduce the concept of gameplay as a useful term in interdisciplinary research settings.

INTERDISCIPLINARITY: COMBINING METHODS, CONCEPTS AND THEORIES

Interdisciplinarity commonly refers to the integration of two or more disciplines tackling a common problem. Interdisciplinarity is also common in complex real-life situations where one research perspective is not enough. In contrast to multidisciplinarity, which denotes a juxtaposition of multiple disciplines each investigating the problem in its own way, interdisciplinarity is about mixing different field-specific methods and developing new methodologies that combine different data, methods, concepts or theories. A considerable amount of academic research is interdisciplinary.

Most interdisciplinary research projects are narrow in scope, integrating adjacent fields, and interdisciplinary research projects are more common in more exploratory contexts than in

This chapter is based on Hansson, K. *Accommodating Differences: Power, Belonging, and Representation Online.* Stockholm University. 2015.

instrumentally oriented ones. Interdisciplinary research projects are also often about concrete problem-solving, they are often especially innovative, and can consist of several sub-projects.

This research project contains all these characteristics. Even though the scope of the project was wide, including people from diverse fields like art, e-participation, urban planning, and decision analytics, the fields that were integrated were narrower, such as art and urban planning, or e-participation and decision analytics. However, our common denominator was participation and democracy, and by focusing on this overall theme and sharing basic democratic theories, disparate fields and sub-projects were kept together on a common ground.

The conceptual distance between research fields is often pointed out as the cause of communication problems and failure in interdisciplinary research, and we were aware of this risk. It is easy to believe that the correlation between the conceptual distance between research fields and failure, is also the explanation for the level of interdisciplinarity. However, we found that much more basic conditions for collaboration were of real importance, such as constraints for participation in time and capital. Especially when involving a large number of people as co-researchers, participants or informants, the differences in their 'gameplay', meaning the rules and cultures for accumulated resources in their field, can be hard to overcome, especially if they are ignored. In the consensus culture of Swedish workplaces these differences can be experienced as conflicts. The tendency is to focus on what participants have in common rather than recognising their differences, hence misunderstandings due to ignorance are often grounds for conflicts that eventually develop.

Another important factor in our projects combining different fields and groups of people has been different attitudes to participation and the power inequalities within the participatory setup in different research methodologies. In the following pages we will therefore look at the role of the participant in different methodologies.

THE ROLE OF THE PARTICIPANT

The differences in ontology and epistemology between research fields may be most clearly expressed in the different attitudes to the data and role of the participant. For example, in the field of decision analysis the data is often taken for granted: it is something you have or do not have, that can be extracted and translated into numbers. Participants in the research are seen as informants who deliver data that is 'out there' and can be extracted if you just ask the right questions. The data can be easily illustrated in diagrams and tables.

In contrast, more qualitatively oriented research fields, such as design research, look at the data more critically as something that is situated in a certain context and made 'in here': co-created by the researcher and the participant in the research situation and produced in a hegemonic discourse. Here the participant is seen more as a co-designer or co-researcher and as the expert on his or her own reality. This data is best presented as a narrative and illustrated as quotes and documentary images and films. These differences are often seen as expressions of two different incompatible belief systems that cannot exist in the same scientific space, or in the same research publication. We have chosen rather to see these differences as different positions in a shared process, where one section of the research process is about creating high-quality data that represents some part of reality in some way, and another section of the research process is about using this data as a starting point for theories and calculations. Both paradigms are needed to describe a complex reality.

The differences in attitudes towards participation can be illustrated by comparing some previous urban planning projects in which members of our research team have been actively involved as researchers coming from the fields of computer science, urban planning, social science, and art. As a way to create a common vocabulary, we used these projects to identify differences and commonalities in the perceptions of the participants and the role of the method. The projects, described in Table 1 on the next page, are fairly typical for urban planning practices in Sweden and show the diversity of research practices represented in the group of researchers' portfolio of methods. They are also typical for interdisciplinary research, as the focus is to solve a concrete problem that needs a diversity of perspectives to be apprehended.

What these projects have in common is that they all involved participants in one way or another. By looking at how they did it, and what role the participants played, we can describe some of the differences between these methodologies. Researchers in the realm of social science commonly use participatory methods, such as surveys, focus groups and interviews. However, some researchers also want the research to be participatory. Participatory research is a general term for the use of participatory methods to change the way research is conducted. It emerged as a response to a research paradigm that alienates the researcher from the researched. Instead, participatory researchers aim to change the power relations between researcher and participants and to create knowledge that clarifies

Table 1. Summary of eight cases of participatory processes in urban planning in Sweden.

Nacka: Infrastructure	The aim was to help the politicians to decide whether services such as roads, water supply, sewerage and marinas, should be in private or public hands. **Method:** Multi-criteria, multi-stakeholder decision analysis to enhance transparency
Örebro: Water quality	The aim was to reach a more sustainable (long-term) solution with improved quality of the water in Svartå River, Örebro. **Method:** Multi-criteria, multi-stakeholder decision analysis to enhance transparency
Stockholm: Transportation	Future development of the infrastructure around Stockholm including new roads and public transportation. **Method:** Multi-criteria, multi-stakeholder decision analysis to enhance transparency
Muskö: Eco Village	The aim was to develop a plan for an eco-village for more sustainable living. **Method:** An iterative dialogue process in three steps with residents and other stakeholders, e.g. the municipality, investors and NGOs.
Stockholm: Central Station	The aim was to develop the central railway station in Stockholm with new premises. **Method:** A dialogue with the two closest stakeholders. The resulting plans were displayed in public and consultation meetings with the public were held.
Högalid: Urban Development	Because of a housing shortage the city wanted to increase the density of centrally located neighbourhoods in Stockholm. **Method:** A design charette was used in the beginning of the plan process, where municipal officials, developers, and residents participated in a consultative and creative collaborative process.
Husby: Urban Development	Municipal development plans included new houses and extensive renovations, and a redesign of the town centre. **Method:** The methods used by the municipal authority to involve residents were surveys, dialogue forums and exhibitions. Residents used town meetings and online tools like blogs, Twitter and social media to create debate.
Upplands Väsby: Vision for Future Development	Municipal plans included an increase of the population, but also an expansion of the number of workplaces and to strengthen public and commercial services. **Method:** Surveys, dialogue forums and interactive exhibitions to involve residents in planning

these relations. Participation in this perspective is not only about how we produce knowledge, but also about how this production empowers the participants. Participatory methods in areas like participatory urban planning and participatory design are used as ways to create more informed planning and design processes, to make the implementation more effective and sustainable. Above all, the participatory practices are based on the democratic idea that everyone has a right to participate in decisions that affect them. Most uses of participatory methods are not this radical — instead, participation is seen as a way to understand a social reality of some sort by inviting the participants of this social reality to contribute. The participant is thus seen differently by different researchers, from the participant as a passive research object to the participant as an active co-creator of data.

One of the more minimal modes of participation is where the participant is viewed as an object that is involved to secure compliance and lend legitimacy to the process. For example, in the district of Husby in Stockholm, one of our research sites, the developers involved a large group of residents in town meetings and workshops where people were invited to give input on the planning of the area. However, the more urgent matters, like who could afford to live in the area after the renovations, were not discussed and when the gentrification plans were presented they were legitimised by the claim that residents had been involved in the planning.

Participants can also be seen as instruments and participation as a way to make projects or interventions run more efficiently, by enlisting contributions and delegating responsibilities, for example, over data gathering. Another of our research cases, the municipality of Upplands Väsby and the plan for development of the railway station and its vicinity, can be taken as an illustration of how a complex planning process can become more informed by including citizens' input in the planning process.

Upplands Väsby in the northern part of the Stockholm region has just over 40,000 inhabitants. Municipal plans include an increase of the population, but also an expansion of the number of workplaces and strengthening public and commercial services. An important feature of the municipality's development strategy is changing its image from a mono-functional dormitory suburb to being part of the region characterised by urban qualities: creating an urban fabric with higher density where different functions are physically integrated. The significance of culture and the promotion of street-life are stressed in the visions for the future. At present, the municipality is engaged in a number of activities to realise these ambitions. A long-term vision is being developed. This activity includes a variety of measures aiming at a more active involvement of the residents. Substantial new construction and 'fill-in' are to be carried out in the central part of the municipality with the aim of creating and strengthening urban qualities. This comprehensive change process is complicated, involving a number of stakeholders with varying interests.

The plan for the development of the railway station illustrates this complexity. Residents living in close vicinity to the railway station, whose local environment will be most affected by the project, consider themselves self-evident stakeholders. But other individuals will also be affected, directly or indirectly, by the project. For example, train commuters from other parts of Upplands Väsby will benefit from improved means for intermodal public transport. For individuals working in the area, the project means that the adjacent outdoor environment will change dramatically, and for current and potential Stockholm residents, suffering from the housing shortage in the Stockholm region, the plans for redevelopment of the railway station and adjacent land could create housing options. Thus, an initial issue is to define groups with an interest at stake. As a way to understand citizens' and other stakeholders' specific standpoints we used a survey to get participants' opinions on different alternatives that also could be weighted in relation to each other. Having done that, it become obvious that these interests were diverse and conflicting. Participants can also be seen as more like someone to consult with, as agents, and participation as a way to get in tune with public views and values, co-create problem definitions and solutions and enhance responsiveness. For example, in Husby we used seminars as an adjunct to an art project in the public room, not only as a way to understand the problems but to develop ideas and strategies.

Finally, data can be seen as something that is created for a purpose, and participants can be seen as creative artists, with political capabilities, critical consciousness and confidence. In the project, artists were invited to explore and interpret the situation in multimodal installations. These artworks played the role of probes, starting discussions with residents and other stakeholders.

It is also important to remember that artefacts such as prototypes and interactive interfaces are important for participation, and also have agency, relations and power. Different modalities and materialisations change the way the research is perceived and used. A prototype can, for example, be a simple abstract sketch that encourages participation as it is open for development. Unlike a detailed CAD drawing that almost looks like a finished product but is easier to criticise, or a computer program that needs a

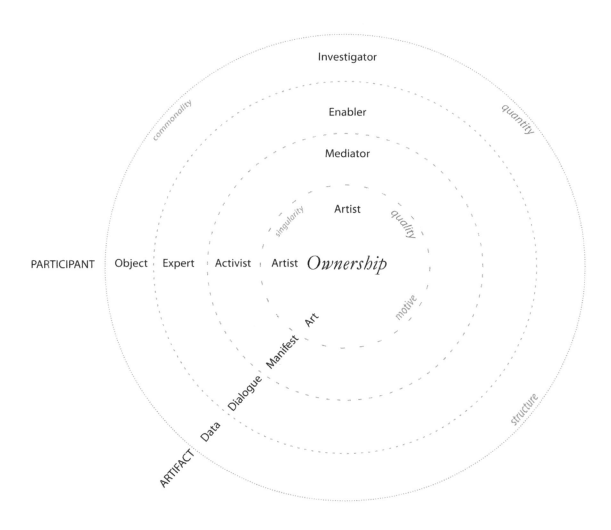

Figure 1. Positions for the researcher, the participants and the data in relation to different epistemologies.

certain expertise to read. Artefacts are also interpreted differently depending on their symbolic value: a performance by an artist, for example, is interpreted differently to a data sheet with values generated by a group of computer scientists.

Combining the scale of different types of participants with a scale of different types of views of the researcher, we get a map (see Figure 1) where one can place the use of different methods, corresponding to different epistemologies, from seeing the researcher as someone who is coming up with general theories looking at participants' common behaviour (commonality), to ideas of the single participant's particularity and subjectivity as a basis for knowledge production (singularity). In this project we have been combining different positions on this map, and used the tension and contradictions between these positions as a source for innovation.

DIFFERENCE IN GAMEPLAY BETWEEN RESEARCH AREAS

It is not only the attitude towards the research subject that differs between different areas, but also the gameplay of the areas. This more basic problem in interdisciplinary research needs careful attention, especially when involving a large number of people as co-researchers, participants, or informants. For example, differences in the parties' time constraints for participation are often ignored and can therefore be a reason for tension or lack of engagement. Research practices, just like games, contain an economy of some sort where the challenge is to accumulate resources. In games, users commonly achieve higher levels and 'score' by doing different activities, so-called game 'challenges'.

In the above-mentioned case from Husby there were three different research disciplines involved, and people at different stages of their career ladders:
- Artistic researchers, most of whom financed their participation as part of a temporary teaching position, also involving students in the research.
- A professor in urban planning, tenured position, full-time employee.
- A professor in computer and systems sciences, tenured position, full-time employee.
- An associate professor in computer and systems sciences, part-time employee.
- PhD students in urban planning.
- PhD students in computer and systems sciences.
- Local actors from the area, participating in the project as co-researchers.

In this group there were thus at least seven different 'game challenges'. For example, the PhD students needed to publish articles in refereed journals in their area of study, in order to complete their education. The artistic researcher needed to show her work in prestigious venues and to win as much attention as possible from gatekeepers in the art world. The associate professor needed to demonstrate evidence of accomplishment with an impressive and extensive publication record containing research articles in referenced journals. In the field of urban planning, the PhD students would write monographs and journal articles. In computer and systems sciences it is more common to contribute to conference proceedings. The local co-researchers might have political motives for participating, for example not only gaining new insights from the collaboration but also a network of contacts that could be useful in the local context.

The fields of urban planning and computer and systems sciences are also differently positioned on the qualitative-quantitative scale. In order to be published, scholars need to adhere to different styles of writing, and style can be especially difficult to integrate in interdisciplinary research. Aesthetics show whether you are part of a group or not: they are an important identifier and can be the reason why, for example, a publication is seriously reviewed or not, or that the artist gets attention from the gatekeepers of the art world. However, these different game rules are not usually clarified, either because participants are ignorant of the differences or because they do not want to give the differences too much space. Unspoken differences can also be reasons for conflict. For example, a person in full-time employment can easily forget that other participants attend working-group meetings in their free time. Co-writing articles can also become difficult for researchers from different paradigms: since they need to publish in the most prestigious journals in their fields in order to advance their careers, they cannot risk using research approaches or concepts inappropriate to their own field.

These differences are not easy to overcome, and there will be conflicts. To create better conditions for interdisciplinary research it is good to have some sort of reflexive practice and to articulate questions about participants' different economic systems, motivations and practical constraints.

The previous map of researchers' and participants' positions can also be useful when navigating between different research paradigms and situations, and aid the establishment of strong research collectives.

FURTHER READING

Björgvinsson, E., Ehn, P. and Hillgren, P-A. Participatory Design and 'Democratizing Innovation', in *Proceedings of the 11th Biennial Participatory Design Conference*, Eds. T. Robertson, K. Bødker, T. Bratteteig and D. Loi. Sydney: PDC '10, The 11th Biennial Participatory Design Conference. 2010.

Cornwall, A. Whose Voices? Whose Choices? Reflections on Gender and Participatory Development. *World Development.* 31(8), pp. 1325–1342. 2003.

Cornwall, A. and Jewkes, R. What Is Participatory Research? *Social Science Medicine.* 41(12), pp. 1667–1676. 1995.

Dearden, A. Participatory Design and Participatory Development: A Comparative Review. *PDC '08: Experiences and Challenges, Participatory Design Conference, Indiana University, Bloomington, Indiana, USA, October 1–4, 2008*, pp. 81–91. 2008.

Gaventa, J. and Cornwall, A. Challenging the Boundaries of the Possible: Participation, Knowledge and Power. *IDS Bulletin.* 37(6), pp. 122–128. 2006.

Hansson, K., Cars, G., Danielson, M., Ekenberg, L. and Larsson, A. Diversity and Public Decision Making. *World Academy of Science, Engineering and Technology.* 6(11), pp. 1678–1683. 2012.

Reason, P. and Bradbury, H., Eds. *The SAGE Handbook of Action Research: Participative Inquiry and Practice.* 2nd ed. Los Angeles, CA: SAGE. 2008.

Wallerstein, N. Power Between Evaluator and Community: Research Relationships within New Mexico's Healthier Communities. *Social Science and Medicine.* 49(1), pp. 39–53. 1999.

The Concept of Democracy

This chapter is based on Hansson, K. *Accommodating Differences: Power, Belonging, and Representation Online.* Stockholm University. 2015.

The concept of democracy can be confusing as there are many implicit ideas and understandings of democracy, sometimes contradictory. In this chapter we develop our thoughts on e-democracy, e-government, and open democracy with the help of political sciences, and we also develop a model for evaluating deliberative democracy.

Digital differentiation and complex, opaque decision processes in collaborative media are threats to representative democracy for many reasons. The participatory dilemma is compounded online, as people who already have a great deal of influence gain even more powerful tools, hence it is important to understand problems and handle them with careful deliberation and representation. The suggested model focuses on these concepts, addressing the problem of lack of supportive tools and venues for broad deliberation, and lack of analytical tools. The model can be used for evaluating how tools and projects support broad deliberative discussion, and to describe how and by whom the data is produced. The aim is to create a better understanding of how the participatory dilemma in online deliberative processes can be handled.

The concept of democracy is generally taken for granted in areas such as e-government, open government, and e-participation. The underlying concept of democracy that form the basis for technological development is usually an unarticulated liberal conception demonstrated in the way researchers address different problems. Democracy in this liberal discourse is an instrument similar to a market economy, where citizens vote for the political parties of their choice, based on how they satisfy citizens' needs and interests. Here, the idea of individual autonomy and transparency is an essential condition for making enlightened choices. Concepts such as collaborative or open government promote a more participatory style of government favoured by proponents of deliberative democracy. Participatory urban planning, established in legal systems, is a further opportunity for participatory democracy.

The central idea of this participatory paradigm is a return to a classical democratic ideal where broad, public, deliberative conversation is essential for reaching a shared understanding of the problems at stake and agreement on the decisions to be taken. Without active and engaged citizens, the gap between them and their representatives creates alienation and turns democracy into a marketplace for political ideas consumed by a passive audience.

The deliberative democracy model has also been criticized, for its dependence on the concept of a neutral public sphere without agonistic interests where all the facts are presented and everyone can share a common understanding. Critics point out that participation in the public sphere is highly unequal, and a hegemonic discourse dictates what is permissible to express in this sphere and what is considered 'political'. As a result real consensus cannot exist, and there is a risk that belief in this idea can in fact undermine democratic institutions. It is also easy to be critical of the central aim of deliberative democracy: creating a neutral sphere beyond self-interest and passion, where 'objective' reasoning and consensus is possible. By contrast, radical democracy embraces a plurality of values and identities, and proposes turning conflicting interests into competing interests rather than seeking one solution that fits all.

In this research project we have turned to Robert A. Dahl's pluralist theory of democracy for finding a common ground for what we mean by democracy. Dahl's theory is a useful starting point as it does not constrain democracy to a particular context, but rather sees it as an iterative and scalable process that includes those affected by its decisions. Dahl's democratic model can thus apply to members of a small group, citizens of a state, or participants in a voluntary organisation. Democracy, in Dahl's perspective, is an ongoing reflective process that is not only about collective decision-making but also about who is a representative 'citizen' in the decision-making processes.

Basic democratic rights to participate in the deliberative processes of agenda-setting, discussion and voting include the aim that everyone involved has an enlightened understanding of the problems and opportunities, as well as the right to express their understanding. Equal representation is important on multiple levels, from setting the agenda to discussion and voting.

We can reflect on the degree of democracy in a situation by analysing how membership is decided; how the members have set the agenda; how discussion around the problem is organised, and who can participate; how, by whom and when the decisions are made, and if a level of understanding is maintained. The situations may look very different: the organisation of an online working group, the government of a country, or the editing of a post on Wikipedia.

In our overviews of research projects on e-participation, e-government and open government we identified problems in the deliberative part of this democracy model, where problems are defined and developed in a reasoning process. We also found problems in the representative part of the model, where membership is defined, and where someone is taking a decision. The available tools often lack structure and sophisticated means to support more complex reasoning in the deliberative process. Participants in many projects also lack democratic legitimacy due to unequal representation: there often is a rather limited group that has the means and the motivation to be fully active members. So let us look more closely at two of the main features in this democratic process: deliberation and representation.

THE DELIBERATIVE PROCESS

A common image for illustrating the democratic deliberative process is the one of groups of men in a café talking in a civilised manner, where different arguments are discussed and every aspect of the problem is explored until a common understanding is developed and consensus is reached. The underlying assumption is that if we just collect the right information from a diversity of perspectives and experiences we will be able to take an informed, rational decision. This decision process can be taught, and it includes weighing pros and cons and predicting the consequences of different actions.

Understanding is a central notion in this communicative process. And in areas such as e-participation, e-government and open government requirements for openness and transparency are also proposed, meaning that the whole decision process, including data gathering and decision mechanism, should be open for inspection. Interoperability is another related concept in the field of computer science, meaning that information should not only be open, but also easily accessible with standards that are simple to reuse and that makes the data sharable. With the concept of understanding we emphasise that access to data not is enough if it is not possible to interpret and process it. Too much information can, for example, sometimes make understanding more difficult and hinder people from participation. Understanding is difficult

Figure 1. N. and G. Urbonas *et al.*, *Husby Chanel*, in *Performing the Common*, Husby, Stockholm, 2012. Photo by Åsa Andersson Broms.

even when it comes to simple decisions. It takes time and energy to gather information and to predict and understand the future consequences of a situation. In the field of decision theory, forms of deliberative reasoning have therefore been developed and instrumentalised. Such instruments are, for example, about structuring the decision procedures, providing quantitative data regarding alternatives and the criteria involved. In this context the deliberative processes are described in different iterative stages:

The first stage is to identify and define the issues at stake: How do we know we have a problem? Why is it a problem? How and where do we think we can find a solution? The second stage is about structure: What are the different aspects of the problem? What do we know about the different perspectives? What are the different solutions identified? The third stage is about opening up the problem and capturing all available information needed to understand what different solutions will lead to: What could happen? How likely is it? What are the consequences of different events? How can they be measured? How are the various criteria related to each other? The fourth stage is about moderating discussion and/or modelling the problem. Different perspectives, goals and criteria are brought together with the help of a moderator. These different goals, criteria, and gathered information can be put together in a model where the outcome of relations between different events, probabilities and weight of criteria can be calculated.

Central to the process is creating a shared understanding of the phenomena involved through transparency and openness. Evaluation of the model is important throughout the process and the process can be iterated in the light of new information. Finally a decision basis is formed, which explains the problems and recommends different solutions.

These stages are of course a simplification. The deliberative process is dynamic and distributed over time and space. It takes place in a variety of contexts and modalities. It also accommodates diverse participants representing different experiences and viewpoints.

REPRESENTATIVENESS IN DELIBERATIVE DEMOCRACY

The deliberative process has been criticised from different perspectives. Most important in our overview is the problem with representation in the political process. It matters who it is that discusses and takes decisions. Feminist scholars especially emphasise the importance of 'situated knowledge' meaning that knowledge is always situated in a person's prior understanding of the information. This is why it is important to have representation not only of different perspectives but also of different people. People have different and sometimes antagonistic interests, but also produce and interpret the information differently, which is why the outcome of information gathering also depends on who it is that produces the information. A democratic deliberative process also needs mechanisms for neutralising and balancing asymmetrical power relations in order to make all perspectives visible. However, this kind of enlightened reasoning may only be possible if there are no major conflicts between different groups. In practice, politics is full of passion and arriving at a consensus on rational grounds is often impossible: the conflicts between different interest groups and world views are simply too great. In addition, the agenda and discussion are governed by a hegemonic discourse. In this dominant discourse there are constraints on what political positions it is possible to take.

Democratic representation is therefore not simply about the people who are affected by the decision also being involved in taking the decision, but also about having the means and the motivation to participate. Democracy is not just about legal rights to vote or to speak freely, it is equally important to have the social, economic, and cultural capital required to participate as a full citizen in political life. Online, this means having the digital literacy needed to participate fully in the production of the information that informs the deliberative process. Democracy is also about the recognition of one's identity, that the questions you feel are important also are acknowledged as political, and that you can identify with the actors in the public arena. Representation is also complicated in a more global system where those affected by decisions made in a certain location might live somewhere else. Therefore the question about representation is increasingly relevant, as the nation state as the basis for the institutionalisation of democracy is questioned.

The above description of the deliberative process and democratic representation can be summarised in the following criteria that can be used when analysing tools and processes for collaboration from a democracy perspective (see Table 1 on next page).

DELIBERATION AND REPRESENTATION IN HUSBY

To exemplify the model we can use it to reflect on our case study in Husby (Figures 1–2), a suburb of Stockholm with around 12,000 residents, where the officials invited residents to a dialogue around a planning process. Politicians along with construction companies wanted to develop the area. Stockholm needed to expand and Husby was conveniently located regionally with good transport links and

Table 1. Model for evaluating democracy: criteria for deliberation and representation.

Deliberation How?	**Representation** Who?
Definition How is the problem defined?	*Power* Who is defining the problem? Who is dominating the discourse?
Structure Are there any means to structure the problem? Are there different aspects presented? Different solutions?	*Diversity* Are there multiple viewpoints from different groups present? (e.g. gender, age, class, ethnicity etc.)
Openness Are there any ways of gathering and sharing information? Are there ways of categorizing and/or weighting information? Is the decision process transparent? Is the data open?	*Differences* How are participants' differences acknowledged and handled? What assets are needed to participate?
Moderation Is there any modelling of the problem? Any ways users can count on probabilities and consequences? Is the discussion facilitated?	*Representation* Who is participating? Is there any means to know the representation of different groups of people? How do we know? Security?
Understanding Is it easy/difficult to take a decision based on the information given?	*Motivation* What is the motivation to participate in the decision process? What types of identities are recognized in the context? How is the problem contextualized? To whom does the aesthetic make sense? For whom are the questions/problems important?

Figure 2. Workshop at Husby Träff as part of N. and G. Urbonas *et al.*, *Husby Chanel*, Husby, Stockholm, 2012. Photo by Karin Hansson.

large unexploited areas. There was also a general idea that the area had problems and that these problems could be solved with renovations and new roads and buildings. But renovation of the area also meant gentrification, forcing some of the current residents out due to higher rental costs. These changes also coincided with changes in the social services in the area due to privatisation of the healthcare system (which was perceived negatively by the residents) and as part of the general development of the area.

In this case, there is already a democratic problem in the very definition of what the 'problem' is, and who takes part in this definition. Strong interests in developing the area for economic reasons are here combined with a dominant media discourse developed by people who do not live in the area and are not directly affected by the development plans. The conditions for a deliberative dialogue including those most affected by the decision were not the best. As the development could threaten some people's entire lifestyles and force them to move elsewhere, it was difficult for them to see the benefits for the whole region and to be understanding and 'rational' from a larger perspective. Even though officials provided participants with means to structure the dialogue, the initial problems the officials invited them to address were not the problems the residents felt were important, and the different aspects that were presented in the dialogue meeting were not relevant for the way some residents framed the issues. For example, there were no opportunities to explore the relationship between different aspects of the development plan and higher rents. Nor were there any means for the public to calculate probabilities and consequences. And the decision process was kept closed to outside inspection.

So who was represented in the Husby deliberative process? For example, the notion that Husby was a problem area that justified intervention: who created this notion? The impression given in the media of Husby and other suburbs on the periphery of Stockholm, or any other large European city, is one of a high proportion of immigrants, low incomes, crime, and social exclusion. But in fact Husby is relatively well-off. For example, if you set the school results against the proportion of new residents and children with languages other than Swedish as their first language, Husby's school results are respectable. Crime is no higher than in some of the more affluent areas in central Stockholm, though in the dominating media discourse these latter areas are not portrayed as problem areas. And when we studied who is represented in the media image of Husby, we found an uneven distribution of identities in terms of gender, ethnicity and age among those voices. This clearly shows the potential for significant inequalities in representation and recognition of identities in the public sphere. And there is a lack of acknowledgement of the existing plurality of identities and world views at the site. Different viewpoints did not exist in the dominant public sphere and were not represented when the problems with Husby were defined by public opinion. However, Swedish newspapers are not the only public sphere in Husby. Many local organisations in Husby use information technology to establish alternatives to the dominant media: for example, a combined e-mail list united several groups in organising a protest against the plans.

But not everyone is interested in participation, and this poses a dilemma for a more deliberative democracy model, as those participating in the discussion are not necessarily representative of those affected by the issue and do not understand the full extent of the problem. The disadvantage of a more participatory government is that those who are involved are often groups of people who are already relatively influential in the community. Most people lack the motivation to participate and the opportunity to gain greater influence is often taken by just a few. Others feel that they have more pressing matters to engage in. It also takes a certain kind of cultural and social capital for one's involvement to feel meaningful and rationally justified. Even in cases where the level of participation might be high, the results may still not be truly representative. This is an example of how the model can be used to analyse democracy in a complex case of broad deliberation around a conflict where the problem and solution are defined in an unrepresentative public sphere. However, the model can just as well be used to analyse a single discussion or the functionality of a collaborative tool (See Figure 3).

The unequal distribution of online participation may produce severe counter-effects when attempting to strengthen democracy through increased use of collaborative media. But the method offers great potential if the problems of deliberation and representation can be more clearly understood and managed. The deliberative model can be used to evaluate how different tools and research projects deal with the questions about how discussion is supported and who is part of the discussion. And this might give us a better understanding of how we can handle the participatory dilemma in online deliberative processes.

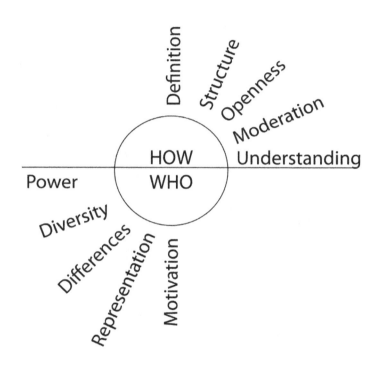

Figure 3. Criteria for evaluating deliberation (how) and representation (who).

FURTHER READING

Dahl, R.A. *Democracy and Its Critics.* New Haven, CT: Yale University Press. 1989.

Dryzek, J.S. Deliberative Democracy in Divided Societies: Alternatives to Agonism and Analgesia. *Political Theory.* 33(2), pp. 218–242. 2005.

Fraser, N. What's Critical about Critical Theory? The Case of Habermas and Gender. *New German Critique* (35), pp. 97–131. 1985.

Fraser, N. Rethinking Recognition. *New Left Review,* pp. 107–120. 2000.

Habermas, J. *Between Facts and Norms: Contributions to a Discourse Theory of Law and Democracy.* Cambridge, MA: The MIT Press. 1996.

Mouffe, C. Deliberative Democracy or Agonistic Pluralism? *Social Research.* 66(3), pp. 745–758. 1999.

Rawls, J. *Political Liberalism.* New York: Columbia University Press. 1993.

Art as a Creative and Critical Public Space

In this research project art functioned as a creative and critical room that created a greater understanding of the significance of discursive practices and the importance of reviewing the information that is the foundation of how we formulate the research problems. Art was also used as a way to enhance participation by initiating public discussion around research related issues and as a way of developing research themes and building theories. As the use of art is not as common in research, as other qualitative methods in this chapter, we will elaborate on the position of art in research and exemplify with cases from one of the projects.

THEMATIC ARTWORK

[The music starts to play. The camera pans across the stage and zooms in on the TV host having her make-up put on. She starts to go up towards the stage. The camera follows her. She stops and looks into the camera.] The host introduces (with an American accent):

"Welcome to the Edge City Talk Show. Today's show is about the desk and the office. Most people have their jobs in Edge City, a fantastic place with business, shopping and entertainment, everything in the same place. Edge City lies outside of the traditional urban environment. It's almost like the city but not in the city, fantastic but with more nature!!! Edge City is a so-called superburbia. You have everything close by!"

[Pause]

"I visited a superburbia once and the idea for today's show came when I was visiting such a place in the US a few years ago" [The host pauses and looks into Camera 3].

"Ah, it was a remarkable experience. Edge City is something totally different from your average suburb. There are at least 4 million square meters for your office. It can fit between 20 to 50,000 employees. So interesting! One of the most interesting aspects is that it's an international place. Since everyone communicates in English it's perfect for me".

This chapter is based on Hansson, K., Ekenberg, L., Gustafsson Fürst, J. and Liljenberg, T. Performing Structure: Fine Art as a Prototype for Participation, *Proceedings of the 17th International Symposium on Electronic Art ISEA2011.* 2011, and Hansson, K., Ed. *Performing the Common [Föreställningar om det gemensamma].* Berlin: Revolver Publishing. 2015.

The described projects are part of CATS Centre in Arts and Technology in Society, a centre at DSV in collaboration with the Royal Institute of Arts and the Royal College of Music in Stockholm (see Figures 1–12 and Scripts 1–2 for documentation of some projects).

[Emma looks into Camera 2. Images of the modern office are shown on the TV-screens in front of the stage while Emma continues talking. The images loop.]

Emma continues:

"When I was in Silicon Valley I got so inspired. It made such an impression on me and it got me thinking about offices. What kind of a workspace do we have?

"What kind of office do we want? How will we decorate it? Will the office be mobile? Will everyone have his or her own desk or can you share a desk?

"We have fantastic guests we will be talking with about their personal experience of work and offices. Today's first guest… Welcome Arash Sofla. A warm welcome for Arash…"

This quote is from a dramatic art performance by Shiva Anoushirvani which consisted of an outdoor television show with invited guests from the area of Rinkeby-Kista (Figure 1). Anoushirvani based her work on how she experienced the location after working with young people in the area in a local youth centre. She formulated the conflicts and tensions she experienced as a TV show, where fictional narratives were mixed with reality. The TV show created a narrative that bound together contradictory images of the place and mixed them in a way that was both surreal and comical, turning the residents into actors and their reality into a television spectacle.

Unlike a more conventional ethnography, where the researcher observes and takes notes and eventually publishes her findings in an academic journal after discussing it with colleagues at scientific conferences, art is a theory made public in a format that is more direct and accessible than academic papers. Art is about giving expression to the situation as one experiences it, clarifying the artist's position and perspective, and enabling a discussion with situation.

Anourshivani's artwork was part of *Performing the Common* (Figures 1–5), an artistic exploration of Rinkeby-Kista, which is a suburb in northern Stockholm. The project, which ran between 2010 and 2012 with sixteen participating artists, was part of a larger research project undertaken at the Department of Computer and Systems Sciences at Stockholm University and the Department of Architecture and the Built Environment at the Royal Institute of Technology, in collaboration with the Royal Institute of Art in Stockholm. The art project dealt with the performance of organisational systems like democracy in a place structured by globalisation through migration and information. An art exhibition in the public space was employed as a way to better understand the conditions for democratic participation and

Figure 1. S. Anoushirvani, *Edge City Talk Show*, in the exhibition *Performing the Common*, 2012. Photo by Martin Hultén.

Figure 2. G. Weibull, 'Nothing is done out there to be evil' – Part I: Speech. Version II, *Performing the Common*. Husby, Stockholm, 2012. Photo by Åsa Andersson Broms.

urban development in the area of Rinkeby-Kista. In this work-in-progress, artists working in relation to research regarding e-democracy used art as a method to explore the context.

The rationale was the need for a more informed discussion regarding the importance of form and structure in democracy in relation to technological developments in the field. Research on e-participation also lacks innovation in the sense that most of the current software is adaptations of existing technologies. Furthermore, the internet is treated as a distinct artefact and technological solutions are mostly taken for granted. These approaches have seldom been successful regarding broad and representative citisen involvement, and particularly not in more socially complex settings. A belief in the ability of technology to shape a neutral place for deliberative discussions is omnipresent in the discourse on the internet and democracy.

We were sceptical about a technology strongly influenced by a liberal notion of democracy as an egalitarian sphere for reasoning, rather than, for example, a Foucauldian notion of hegemonic discourse shaped by power relations. The question then arises whether there are other complementary approaches to the field. Our approach is more along the lines that socially embedded research could give way to more robust forms of knowledge production. We initiated an art and research project to explore how an unconditional conversation about the common and socially shared space can take place in practice. In contrast to a technology-driven approach, the argument is that art projects can be used for both investigating and creating multimodal mediated participation. Furthermore, thematic art projects can be used as a way of prototyping for participatory democracy. Artists' actions, installations and role-playing create a direct confrontation and interaction with a specific place and its inhabitants to explore the dynamic relationships that constitute its context. The notion of art creates a certain focus and expectation of seeing something beyond the everyday perception. We would like to see art as an informal context that provides an unconditional opportunity to try different positions and opinions.

Since the participatory movement of the 1960s, art that more directly includes its audience in the performance or process has been widely explored, and today participation as an aesthetic component is common in the nomadic context of contemporary art. However, we believe that too often the critical potential of participatory art is reduced to symbolic gestures. We aimed to overcome this by situating a participatory art project in a local context and connecting it with research on e-democracy, thereby creating opportunities for the art project to inform the research, and vice versa. The conceptual starting point for *Performing the Common* was a recognition of the need to examine the norms and beliefs forming the basis of the structures and communication patterns that current technologies co-create. We were interested in the "doing" of democracy within science, and what the basis for democracy looks like.

THE CONCEPTS OF ART AS TECHNIQUES

In participatory design, multiple genres of art are used as a way of involving users in the process, such as probes, scenarios and role-playing. In this art project we did not emphasise any particular artistic genre; instead we used different concepts of art as a way of exploring the conditions for a participatory democracy grounded in a particular context. Our techniques for exploring different perspectives on e-democracy included:

Subjectivity	comparing the site with other global nodes through artists' personal experiences
Conflict	emphasising diversity and conflict rather than consensus
Pain	using the artwork as a memory-work, a technique for understanding underlying conflicts and detecting norms and behaviours

SUBJECTIVITY

The notion of subjectivity is strong in the avant-garde concept of art. We can reach a contextual understanding beyond statistical generalisations by departing from the individual artist's subjective understanding of a certain situation. We situated the art project in Rinkeby-Kista, which is the home location for the Stockholm University Department of Computers and Systems Sciences and the researchers in this project. It is also the location of Centre in Arts and Technology in Society (CATS). This is one of Stockholm's more expanding suburbs, and a central location for global companies primarily in the information industry, and both Stockholm University and the Royal Institute of Technology in Stockholm have chosen to place parts of their operations here. It is also home for programmes, such as the government funded SPIDER (The Swedish Program for ICT in Developing Regions) which, among other things "exports" e-democracy to developing countries. Rinkeby-Kista is characterised by extreme local segregation; those who live there are not generally the same as those who work there. The unemployment rate among the

Figure 3. Åsa Andersson Broms, *Façade*, and S. Shahabi, *Local Composing*, in the art exhibition *Performing the Common*. Husby, Stockholm, 2012. Photo by Åsa Andersson Broms.

local residents is high, as is the proportion of immigrants. The place illustrates the new divisions created by globalisation, where diverse socio-economic worlds become wrapped up in each other and where the state's ability to balance differences has declined. Here, technology has not decreased but increased disparities as the importance of social and cultural capital has increased in the networked economy in general.

The latter is not unique to Rinkeby-Kista and, in order to compare the site with other global nodes through artists' personal experiences, we invited artists from different peripheral nodes heavily restructured by the global system, such the Moldavian artist Stefan Rusu who uses art as a way to talk about social and political phenomena. He is also the leader of the KSAK Center for Contemporary Art in Chisinau, Moldova, and has developed art projects throughout Europe, the Middle East and Asia, focusing on processes and changes in post-socialist societies. The Lithuanian artists Nomeda and Gedimina Urbonas also explore post-Soviet notions of changing national identity, and the conflicts and contradictions caused by the new economic and political conditions. They started JUTEMPUS, an interdisciplinary program for art in Vilnius, and VOICE, an online publication on media culture. In Rinkeby-Kista these artists worked in close relation to local Swedish artists and local organisations.

Unsurprisingly, and as various social media have demonstrated, communication technology is not necessarily alienating. It can instead support previously fragmented groups to keep together and provide the means for new communities with a shared interest to form and interact. Technically, it seems to be easier to lump together similarities rather than differences, and to design services that offer us new products and friends based on our previous choices. The technology thus niches us, scatters us, and makes the common areas of understanding fewer and easier to avoid. It is difficult to get along with "the other".

CONFLICT

In order to develop an understanding of the common it is not enough to talk only to people who think and act like us. A technique that is not based on combining equals but different varieties appears here as a discursive democratic utopia. In the choice of artists, we therefore tried to see beyond our own aesthetic practices while creating a heterogeneous group of artists. By bringing together artists with different experiences and modes of expression, we promoted a situation of conflict where the individual artists' subject positions were questioned.

Figure 4. I. Jansson, *Conversion in Progress*, in the art exhibition *Performing the Common*. Husby, Stockholm, 2012. Photo by Björn Larsson.

Conflict is also a recurrent theme in art, where the individual artist is in conflict with the collective system. An avant-garde artist breaks with the norms and differentiates him – or herself from ordinary people and previous art. It is accepted in these settings that an artist's role is created through a differentiation process, where an outsider is opposed to the norm: avant-garde in contrast to the conventional; painting in contrast to performance, and so on.

We take another direction in this project and depart from our different perspectives, deconstructing the norms that create difference while looking for a common denominator. To avoid being locked into just one perspective, sixteen invited artists and artists groups approached the subject from a multitude of angles such as community art, urban installation art and activist art. The artists used locative and interactive media, as well as more traditional artistic techniques. The particular genre of art was not important here; a common denominator was that the artists worked with situation-specific emancipatory art projects that in various ways related to the physical and mediated public sphere. We did not emphasise a particular artistic method, but rather the actual meeting between artists and the procedures for dealing with differences. Using the thematic exhibition as a framework, different artistic perspectives created a triangulation of methods where a more diverse and complex picture of the situation could emerge.

PAIN

The group exhibition worked as a special form of knowledge building through the joint development of a theme. This has similarities with a qualitative method called memory-work which uses the memories of a group of researchers to investigate norms and social structures. This use of personal experience as a tool for academic analysis is based on Husserl's systematic attempt to examine the subjective unconscious where he argues that we can reach a general understanding of a phenomenon by understanding the individual's experiences. The idea behind the memory-work method is that memories often derive from situations where we have experienced a taboo or a cultural constraint that caused a sometimes painful conflict. To get to the underlying experience that caused the memory, one must see through cultural norms and behavioural patterns. The memory-work method is specifically intended to reach the underlying experience. To achieve this, one begins by describing the individual's own conscious memories. The collective analysis of each memory is then intended to identify the underlying conflicts and to detect the cultural norms and

Figure 5. A. Hesselgren, *Open Space*, in the art exhibition *Performing the Common*. Husby, Stockholm, 2012. Photo by Anna Hesselgren.

behaviours involved, that is, the very reasons why the memory has become a memory.

In the project, we considered the similarities between the memory-work approach and the thematic group exhibition, and developed our own method of collective knowledge production. Within the framework of the arts organisation Association for Temporary Art [a: t] Åsa Andersson Broms, Nils Claesson and Karin Hansson previously carried out a series of thematic art projects and exhibitions related to the information society and the changing conditions for democracy: *Best Before – on the Information Society*, Tensta Konsthall (1999), *The Art of Organizing*, Gallery Enkehuset (2000), *Money – a commentary on the new economy* and *Public Opinion* at Kulturhuset in Stockholm (2001, 2002). Central to the work is the collaboration between the artists and the ambition to create something beyond the sum of the single parts. This way of working with a thematic art exhibition has many similarities with the qualitative research method of memory-work. The artist most often departs from his or her subjective experience of the chosen theme and focuses on the elements that he/she thinks are interesting. What is interesting most often means some form of unresolved conflict that chafes at an individual or societal level. The motivation for making art is to a great extent about the need to express a subjective experience/interest on a structural level where others can read it. The collective process in a group exhibition, where artists share their ideas and reflections with each other, works at its best as a collective memory-work where the discussion of ideas creates an understanding of underlying conflicts and detects the inclusion of norms and behaviours – the very reason that the art has become an artwork.

ART AS A PARTICIPATORY METHOD

When we claim that art is a participatory practice we do not mean that it has to be concerned with participation, or be interactive in a situation where a work of art is created by a group of participants. Our point is that it is precisely the artist's position as an individual subject that makes further dialogue with the situation being investigated a possibility. If the researcher/artist is a person who is committed, with clear views and an ability to express them, then one can meet and criticise her. Unlike ordinary research data, the artist's results are communicated more directly, as a reaction to the situation, and this creates the conditions for further dialogue. Here an individual work of art can be the starting point of the dialogue, or the dialogue can be the starting point for the work process itself.

In the field of participatory art, the aim can also be to diminish the authority of the artist/designer to make the participant a co-designer. In the art project *Performing the Common* we rather wanted to emphasise the authority of the artist/designer as a precondition for dialogue; the artist is someone who tells her or his story as an invitation to others to tell theirs. Participatory methodologies always entail unequal power relations. Artistic practice is no exception, but involves a different kind of relationship which allows other types of conversations. The modern art concept is in a way anti-authoritarian, as it does not pretend to report the truth about a phenomenon, but just the expression of the subjective perspective of one or a few individuals. At the same time art and the artist are highly authoritarian. One of art's most important claims is that it is different and special, valuable enough for museum collections, something unusual that requires extra concentration and ability. The artist is a co-creator of this aura and is also expected to have specific characteristics, a particular sensitivity and expression. Here there are similarities with the researcher who is expected to be someone who stands outside politics and the social and economic relations of a situation. But while the designer legitimises her- or himself by referring to design expertise and user studies, the artist never represents anyone but her- or himself, which means there is another kind of opportunity for others to disagree, think the opposite, or ignore this person.

Nomeda and Gediminas Urbonas' work in the art exhibition is an example of this. Their contribution was a subjective investigation of the site using visual images, interventions, discussions and study visits. They formulated and shared their experiences in a guided tour around Husby, in a symbolic burning of a car model outside the art hall, and in a communal meal. Fictional narratives were mixed with affirmations and exaggerations in a concretisation of a dream of the suburb, a dream in which the image of burning cars is mixed with utopian ideas about community. Just as conflicts in Husby pertaining to increased rents and cuts in social services strengthened the local sense of community, the ritual conflagration of the car provided a cooking stove and a gathering place. The guided tour created a narrative that bound together contradictory images of the place and turned the spectators into tourists visiting a social system in a state of transition.

Nils Claesson's video sliN is another artwork in the exhibition. Most of the descriptions we have of Husby are from an inner-city perspective or by someone who does not have a personal experience of living in that locality. Claesson's work gives this description a body, a subject. In sliN the artist goes backwards, all the way from his home in central Stockholm to the art gallery in Husby on the city outskirts. The artwork was created by filming Claesson travelling from the gallery to his home by foot and playing the film backwards in the Husby art gallery. Thus, the artist uses his body and his experience literally to understand the distance between his own subjective position and the other. Instead of accepting a "general idea" about Husby, we see how this view is situated in a body that walks backwards and primarily describes his own experience.

In the research context the artists' various individual projects created a more complex and nuanced picture of the setting and the conditions for communication. Instead of just observing the place, the artwork helped to create an active dialogue with citizens by materialising impressions and conclusions. In this way the artistic works functioned as a participatory method and a public sphere for the issues that emerged in the research project as a whole. In parallel with the art projects we conducted public seminars and also more conventional qualitative and quantitative studies that together with the art projects gave an understanding of site-specific communication structures.

The art was used as a participatory practice, but not primarily by involving a variety of participants in artistic production. Rather, participation was enabled because the artists were clear about their own motives, ideas and conclusions. By communicating this directly as a reaction to the location and the theme, either in the exhibition or in the work, the art established a public sphere for dialogue. Here the artist's persona was important as a personification of ideas and as someone with whom to engage in dialogue, directly or indirectly.

To conclude, this project contributed to the discussion about artistic research by showing how situation-specific art can be viewed as a qualitative method for highlighting and exploring discursive practices. Through a triangulation of different artistic perspectives the themed and collectively generated art exhibition created a diverse and complex picture of notions such as participation and democracy. The artistic work was an iterative process where concrete images, scenarios and situations created a direct communication with the site. We wanted to see the project as a construction of prototypes for alternative societies as well as a laboratory for participation. Following a rich tradition of participatory art, we emphasised the artists' capacity to listen, interact and respond.

Figure 6. R. Forsberg and J. Gustafsson Fürst, *The Diary of Antigone*. Husby, Stockholm, 2011. Photo by Johanna Gustafsson Fürst.

Figure 7. K. Hansson, *The Affect Machine*, in *Performing the Common*. Internet and Husby Konsthall, Stockholm, 2012.

Figure 8. In L. de Betou and K. Hansson, *The Affect Machine Historical Archive*. Digital Art Centre, Kista, Stockholm, 2015. Photo by Ingvar Sjöberg.

Script 1. Hansson K. The Affect Machine Historical Archive. 2014.

In our relational society no one can own anyone else's work, or even their own work, as their own subject is dependent on all the others, and can therefore not exist outside of this relationship. For us this is the norm and something completely natural.

But society has not always been organised in this way.

[Moving and still pictures of the solitarian individual: Instagram selfies, advertising, politicians, business leaders etc.]

NARRATOR

In the un-relational age, or Capitalism, the solitarian individual was emphasised and there was a division between men. Maintained by segregation. Segregation between men and women, black and white, old and, young, public and private, production and reproduction

Production was based on this division of people, places, and practices.

[Mark sitting in a futuristic, ergonomic chair.]

MARK

The lonely individual was emphasised, and he... his relation to others was described as a competition instead of collaboration, a survival of the fittest instead of a survival through the care of others. It was mostly a man.

[Maria walking in the park. People strolling.]

MARIA

Today our extended social network is our life basis, and it is difficult to think of a life without this community.

We say "I am we".

We believe there is no sustainability outside the group, Without our relations to others we wouldn't be able to survive, there would be no food, no houses, no culture, no language.

[Children playing football in the park]

In the capitalistic system competition was not only a child's game, and something you learn not to do when you become older, but was seen as an essential way of organising society. And that was called "the market mechanism".

The basic idea behind this was to divide people's demands for goods and services from the wider contexts, and do the same with the supply of the goods and services. Then these demands and supplies would meet in an abstract market, that would enable a more efficient matchmaking between supplies and demands and thus create equilibrium and harmony. Instead of organising society along extended mutual relations, the organising was based on categorising, comparing these categories, creating markets for certain goods and services. The categorising was made on all levels: on the individual level, on the level of functions, and on the levels of organisations.

[Astrid is the School expert so maybe she is standing in a school yard or walking in a school corridor]

ASTRID

On the individual level, people were lumped together in groups based on their attributes rather than their mutual relations.

ASTRID

E.g. teachers were lumped together with other teachers, to create a so-called "market" for teachers. The idea was that the individuals would go to this market when they were in need of teaching. Then they would be able to choose between different types of teachers. The idea was also that this comparison would make the teachers compete (instead of collaborate), and produce the "best" piece of teaching, as if teaching was a commodity. The potential students, looking for teachers, were also a sort of market, where teachers could look for different kinds of students. The market for students was also the place where students competed to win the best education. The idea with the competition was that the high achieving teachers would "win" the high achieving students, and vice versa.

ASTRID

For us it might sound strange not to pair the low achieving students with the best teachers, as they have a greater need for education, but the belief was very strong that this incitement "to win" a competition would benefit the society as a whole, by making everyone more competitive instead of supportive.

[Archive pictures from different parts of the world.]

NARRATOR

Another concept that was valued was the right to "choose", and the idea that the logic of the market would make a variety of possible choices available. The system was called "freedom of choice", but did not in fact give freedom of choice, as the choices were restricted to what value the individual could contribute to the market.

MARIA

This paradox, the amount of choices available, and the value restriction that in practice made most "choices" unavailable, was difficult for some people to handle. Often they tried to force their will on the situation by acts of violence. Thus, the market needed armed forces, to protect it from those who didn't have the means to participate.

Back to Clint who walks around in his calm big kitchen. He is making food for his grandchildren that sit at the table.

CLINT

It was all about division those days. The private versus the public was the main paradigm. The private where everything had something to do with reproduction, like childcare, eating, sleeping, care of the elderly. The public was where production took place, like building cars, or making bread. They believed that division and alienation was something good. They worshiped alienation!

The main character in the movies was a lonely man with poor or no contact with his network

NARRATOR

How strange this can sound. We have to put it in a historical context where communications were not developed, and where economics didn't count time (as if there were no children or elders), and resources were seen as unlimited. Of course this was also why this system finally collapsed, as there was no sustainability.

TEXT

The first Affect Machine was developed during this era as a participatory art project that engaged a small but committed community of people searching for alternatives. When all other system s broke down it already existed as an alternative, which is why it was possible to overcome the crisis.

Today we have communication systems that allow the social and private and economic and public sectors to be one. Communication technology brings about the possibility of reducing the alienation between producer and consumer by establishing direct relations without any tangible intermediary.

In this our relational economy everyone is a consumer and producer, and resources are distributed according to the logic of the network "From each according to his ability, to each according to his need".

Figure 9. K. Hansson, *The Affect Machine*. Digital Art Centre, Kista, Stockholm, 2015. Photo by Ingvar Sjöberg.

Promoting a personal brand in the form of taste, education and social relations is central to every career in an insecure and flexible labour market. Accordingly, crowd funding of humanity, rather than of production of commodities, is a possible and reasonable scenario for a future social system, where people are deeply interconnected in collaborative networks. The Affect Machine explores the design of such a market place for social relations.

Figure 10. K. Tollmar and M. Wrange, *Opiner* in the exhibition *Research in Progress*. The National Museum of Science and Technology, Stockholm, 2014. Photo and exhibition production: Igor Isaksson, MU AB and Mats Gus Gustavsson, 100g AB.

Opiner is a project which explores how smartphones in combination with a web-based platform and digital visualisations in the public domain, can used to increase the involvement of citizens in political decision-making processes.

Figure 11. R. Forsberg, *Women in science – Lise and Otto*. Kista, Stockholm, 2015.

Lise and Otto is the first set of the trilogy *Women in Science* in which the RATS Theatre focuses on female researchers. *Women in Science* highlights personal destinies, scientific discoveries, and also problematises the conditions in research today.

Figure 12. R. Forsberg, *Maryam*. Dramaten, Stockholm. 2013.

Maryam is a theatre performance that takes place on mobile phones. Using GPS coordinates and a nonlinear digital map, the audience can follow young Maryam al-Ijliyas life. The audience get to know both henna and astrolabe, predecessor of today's GPS. The visitor wanders through the city and can meanwhile share ideas and learn from others' reflections.

Script 2. Forsberg, R. Maryam. 2013.

Maraym is a young woman of science in tenth century Aleppo, Syria. She has developed the advanced, pocket sized, astrological instrument the astrolabe, which, using the stars, is capable of measuring time, place and position. She struggles for a seat in Bayt al-Hikma, The House of Wisdom.

When you press play a map will appear on the display, showing a place where you both start and finish. Visit the different sites to have the story told. You navigate freely and in your own chosen order between the six scenes. Maryam is being performed in several cities simultaneously. The dramaturgy is affected by your position in the city. At the end of the play a question is posed. Your answer will become a star on a mutual firmament.

Prologue

Maryam

My university is the square, the street and the vantage point of the brick wall. Here I draw my ideas before the infinity's firmament and etch my longing into the sphere.

Maryam's father

The father counts the stars around the Great Bear. Dubhe, Megrez, Alkoth, Mizar, Alkaid, Dubhe, Megrez, Alkoth, Mizar, Alkaid.

The Choir

The calling voices of the choir mix with the sounds of the square.

I dream of my land in liberty, I dream of having a child, I dream of learning to read and write, I dream of marrying whomever I want, I dream of speaking freely.

Maryam

Arabs, Persians, Muslims, Christians and Jews gather here to share prayer under the heavens. The university of life is here, where I follow the changes happening over time. I am an artisan carving scripture into the gleaming brass, turning results into practice. I am an artist shaping a piece of jewellery, irresistible and nigh inseparable from our cosmos.

In my dreams I burst the shut gates of The House of Wisdom. In my dreams I roll out the great maps of the celestial bodies and press them to my chest. In my dreams I follow the wandering of the sun and the moon and let my hair fall freely over the steps of stone.

Scene 1 Along the wall

Maryam

The Great Mosque throws cool merciful shade where I stand. Far ahead I see you. You are heading in to the scholars with my sketches under your arm.

Maraym's father

I do not just wish to give you the opportunity to interpret time, to calculate your position on the surface of the earth, to understand the beginning and the end of the day.

Maryam

Surreptitiously my fingers move over the instrument, I want to roll around on the star map and like the star cursor I want to aim for the heavens.

Maryam's father

Child, I would show you how closely your soul is to the firmament.

Maryam

You pause for breath on the steep hill, your body is ageing now but you are reluctant to admit it. You do not know I followed you here, you do not know I plan to go further, you do not understand why I so wish to share my knowledge beyond the already initiated, I long out, I long to, I want to be less alone.

FURTHER READING

Evans Hyle, A. (Ed.), *Dissecting the Mundane: International Perspectives on Memory-work.* Lanham, MD: University Press of America. 2008.

Frieling, R. (Ed.), *The Art of Participation: 1950 to Now.* San Francisco, CA: Museum of Modern Art. 2008.

Metzger, J. Konstnärliga rum i samhällsplaneringens processer [Artful spaces in the processes of spatial development]. Ann Magnusson (Ed.), *Att dela ett samhälle.* Stockholm: Konstfrämjandet. 2010.

Stimson, B. and Sholette, G. (Eds.), *Collectivism after Modernism: The Art of Social Imagination after 1945.* Minneapolis, MN: University of Minnesota Press. 2007.

4

Plural Democracy

This chapter has its basis in so-called cultural theory which criticises many other ideas, including many of those put forward elsewhere in this book. It elaborates upon alternatives to these ideas and emphasises the concept of a plural rationality approach instead of methods based on single metrics, such as cost/benefit analysis, general equilibrium modelling, probabilistic risk assessment and, in particular, approaches that assume that uncertainty is merely the absence of certainty.

CLUMSINESS BY DESIGN

About 14 years ago, Arsenal Football Club decided they really would have to do something about their Highbury stadium. It only held 30,000 spectators and they needed double that. Also, the pitch was slightly undersized and this detracted from their status as one of the premier clubs in the world. Thus it was that Arsenal (I'll call it the market actor) sidled up to Islington Borough Council (I'll call it the hierarchical actor) with the suggestion that the council give the go-ahead – 'outline planning permission' – for Arsenal to acquire, and demolish, the two streets of houses immediately adjacent to its stadium, thereby enabling it to expand its capacity to 60,000, along with a full-sized pitch.

Most of social science (especially in relation to public policy and urban governance) assumes that is it: if it is not the market it is the hierarchy, and vice versa (as, for instance, with financial sector firms and financial regulators, or Margaret Thatcher's attempt to create an 'enterprise culture' by laying into the unions, the professions and other bastions of privilege and restrictive practices).[1] But it isn't! Within less than twenty-four hours of Arsenal's approach to Islington Council becoming public knowledge, a third actor emerged: the Highbury Community Association. Its members

This chapter is based on Thompson, M. *Coping with Change: Urban Resilience, Sustainability, Adaptability and Path Dependence.* UK Government Foresight Future of Cities Project. 2015.

were implacably opposed to the solution Arsenal was proposing: the only solution, Arsenal insisted, playing what it thought was its trump card, if the club was to remain in the borough.

So this third actor – I'll call it the *egalitarian actor* (its arguments being largely couched in terms of the unfair treatment of residents, small local businesses, the unemployed and so on) – really put the cat among the pigeons. An enormous controversy blew up, a petition with thousands of signatures was delivered to Islington Town Hall, and there was a vigorous television debate (chaired, very well, by the former government minister, Ann Widdecombe). It soon became clear, trump card or not, that there was no way Arsenal was going to get permission to expand on its Highbury site. Various alternatives were then proposed – one of which was to re-locate to a vast regeneration project, just a couple of miles away, around King's Cross and St. Pancras stations – but none proved to be feasible. So it began to look as though Arsenal had indeed been right and that the club, to the dismay of both the council and its loyal supporters, would indeed have to move right out of the borough: all the way out to near the M25 orbital motorway.

But then two commercial property surveyors, who also happened to be fanatical Arsenal supporters, got out their maps. To everyone's surprise (including theirs) they found a triangular piece of rather low-rent and under-used land, bounded on two sides by busy railway lines, that would comfortably take a 60,000-seat stadium. Even more amazingly, as well as being already owned by the council, it was less than half-a-mile away from the old stadium and its hallowed (but under-sized) turf! Cutting a long story short, in August 2006 – just four years later, on-time and on-budget – Arsenal moved into its new stadium: onto this near-ideal site, the very existence of which had remained entirely unnoticed until the three-cornered battle – the market actor, the hierarchical actor and the egalitarian actor – had been joined.

So this is a nice example of what is now called (with tongue in cheek) a *clumsy solution*: a solution that, in contrast to the familiar *elegant solutions*, emerges only in those situations where each of these three kinds of actor is (a) able to make itself heard (*accessibility*) and (b) then responsive to, rather than dismissive of, the others (*responsiveness*). Things, we can now see, started off over-elegant (just Arsenal and Islington Council); they only became clumsified when the third actor – the Highbury Community Association – managed to force its way in.

Moreover, in a clumsy solution – and this is the counter-intuitive bit – each actor ends up with more of what it wants (and less of

[1] Her mistake, in line with social science orthodoxy, was to assume that if people were knocked out of hierarchy they would end up in individualism (markets). But of course, and as we will see, there are two other possible destinations: egalitarianism and fatalism.

what it doesn't want) than it would have got if it had somehow managed to achieve 'hegemony' and impose its distinctive (and elegant) solution.

- *Arsenal* (the market actor) has got its state-of-the-art stadium (and a handsome price for its old stadium, which has now been re-developed, mostly for housing).
- *Islington Council* (the hierarchical actor) has kept the club in the borough (and extracted a colossal 'planning gain': thousands of new houses, a futuristic waste-transfer and re-cycling centre, some badly-needed public open space and so on).
- *The Highbury Community Association* (the egalitarian actor) has saved the streets and houses around the old stadium, and forced the council to ensure that those businesses displaced by the new stadium were re-located within the borough, and without any loss of jobs. Of course, they are still critical, especially over the failure to build a new tube station within the stadium (the Piccadilly Line passes directly beneath it) but they do have the satisfaction of knowing that the new stadium is the greenest in the world!
- Even the disregarded *fatalist actors* – the 'cannon fodder' supporters who find their way on foot, stopping off at their favoured pubs and chip shops – have done quite well. Reaching the new stadium is still feasible, whilst they could never have made it to an out-of-the-borough venue.

So the argument, in a nutshell, is that we need to ensure that every decision – every essay at environmental governance – mimics what happened with Arsenal's new stadium. In that case, of course, the clumsy solution came about *by accident*: the rude intrusion of the initially excluded egalitarian actor turning out to be so constructive. The challenge is to get it to happen, every time, *by design*!

But why, it might be objected, if it is as easy as this, do we not see clumsy solutions all over the place? The answer is that the two necessary conditions – accessibility and responsiveness – are not easily achieved. Indeed, the four time-honored precepts of policy analysis – (1) insist on a single agreed definition of the problem, (2) clearly distinguish between facts and values, (3) set up a 'single metric' (pounds, lives saved, etc.) so as to be able to compare and evaluate options, and (4) optimise around the best option – together ensure the silencing of all but one actor. So, if we want to find our way to clumsy solutions, we will have to insert the words 'do not' in each of those precepts. And that, outrageous though it may appear, is what is being proposed.[2]

[2] These four actors, I should stress, have not been plucked out of thin air; they emanate from forms of social solidarity. Since two of these – hierarchy and individualism – correspond to the familiar 'hierarchies-and-markets' framing, plural rationality's novelty lies in its addition of the other two – egalitarianism and fatalism – and in the making explicit of the different 'social constructions of reality' that render each of these four solidarities rational and justifiable.

THE PLURAL RATIONALITY FRAMING: WICKED PROBLEMS, UNCOMFORTABLE KNOWLEDGE, CLUMSY SOLUTIONS

With *wicked problems* (climate change is currently the prime example), and in marked contrast to *tame problems* (the hole in the ozone layer, for instance, to which climate change is often, and erroneously, compared), there are contending and mutually contradictory definitions of the problem-and-solution, and these do not converge as the policy process gets under way. If they are treated as tame problems then the assumption of a single definition imposes elegance, but at a cost: the exclusion of those actors who subscribe to the other definitions. The valid and useful knowledge generated by these excluded actors, since it inevitably calls into question the knowledge that is generated by the 'hegemonic' actor, is then seen as *uncomfortable* and is ignored or marginalised (for instance, by labelling it 'voodoo science'). If that is to be avoided then things will have to be arranged institutionally so that each of the 'voices' is able to make itself heard and is then responsive to, rather than disdainful of, the others. Only then will we see the emergence, as happened with Arsenal's new stadium, of those more robust, consent-preserving, surprise-lessening and inherently democratic outcomes: clumsy solutions (see Box 1. The framing's origins and underpinnings).

Another way of casting this framing is by way of the distinction between the well-known methods of DMUU (Decision Making Under Uncertainty) and the as yet largely unacknowledged DMUCC (Decision Making Under Contradictory Certainties). In the former, uncertainty is simply the absence of certainty (and its methods proved most effective in dealing, via the Montreal Protocol, with the hole in ozone layer); in the latter, there are different 'social constructions' of the problem that are mutually irreducible and mutually sustaining (those, like Kofi Annan and Nicholas Stern, who see climate change as a massive instance of market failure, have no common ground with those, like the members of the uncompromising environmental group Earth First!, who pin the blame on the capitalist system itself. However, these contradictory certainties do not require that water flows uphill, or that the laws of thermodynamics be re-written; they are all (usually) contained within the wide uncertainty that typically accompanies wicked problems.

So we need methods that are very different from those that have been developed in terms of those afore-mentioned precepts of policy analysis. Those familiar tools – tools that the plural rationality approach suggests should be discarded – are all based on single metrics: cost/benefit analysis, for instance, general

Box 1. The framing's origins and underpinnings.

Wicked problems were first delineated more than 40 years ago. They have several inter-related characteristics and, as a result of these characteristics, people typically clash over how to *define* them and over how to *resolve* them:

- The range of possible causes is large and uncertain (as are the possible interactions of those causes).
- The range of possible solutions is equally large and uncertain.
- Every solution is a 'one-shot operation' and will have serious consequences (there are, in other words, considerable 'sunk costs', and this means that a decision – to build a super-sewer, say, or a high-speed rail link – cannot easily be backed out of if things do not go quite as expected).
- Many people, organisations and social domains are involved.
- Wicked problems are essentially unique and novel.
- They have no 'stopping rule' (every attempt at resolution leads to new problems).
- There are no absolutely right solutions.

In his book *Clumsy Solutions for a Wicked World* Marco Verweij checks climate change and the ozone hole against these seven characteristics, thereby confirming that the former is a wicked problem and the latter a tame one. That is the copper-bottomed test for this crucial distinction; usually the existence of plural and mutually incompatible definitions of problem and solution, together with their non-convergence as the policy process gets under way, suffices.

Uncomfortable knowledge: The well-known academic response 'New not true; true not new' nicely captures the way in which the members of a scientific establishment tend to deal with knowledge that threatens the paradigm around which they are stabilised. The philosopher of science, Imré Lakatos, in his book *Proofs and Refutations*, showed that 'monsters' – pieces of knowledge that cannot be accommodated within the prevailing paradigm – can occur even in mathematics, and he went on to tease out the various ways in which this sort of uncomfortable knowledge can be handled: by *monster-adjusting*, for instance (in which both the paradigm and the offending piece of knowledge are progressively modified until a fit, of sorts, is achieved) or by *monster-barring* (in which the offending knowledge, and its carriers, are rejected out of hand, as happened with the first attempts to publish Ohm's law: 'these preposterous theories of Professor Ohm' was the response, and Ohm lost his university position). An example (as I have just mentioned) is the response, back in 2010, by the then head of the IPCC (the Intergovernmental Panel on Climate Change), Rajendra Pachauri, to the glaciologists who helpfully pointed out that a

recent IPCC report had made a serious mistake in its predictions about the rate at which Himalayan glaciers are retreating. He called them 'voodoo scientists' (others have even found themselves stigmatised as 'climate change deniers').

Quite independently of Lakatos, the anthropologist Mary Douglas, in her book *Natural Symbols*, also homed-in on monsters: in her case these were animals – such as the pangolin, among her people, the Lele in the former Belgian Congo – that simply could not be fitted into the indigenous typology. A few years later David Bloor, a philosopher, in a celebrated article 'Polyhedra and the abominations of Leviticus', synthesised these approaches, thereby establishing a thorough-going theory of uncomfortable knowledge. The books [*Proofs and Refutations and Natural Symbols*] have a common theme: they deal with the ways men respond to things which do not fit into the boxes and boundaries of accepted ways of thinking; they are about anomalies to publicly-accepted schemes of classification. Whether it be a counter-example to a proof; an animal that does not fit into the local taxonomy; or a deviant who violates the current moral norms, the same range of reactions is generated.

Clumsy solutions originated, back in 1988, with Michael Shapiro, a lawyer at the University of Southern California. To be precise, he used the term 'clumsy institution' so as to stress the good sense inherent in the seemingly messy way in which new members of the US Supreme Court are chosen. It is a way of escaping from the commonsensical prescription (enshrined, as we have seen, in those four precepts of policy analysis) that, when faced with contradictory definitions of problem-and-solution, we must choose one and reject the rest. The idea was subsequently picked up by a number of anthropologists and policy analysts and the term clumsy institution is now used to characterise the sort of 'policy sub-system' in which those who speak with the four voices – the three we have encountered in the Arsenal story plus the somewhat muted fatalist voice – that are predicted by the theory of plural rationality (also called cultural theory) all enjoy both accessibility and responsiveness. Clumsy institution is thus the polar opposite of what Robert Dahl in his *theory of pluralist democracy*, called 'closed hegemony': the hyper-elegant situation in which just one voice drowns out the others. But, where Dahl had just his dualistic distinction – closed hegemony versus pluralist democracy – our typology of four voices gives us four distinct varieties of closed hegemony. It also enables us to recognise the fourteen different kinds of policy sub-system that populate the 'excluded middle' between Dahl's two extremes. And, for good measure, this refurbishment of the classic theory of pluralist democracy makes clear that it is *discourse* – contending voices, narratives, storylines and so on – that is key.

equilibrium modelling, probabilistic risk assessment, and all those approaches that assume that uncertainty is merely the absence of certainty.

Instead, we need methods that, by zeroing-in on policy discourses (and on the contradictory certainties that they embody), can tell us which voices enjoy accessibility and responsiveness and which ones, like Sherlock Holmes' dog that did not bark, are missing. In other words, it all comes down to *democracy* (see Box 2. Three contending models of democracy) and this means that the methods we need are all going to be methods for getting things to happen more democratically. The four by four typology of policy sub-systems, to give just one example, is now up-and-running, as a device for shifting *corporate governance* away from closed hegemony and towards clumsy solution, in a number of insurance companies. One perhaps disconcerting implication of this is that all those familiar single metric methods are actually working in the opposite (i.e. closed hegemony-ensuring) direction; they are inherently *un*democratic. So what, in addition to the four by four typology, are the tools that make up 'the new policy tool-kit'?

THE NEW POLICY TOOL-KIT

The old tool-kit, as has already been argued, is fine for tame problems, and this means that we must first ascertain (by applying those seven characteristics that are set out in Box 1) that the problem we are addressing is a wicked one (and most problems, these days, are).[5] In a first attempt at pulling together this new tool-kit, almost twenty years ago, there were just eight tools, arranged into three compartments: *reflexivity aids*, *scenario planning* and *macro and micro: each as the cause of the other.* Since then, there have been at least four more: a case study method capable of circumventing those two great drawbacks: valid comparability and a 'small n', the afore-mentioned four by four typology and, most recently, a deliberative participatory process in which the public and the experts co-produce clumsy solutions and a set of methods – MFA (Material Flow Analysis), MSA (Multi-sector Systems Analysis) and eight indicators of technological inflexibility – for the re-engineering of city infrastructure. There is not the space here to lay out those various tools in any detail, but I can conclude by quickly running through the tool-kit's three compartments so as to give a feel for what is entailed in this 'democratic turn' in relation to policy and governance.

REFLEXIVITY AIDS

If we are to avoid elegance and embrace clumsiness we will have to find some way of resisting the almost irresistible urge to pronounce

[3] Coined in the 1980s, by Bernard Levin: a British journalist justly renowned for his regular political column.

[4] There is, of course, a fourth model – a 'non-model' really – that justifies the resignation of those who constitute the fatalist solidarity. 'It doesn't matter who you vote for', they reassure one another, 'the government always gets in'. Since constant vigilance is unlikely to emanate from this quadrant, a high level of fatalism will increase the probability of things drifting out of the feasibility space. Hence the valid concern when a high level of apathy results in a low electoral turn-out.

[5] This is in part a consequence of what is called 'the differentiated polity'. In addition, tame problems, being soluble, tend to disappear, while wicked problems, being solution-resistant, persist.

Box 2. Three contending models of democracy.

Different models (or images) of democracy have long been familiar to political scientists, most of whom have thrown their scholarly weight behind one or other of them. More recently, there has been a growing awareness that there is nothing fruitful about this struggle to decide which model is the right model, and that the fruitfulness is in the struggle itself. In other words, the essence of democracy is in its contestation: a nice insight that simultaneously explains 'Levin's Law' (which states that any country with the word 'democratic' in its title is not)[3] and the non-convergence of countries that are undoubtedly democratic (Britain, for instance, bending rather more towards the guardian model than the United States, Switzerland more towards the participatory model and so on). Not, I hasten add, that other desiderata – universal adult suffrage, a free press, governments dutifully leaving office when they lose an election and so on – are irrelevant. The argument, rather, is that those indicators of democratic health would soon disappear if one model of democracy were to win out over the others.

This triangular scheme helps clarify the normative claim that it is always desirable to open up the plurality: always better, that is, to move things away from closed hegemony and towards clumsy institution. Surely, it can be objected, it is desirable – indeed essential if democracy is to survive – that

plurality be closed down. Terrorists, fundamentalist groups, parties (such as the Nazis in Weimar Germany) who say 'Vote for us and we will get rid of the other 27 parties' and so on, if not closed down, might well destroy democracy. Such groups are often minorities, but what is particularly interesting is the way in which these triangular dynamics can even close down a democracy-threatening majority. Take, for instance, the situation – crude majoritarianism, as it is called – in which 51% of the electorate think it would be a spiffing idea to get rid of the other 49%, and run it round the three models below. You will find that it is supported by none. Upholders of all three models, despite their irreconcilable differences, can therefore all agree that, in situations such as this, things should be closed down, not opened up. Hence all the talk about constant vigilance being the price of freedom, good men having only to stand idly by for evil to triumph and so on.[4]

The three contending models, we can now see, set up a 'feasibility space' for democracy. Within that triangular space, the plurality should be opened up: all three models need to be evident and argumentatively engaged with one another (otherwise the feasibility space itself will shrink). But that triangular engagement can also readily identify groups that are hell-bent on moving the totality out of the feasibility space, and can then work to close down that sort of plurality.

HIERARCHY
The Guardian Model

Sides with Plato and his 'philosopher-king'. Only right that those with superior insight and virtue should make the decisions. Democracy should be indirect, representative and majoritarian, the political class being given primacy over public affairs on the basis of popular elections every few years. This elite should act as 'trustees' (Burke) focusing on the long-term general interest, not short-term individual or factional claims and interests. Loyalty and complaisance are the crucial virtues.

INDIVIDUALISM
The Protective Model

Self-determination is crucial. Paternalism is therefore anathema and plebiscitary processes attractive at first glance. But such processes tend to crude majoritarianism, which can result in even large minorities being denied self-determination. Hence need for measures to protect individual and minority rights and interests. Government's raison d'etre is 'the protection of individual rights, life, liberty and estate' (Locke).

EGALITARIANISM
The Participatory Model

No place here for deference and no support for indirect or majoritarian modes of decision making. Choice must be by direct and broad participation. Decisions should be agreed by all, ideally in a small-scale face-to-face way and at a single level: the grassroots. Leadership is resisted and equally prized. The equal right to self-development is the overriding principle.

one social construction – one certainty – true and reject the others (which, of course, is what the first precept – ensure a single and agreed definition of the problem – does). Reflexivity – the self-conscious examination of the assumptions that underlie any analytical approach – is the modish word for this difficult feat in which we bend over backwards to avoid doing something that is virtually a precondition for conventional science-for-public-policy. Fortunately, there are many sets of predictions from the theory of plural rationality – around sixty at the last count – and some of these are particularly helpful in clarifying the assumptions behind that which we find credible, and in pin-pointing the various assumptions that lie behind other positions that we find incredible.

- *Myths of nature*. For upholders of individualism, nature is *benign* and can be counted on to bounce back from any insult: a mean-reverting world that can be depicted as a ball in a basin (as in 'if something is unsustainable it will stop'). With the egalitarian solidarity we have almost the exact opposite – a ball perched precariously on an upturned basin. This is an *ephemeral* world in which the smallest jolt may cause catastrophic collapse (as in Earth First!'s warning that we are currently heading towards a future composed of just 'cockroaches and Norway rats'). With hierarchy, we have a world that is *perverse/tolerant* – stable within limits: a ball nestled in a trough between two peaks (as in notions such as 'safe limits', 'assimilative capacity', 'dangerous climate change', 'a safe operating space for mankind' and so on). In these three worlds learning is possible: individualist actors quickly come to rely on trial-and-error, egalitarian ones soon realise they need to tread lightly on the earth, and hierarchical ones are led to trust their certified experts to determine just where the limits are located (and then to enact statutory regulations to ensure that everyone stays within them). But, in the fatalist's *capricious* world – a ball on a flat surface – learning is simply not possible: push the ball this way and that and the feedback is everywhere the same ('Why bother?' is the rational response here). 'Sustainable development', we can now see, is far from a neutral goal that we can all sign up to. Indeed, it really only makes sense in terms of the hierarchical *myth*: development that lies in the trough between the two peaks will be sustainable; development that lies beyond those limits will be unsustainable. But if there are no limits, as in the individualist myth, *all* development is sustainable. And if there are no safe limits, as in the egalitarian myth, then *no* development is sustainable. In other words, sustainable development is an 'essentially contested concept' and needs to be treated as such. There are numerous applications of this reflexibility aid, most notably in relation to climate change.

- *Models of consent* is another useful reflexivity aid. Egalitarian actors insist on *direct consent*: a decision is justifiable only if everyone concerned accedes to that specific decision. They therefore favour the method of *expressed preferences*. Individualist actors, however, keenly aware of trade-offs, opportunity costs, fungibility and so on, will readily go along with the proposition that existing consent in one area (smoking, say) be taken as justification for a choice in some other area (nuclear power, for instance). This is indirect consent: a model that can be made operational by the method of *revealed preferences*. In *hypothetical consent* – the hierarchical model – the individual and his or her preferences (whether expressed or revealed) disappear and are replaced by an idealisation: a 'reasonable man', for instance, or some supposedly natural standard, such as the level of background radiation. And, finally, there is *non-consent*: the model that fits the fatalistic solidarity: a setting in which the hierarchical ideals cannot be realised and in which preferences are neither expressible (egalitarianism) nor transitive (individualism). This translates into a method (if you can call it that) that I once heard enunciated by a senior French civil servant: 'You don't consult the frogs when you decide to drain the marsh'.

- A related reflexivity aid is the typology of *ideas of fairness*: related because people are unlikely to consent to something that they perceive to be unfair. This is a somewhat complicated typology because each solidarity generates (and is sustained by) two kinds of fairness: outcome fairness and procedural fairness. Put simply, however, individualistic actors see it as only right that (as in the joint stock company) those who put most in should get most out, hierarchical actors favour distribution by rank-and-station, and egalitarian actors reject both these ideas because of the inequalities that they either create or perpetuate. Egalitarian actors are 'levellers': people they insist should start off equal and end up equal. Absolute *parity* – before, during and after – is their idea of fairness, whilst their individualist counterparts opt for *proportionality* and their hierarchical ones for precedence. Fatalistic actors, for their part, find all these rival ideas of fairness irrelevant. 'Not in this world' is their verdict on distributional justice: *potluck*, you might say.

Each of these typologies is capturing a part of what is called the *contested terrain* and, when added together (along with several others: the discount rates, for instance), they generate *the two-dimensional map of institutional discourse and human values*: a tool that has now been widely applied, especially to climate change. This map, in alerting us to our unquestioned assumptions, and in encouraging us to ensure that we do not ride roughshod over the other sets of assumptions that it also reveals to us, then points us in the policy direction – clumsiness – that is ruled out by those orthodox precepts of policy analysis. Towards policies, that is, that in harnessing the wisdom and experience that are captured by each of the contending positions, husband consent, avoid avoidable surprises and provide us with a learning system that draws on all four of the ways of knowing that our solidarities make possible.

SCENARIO PLANNING

Scenarios, in scenario planning, are little stories: colourful, and often rather alarming, fleshing-outs of different 'visions of the future'. The aim is to preserve and enrich the plurality that is inherent in the various contradictory certainties so that different policy options can be tried out against them. Those that are marvellously successful in one future, but disastrous in the others, can then be assessed against those that exhibit a certain robustness across them all. Scenario planning does not tell you which policy you should choose but it does lead you, in a simple and instructive way, through the risks that exist within the *irreducible ignorance* that is so poorly handled by the conventional uncertainty-as-a-merely-the-absence-of-certainty approach.

Scenario planning, as originally practiced, relied for its plurality on the practical skills of the consultants, sometimes with results that were none too satisfactory. The Anglo-Dutch multinational Shell, for instance, has long relied on scenario planning and yet it found itself in an unanticipated mess over its attempt to dispose of its Brent Spar oil storage structure (after Greenpeace daringly and very publicly landed a helicopter on it as it was being towed out to its planned final resting-place in the Atlantic) and, some years later, in an even worse (and still continuing) mess with its oil extraction operations in the Niger Delta. However, an analysis of Shell's published scenarios reveals that they are all either individualist or hierarchical. Just one egalitarian scenario would have alerted Shell to the presence in its environment (be it the Atlantic or West Africa) of a social construction that, for fairly obvious organisational reasons, was absent from its own decision making levels. There are two tools that can help remedy those sorts of inadequacies.

- *Typology-Based Scenario Planning.* The plural rationality typology can ensure that the scenarios (as well as avoiding duplication) encompass the 'requisite variety'. One complete set of scenarios has been generated in this way. It took six people just one day to do it, and it is immediately usable. For instance, it quickly reveals that the 'liberation of the environment' thesis is perfectly plausible under the individualist scenario. Indeed, Ausubel himself concedes that his prescription – putting our faith in 'human culture'[6] – will pan out like this only if 'development has succeeded and peace holds': conditions that obtain only in the individualist scenario. Try out the same prescription in relation to the egalitarian and hierarchical scenarios and the results are far less reassuring!

- *The Perspectives Approach in Integrated Assessment Modelling.* Sailors are familiar with the idea of taking a particular vessel and then rigging it in different ways, and much the same can be done with models (or, at any rate, with some models). We can rig a model, drawing on our 'two-dimensional map of institutional discourses and human values', so that it is fairly consistent with the egalitarian convictions as to how the world is, and then we can re-rig it so that it is fairly consistent with the hierarchical convictions, and so on. This, in essence, is what certain integrated assessment modellers have been doing: letting policy actors try out their variously preferred solutions against a small fleet of differently rigged models. You could not do this without first building the models, but the models themselves are no longer the aim of the exercise: just hulls that can be rigged, this way or that, and then launched across a number of remarkably different oceans. In this way, the perspectives approach, by incorporating the insights from plural rationality, becomes a model-based form of scenario planning.

MICRO AND MACRO, EACH AS THE CAUSE OF THE OTHER

Where conventional social theory starts from an assumed dualism – the individual and the society – plural rationality's focus is on the various forms of solidarity. The individual, this theory insists, is *inherently relational*: individuality, far from being something that is inherent to each of us (like our fingerprints) is something that, to a large extent, we get from our involvement with others. There is, therefore, no need to make the time-honoured distinction between micro and macro. Indeed, there is a need not to, because to do that would be to slice right through the forms of solidarity that lace the whole caboodle together.

[6] The argument is that science and technology are our culture's most powerful tools, and that they increasingly de-couple our goods and services from demands on planetary resources.

Most policy analysis (and modelling) focuses on the large-scale political and economic institutions: the markets in coal, oil, foodstuffs and so on, and the governments and regulatory agencies that strive to maintain some sort of overall framework within which those markets must function. But it is very small actors – households – that actually consume the petrol, the electricity, the fish-fingers and the mung beans, and if all these tiny acts of consumption were not happening then the gigantic actors would soon cease to exist (the beef industry in Britain, in the wake of 'mad cow disease' came close to this). Nor, if households are heterogeneous (as plural rationality theory predicts they will be), is it valid to handle this micro-level in terms of the homogenising notion of *per capita consumption* (which, if you pause to think about it, is just one macro-number – national consumption divided by another macro-number – national population).

In other words, we need to see consumption as a 'moral activity', with each solidarity shaping its distinctive *household consumption* style. These styles translate into very different purchasing preferences: egalitarian households going for the mung beans, hierarchical ones favouring 'traditional' products, individualist ones concerned that they be seen as successful, and so on. And, as they consume in these different ways, they cause a corresponding heterogeneity within the markets that make those styles possible. For instance, 'up there' we see the interactions (over the Brent Spar) of Shell, the UK Government and Greenpeace closing down certain paths of technological development and opening up new ones; 'down here' we see the upholders of egalitarianism causing their individualist counterparts to delete fur coats from their list of status symbols (and their hierarchical counterparts to ease up on the *fois gras* if they are British, and on the ortolans if they are French). And it was the increasing concern, among egalitarian households 'down here', that products should have 'zero environmental impact' that stimulated Unilever 'up there' to develop its new (and highly profitable) Dove range of toiletries. But all these crucial dynamics – dynamics, moreover, that have profound and highly constructive implications for policy concerns such as climate change – are entirely beyond the ken of those who assume homogeneity and who opt for the micro-macro dualism. Fortunately, there are some policy tools that can extricate us from this seriously blinkered state.

- *Political Cultural Methods.* A reflexive policy maker – a policy maker, that is, who is eager to take account of the heterogeneity – will be less interested in the economic efficiency of the available options (i.e. with conventional policy analysis) and more and more interested in the levels of consent they are likely to command (i.e. with the design of clumsy solutions). She would therefore like to know something of the relative strengths of the solidarities within the population on whose behalf she is, after all, assessing and choosing between those options. She would also like to know something of how those relative strengths are changing: which solidarities are on the way down and which are on the way up? On top of that, she would like to be forewarned of any mismatches in the patterns of allegiance as between elite and lay publics (topical examples, in Europe, are the preferences of various experts on biotechnology and nanotechnology, which seem not to line up too well with the hopes and fears of ordinary citizens). A number of instruments for providing this vital information are already operational. They include household survey questionnaires double-blinded with informal guided interviews, methods for re-analysing in plural rationality terms 'unintended data' – existing surveys that are designed on other theoretical bases, questionnaires on ideas of nature, survey and focus group methods for exploring risk perceptions and structured interviews for eliciting ideas of fairness. To these can now be added fuzzy cognitive mapping methods, questionnaires that also tap into the patterns of social relationships and, most recently, the afore-mentioned participatory process for the co-production by experts and citizens of clumsy solutions.

- *Agent Based Modelling.* Where conventional policy analysis, as we have seen, requires there to be a single and agreed definition of what the problem is, a plurality of problem definitions is a prerequisite for agent-based modelling. Nor does the agent-based modeller have to write any equations or solve them for equilibrium conditions: essential features of the kind of 'top-down' modelling that is commonly relied on in policy work. All he has to do is find some plausible strategies, specify some simple 'bottom-up' rules by which the 'automata' (households, farms, firms, investors or whatever) can latch onto those strategies (thereby becoming 'agents'; hence 'agent-based modelling') and then put the whole lot into a computer simulation and let them get on with it: evolve. Then, after a few hundred 'generations', you look to see whether any whole-system behaviour has emerged. This, clearly, is something to which the plural rationality approach can readily lend itself: the plurality is there (in the forms of solidarity), the strategies are there (in, for instance, the household consumption styles and their moral underpinnings) and the various irreversibilities (costs sunk into one management style – 'big is best', say – rather than some other – 'small is beautiful', say) are there.[7] Such models are not predictive, but they do capture, in a useful way, the sort of dynamic interactions by which micro and macro are each the cause of the other. And they have now been applied to issues as varied as lake Eutrophication.

Though it might appear that we have ended up a long way from where we started – Arsenal Football Club and its new stadium – there is a single, and essentially democratic, theme running through all the methods and applications that have been set out in this chapter. That theme is that, if we want to find our way to the best possible outcomes, we will need to ensure that our decision processes are designed in such a way that, as with Arsenal (where, of course, it happened by happy accident) each solidarity's voice is heard, and responded to, by the others.

FURTHER READING

Dahl, R. *Polyarchy: Participation and Opposition.* New Haven, CT: Yale University Press. 1971.

Douglas, M. *Natural Symbols: Explorations in Cosmology.* London: Cresset Press. 1970.

Hofstetter, P. *Perspectives in Life Cycle Impact Assessment.* Dordrecht: Kluwer Academic Publishers. 1998.

Ingram, D., Taylor, P. and Thompson, M. Surprise, Surprise: From Neoclassical Economics to Elife. *ASTIN Bulletin (Journal of the International Actuarial Association).* 42(2), pp. 389–412. 2012.

Lakatos, I. *Proofs and Refutations: The Logic of Mathematical Discovery.* Cambridge: Cambridge University Press. 1976.

Ney, S. *Resolving Messy Policy Issues.* London: Earthscan. 2000.

Schwarz, M. and Thompson, M. *Divided We Stand.* Philadelphia, PA: University of Pennsylvania Press. 1990.

Schwartz, P. *The Art of the Long View.* London: Doubleday Currency. 1991.

Thompson, M. Decision Making under Contradictory Certainties: How to Save the Himalayas When you Can't Find out What's Wrong with Them. *Applied Systems Analysis.* 12, pp. 3–34. 1985.

Thompson, M., Ellis, R. and Wildavsky, A. *Cultural Theory.* Boulder, CO: Westview. 1990.

Verweij, M. *Clumsy Solutions for a Wicked World.* Basingstoke: Palgrave Macmillan. 2011.

Young, H.P. *Equity in Theory and Practice.* Princeton, NJ: Princeton University Press. 1993.

---

[7] Without irreversibilities the system will not evolve. So the plural rationality approach comes out of a very different stable – we can call it institutional evolutionary economics – from the one conventional policy analysis comes out of: neoclassical economics.

ELICITATION

The fact that people often have difficulty making decisions has been noted in a wide range of areas. It is obvious that the cognitive limitations of the human mind make it difficult to process the large amounts of complex information intrinsic in many decision making situations, and that unguided decision making easily ends up as something very sub-optimal. During the last few decades, the field of decision analysis has developed as a structured approach to analyse decision situations formally, based on research within disciplines including psychology, mathematics, statistics, and computer science.

At the same time, quantitative decision making has moved from the study of decision theory founded on a single criterion towards decision support for more realistic decision making situations with multiple, often conflicting, criteria. When such decision analysis applications are used to aid prescriptive decision making processes, additional demands are put on these applications to adapt to the users and the context, where the issue of elicitation is already crucial. This is a really demanding cognitively task, subject to different ambiguities and biases, and the values elicited can consequently be heavily dependent on the particular method of assessment.

A number of methods for assessing and weighing criteria have been suggested, but there are still no generally accepted methods available and the process of eliciting adequate quantitative information from people is still one of the major challenges facing research and applications within the field of decision analysis. In order to study and analyse suggested elicitation methods more explicitly, they can be categorised into the following.

- *Extraction*: dealing with how information (probabilities, utilities, weights) is derived through user input.
- *Representation*: dealing with how to capture the retrieved information in a structure, i.e. the format used to represent the user input.
- *Interpretation*: dealing with the expressive power of the representation used and how to assign meaning to the captured information in the evaluation of the decision model used.

Independent of this, it is still the case that elicitation methods in decision analysis are often demanding and require too much precision, and too much time and effort. Some of the issues may be remedied by connecting elicitation methods to an inference engine that facilitates a quick and easy method for decision-makers to use weaker input statements, while being able to utilise these statements in a method for decision evaluation. More specifically, within the realm of e-governance the development has moved towards testing new means for democratic decision making: e-panels, electronic discussion forums and polls. Although more formalised process models might offer promising potential when it comes to structuring and supporting the transparency of decision processes in order to facilitate the integration of the public into decision making procedures in a reasonable and manageable way, it should be realised that the method is very complicated, particularly when it comes to incorporating citizens' input into the decision process. Being content with only enabling more participation will definitely not result in enhanced democracy by itself, and an adequate mechanism for participation exercises is vital, regardless of the democracy model. What's more, such methods are to a large extent locked into traditional ways of using computer-based texts and images that often hamper clear communication.

In the next few chapters, we discuss these issues with a focus on elicitation processes for public decision making as a background for later providing tools for citizens to organise discussion and create opinions; enabling governments, authorities and institutions to analyse these opinions better as well as to account for this information in planning and societal decision making. The criteria weight elicitation is of utmost importance since this has to be carried out by having the user express subjective preferences, and several techniques for deriving criteria weights from preference statements have been proposed. *Chapter 5* is a comparative study of criteria weight elicitation providing a thorough survey of prevailing techniques for elicitation of criteria weights in multi-criteria decisions.

Chapter 6 then suggests an integrated framework for public decision making, trying to remedy some of the problems that were highlighted in *Chapter 5*. It also covers some more general aspects regarding elicitation in public settings, as well as some of the technical issues involved. It discusses how the general ideas regarding elicitation of decision components can be useful for evaluation purposes when the information involved is numerically imprecise, which is often the case. In these situations, conflicts are both fruitful and inevitable and in *Chapter 7* we suggest and utilise a preference elicitation questionnaire where the stakeholders state negative, neutral or positive attitudes towards how different actions on the agenda perform against comprehensible objectives. We then use this in a computational framework demonstrating the intensity of conflicts and how they can be visualised.

Chapter 8 utilises elicitation techniques and methods for handling vagueness in a model and demonstrates how this can be used in practice for enabling systematic evaluations, exemplified by an evaluation strategy for contributions of ICT to development. Finally, *Chapter 9* describes how an alternative elicitation method in the form of a theatre performance can contribute to the intricate elicitation, modelling and development of e-democracy. The performance shows how such interaction can be organised and also highlights the conditions under which the interaction can become successful.

5

Criteria Weight Elicitation – A Comparative Study

Although many decision analysis methods have been proposed, few of them have been widely used in actual practice. However, some of the proposed methods and approaches have been employed more than others. A reason for this is that when decision analysis methods are actually applied additional demands are put on these methods with respect to how they can be adapted to the user's practices and the context at hand. When it comes to decisions with multiple criteria, *weight elicitation* is of utmost importance since this has to be carried out by the user expressing subjective preferences and several techniques for deriving criteria weights from preference statements have been proposed. Expressing preference statements in order to reveal criteria weights is a cognitively demanding task. It is typically subject to biases, and the resulting weights can be heavily dependent on the technique used.

The study of decision making has traditionally been divided into normative and descriptive disciplines. Within the *normative* discipline, the theories describe how decision-makers should make choices when considering risk, focusing on the choice activity. It is based on the notion that decision-makers systematically gather information, objectively analyse, and select alternatives consistent with the decision-makers' attitudes to risk and preferences. The rational model has been criticised with respect to its strong assumptions about human decision-makers' cognitive abilities. The *descriptive discipline* instead, where models describing how people actually do make decisions, have put emphasis on why and how people do not act in accordance with the normative ideal. This has led to the development of other models, where organisational characteristics, such as context, societal structures, and conflicts among stakeholders or hidden agendas cause decision-makers in organisations to deviate from

This chapter is based on Riabacke, M., Danielson, M. and Ekenberg, L. State-of-the-Art in Prescriptive Weight Elicitation. *Advances in Decision Sciences*. Vol. 2012. 2012.

rational choice. However, the descriptive models do not provide guidelines or complementary tools for applied decision making. Although real decision-makers do not act rationally, they might still desire decision support to assist them to make more rational choices since those are easier to defend and explain. Yet, when it comes to decision making processes, structured methods are still seldom applied in real situations, and decision-makers often act on rules of thumb, intuition, or experience instead. Over the years, research on quantitative decision making has moved from the study of decision theory founded on single criterion decision making towards decision support for more complex decision making situations with multiple, often conflicting, criteria. In particular, Multi-Criteria Decision Analysis (MCDA) has emerged as a promising discipline within decision support methods that can provide decision-makers with a better understanding of the trade-offs involved in a decision, e.g. between economic, social, and environmental aspects (criteria). Despite the number of MCDA applications having increased during recent decades, behavioural issues have not received much attention within this field of research. The identification of such problems and the call for research on behavioural issues have been recognised for a while. Moreover, current software applications provide relatively good support for decision analytical calculations but less support for the decision making process itself. Some researchers in the field suggest that this functionality is something that needs to be included in further developments of MCDA methods, and point out that, regardless of the progress made within the instrumental dimension of multiple criteria approaches, the problem of under- or non-utilisation will continue until parallel research is conducted on the socio-political context in which these MCDA methods are to be applied.

DECISION ANALYSIS

Although there have been significant developments within the decision analysis area, including different ways of utilising computers to support the analysis, decision-makers rarely perform decision analyses of complex problems in practice. Some authors say that this is because of the low level of attention given to prescriptive decision support research studying real settings. This means that the tools developed still deviate too much from the real requirements, and that the utilisation of these tools as aids in real decision making processes will not substantially increase unless we learn more about real decision making and the role of decision analysis support. Another explanation for their limited usage within businesses today is the fact that the tools and methods are too demanding or too difficult for lay persons to use. Tools consume too much time (especially first-time use) and effort. Many decision problems have a large number of possible outcomes, making the representation and elicitation of preferences and beliefs for all outcomes a time-consuming activity. But even in situations where the outcome space is manageable, there is a need for elicitation methods better adapted to the real-life circumstances of usage. Suggested techniques for elicitation are to a great extent a matter of balancing the quality of the elicitation retrieved with the time and cognitive efforts demanded from the users.

DESCRIPTIVE AND PRESCRIPTIVE MODELS

Descriptive models of choice behaviour, that is, models describing and explaining how people actually make decisions, have been proposed. It is often claimed that people make decisions not only based on how they judge the available information, but also influenced by more subconscious factors. One result from descriptive studies is the *principle of satisficing*. It says that people attempt to find an adequate solution which satisfies their needs or is sufficiently good, rather than requiring an optimal solution. People will then choose the first course of action that is satisfactory on all important attributes. This finding is attributed to Herbert Simon. Simon also coined the terms substantive and procedural rationality. Substantive rationality has to do with the rationality of a decision situation, that is, the rationality of choice. Procedural rationality considers the rationality of the procedure used to reach the decision. Prescriptive decision theory should then address both these aspects of rationality.

Another result of descriptive studies is prospect theory. In prospect theory, utility is replaced by a value separated into gains and losses. The value function is S-shaped and passes through a reference point, representing no loss and no gain. It is asymmetric (steeper for losses than for gains) and implies that people are loss averse. This means that the loss of $1000 has a higher impact than the gain of $1000, or that a loss of $1000 is farther away from the reference point than a gain of $1000. The theory also suggests that decision-makers are risk averse when it comes to gains and risk seeking when it comes to losses. Prospect theory also expects preferences to depend on the framing of the problem, that is, how the problem is formulated, and experiments have shown that people select differently when mathematically equivalent decision problems are presented using different words. Another alternative to model how humans make decisions is regret theory. Regret theory suggests that people avoid decisions that could result in regret, and therefore include regret as a variable to the regular utility function.

According to rational theory, decision making processes are based on four parts:

1. Knowledge of alternatives (a set of alternatives exists).
2. Knowledge of consequences (probability distributions of the consequences are known).
3. Consistent preference order (the decision-makers' subjective values of possible consequences are known and are consistent).
4. Decision rule (used for selection among the available alternatives based on their consequences for the preferences).

Since we cannot claim to have knowledge of all possible alternatives – we do not know all possible consequences – we have problems in expressing our preferences. We do not select the best alternative in accordance with the normative decision theory that human decision-makers experience 'bounded rationality'. This limits the rationality of identifying all possible alternatives as well as all their consequences.

PRESCRIPTIVE DECISION ANALYSIS

Given that we want to act rationally, a systematic approach for information processing and analysis of some kind is needed. This is of great importance when the problem at hand is complex, for instance, if it involves uncertainty or conflicting goals and is not of a repetitive kind so we cannot learn from experience.

As early as 1966, Ron Howard coined the term 'decision analysis' when he referred to a systematic procedure using formal decision rules for preparing and deliberating upon decision problems. Since we use a decision rule, we can say that decision analysis is the applied form of decision theory, in which we develop theories prescribing how we should make decisions. In essence, decision analysis promotes decision processes where we identify the primary objective(s) or goal(s) of the decision-maker(s), the different alternatives (the available courses of action), and the possible consequences of each alternative. Then we use a decision rule to point out the alternative having the best fit with our preferences and risk attitudes.

Prescriptive decision analysis is more pragmatically oriented than purely normative theories. Prescriptive decision analysis aims to combine the normative and the descriptive theories into guidelines for real decision making, providing aid to decision-makers for investigating and solving real-life decision problems.

As such, developments within prescriptive decision analysis focus mainly upon the applicability of decision analysis practices and tools to real problems in real contexts, with real decision-makers. It deals with tailoring decision analysis processes and tools for specific problems and problem domains, such as corporate strategy in a specific business segment. Consequently, when judging the goodness of prescriptive decision tools and decision process designs, we should assess their usefulness and pragmatic value in addition to assessing how the tools conform to normative theories of procedural and substantive rationality, which they should.

One such influential decision process design is 'value-focused thinking', advocated by Ralph Keeney. He holds the position that the objectives of the decision-makers should be understood before the formulation of alternatives, since this stimulates the decision-makers to be more creative and more open minded when discussing ways to achieve those objectives. Value-focused thinking is then put in contrast to 'alternative-focused thinking', where the decision-maker initially finds the available alternatives first and thereafter evaluates them. The prescriptive decision analysis process is also iterative. It includes iterations between the steps of setting the objectives, identifying alternatives, identifying uncertainties and evaluating alternatives. During this iterative process, perceptions may change and new may evolve. This is called 'requisite modelling', and a model is said to be requisite when it is sufficient for the decision situation at hand. Since a decision analysis should encompass decision-makers' preferences, these must be elicited. The techniques and methods used for elicitation should be practical and should not require too many inputs from the decision-makers as well as providing adequate judgments from decision-makers.

MULTI-CRITERIA DECISION AIDS

Multi Attribute Value Theory (MAVT) and Multi Attribute Utility Theory (MAUT) are the most widely used MCDA methods in practical application. The relative importance of each criterion is assessed, as well as value functions characterising the level of satisfaction by each alternative (according to the decision-maker) under each criterion. Thereafter, the overall score of each alternative is calculated. The main difference between the two is that MAVT is formulated to assume that outcomes of the alternatives are known with certainty, whereas MAUT explicitly takes uncertainty (relating to the outcomes) into account (and thus uses utility functions instead of value functions). Both MAVT and MAUT rely on so-called measurable value functions, or cardinal utilities, meaning that the value difference between two alternatives has a meaning. However, in many practical situations, it is hard to distinguish between utility and value functions elicited with risky or riskless methods due to factors such as judgemental errors and response mode effects. Basically, MAUT methods contain the following five steps:

1. Define the alternatives and the relevant attributes (criteria).
2. Evaluate each alternative separately on each attribute, i.e. the satisfaction of each alternative under each criterion represented by a value/utility function.
3. Assess the relative importance of each criterion, i.e. assign relative weights to the attributes.
4. Calculate the overall score of each alternative by aggregating the weights of the attributes and the single-attribute evaluations of alternatives into an overall evaluation of alternatives.
5. Perform sensitivity analyses on the model and make recommendations.

Examples of MCDA methods other than the MAVT/MAUT approach include the Analytic Hierarchy Process (AHP) which is similar to MAVT but uses pairwise comparisons of alternatives (utilising semantic scales) with respect to all criteria, and outranking methods based on partial ordering of alternatives, where the two main approaches are the ELECTRE family of methods and PROMETHEE.

ELICITATION

The process of eliciting adequate quantitative information from decision-makers, representing their preferences and beliefs, is still one of the major challenges when using decision analysis in practice. There is still no universally generally accepted method for weight elicitation. One common agreement among decision analysis researchers, however, is that in real applications of decision analysis, decision-makers and analysts should be concerned not only with what experts are asked to assess, but also how they are being asked. The study of elicitation has been greatly influenced by psychological findings on how people represent uncertain information cognitively, and how they respond to queries regarding that information. The different elicitation methods suggested from the decision analysis community have distinct features which impact their applicability in practice. In order to study and analyse suggested elicitation methods more explicitly, we need to categorise them. In order to study them and compare them, the following division of the elicitation process into three conceptual components is made in this chapter:

Extraction: This component deals with how information (probabilities, utilities, weights) is derived through user input.

Representation: This component deals with how to capture the retrieved information in a structure, i.e. the format used to represent the user input.

Interpretation: This component deals with the expressive power of the representation used and how to assign meaning to the captured information in the evaluation of the decision model used.

These categories will be used in the following to analyse elicitation methods in order to discuss their characteristics and identify elements that can impact their practical applicability.

PROBABILITY AND UTILITY ELICITATION

In decision situations with uncertain consequences, numerical probabilities are assigned to the consequences representing the decision-maker's degree of belief with respect to the future. Each consequence is also assigned a utility value. The best alternative is then the one with the combination of probabilities and utilities such that the expected utility is the highest. Needless to say, this means that, when using this model, we must have access to both the probabilities and the utility values of each consequence. Although probabilities can be obtained by using historical data or statistical models, they still represent degrees of beliefs. Probability is commonly elicited from domain experts, and the experts have to express their knowledge and beliefs in probabilistic form during the extraction. This task sometimes involves a 'facilitator', a person skilled in decision analysis and with insights into the decision problem at hand, leading the elicitation to assist the expert. The objective is to find probabilities providing an accurate representation of the expert's present knowledge, regardless of the quality of that knowledge, meaning that the probabilities sought are subjective and not objective. Subjective probability is thus one of the prime numerical inputs in current extraction procedures.

Methods for utility elicitation are similar to probability elicitation processes, but are in a sense more complex since the focus is on the preferences of the decision-maker. Probabilities can be elicited from experts (and should remain the same regardless of who makes the assessment), but can also be learned from data, whereas utility functions are meant to accurately represent decision-makers' individual risk attitudes and are thus required for each decision-maker. Utility can be seen as the value a decision-maker relates to a certain consequence. In the decision analysis field, it is also common to distinguish between a value function and a utility function, where the latter also should model the risk attitude of a decision-maker besides value differences between consequences. Most of the techniques for specifying a value function rely on having the decision-maker judge how big the steps are between different consequences, but without taking uncertain consequences into account, which it should be the case when eliciting utility functions.

Several techniques for utility elicitation have been proposed and used, with gambling methods being the most commonly used techniques. Capturing utility assessments in terms of hypothetical gambles and lotteries may not successfully map people's behaviour in all real situations. Some people have a general aversion towards gambling, and people often overweigh 100% certain outcomes in comparison with those that are merely probable (< 100%) which complicates matters further.

Moreover, the classical theory of preference assumes that normatively equivalent procedures for elicitation should give rise to the same preference order – an assumption often violated in empirical studies. People do have well-articulated and preconceived preferences regarding some matters, but in other settings they construct their preferences during the process of elicitation, which is one cause of these violations. They suggest that the need for preference construction often occurs in situations where some of the decision elements are unfamiliar. Such circumstances make decision-makers more susceptible to influence by factors such as framing during the elicitation process, and could explain some of the problems related to extraction.

RATIO WEIGHT PROCEDURES

Ratio weight procedures maintain ratio scale properties of the decision-maker's judgements from extraction and use exact values for representation and interpretation. Common to all these methods is that the actual attribute weights used for the representation are derived by normalising the sum of given points (from the extraction) to one. Methods adopting this approach range from quite simple rating procedures, like the frequently used direct rating (DR) and point allocation (PA) methods, to somewhat more advanced procedures, such as the often-used SMART, SWING and trade-off methods. As already mentioned, these methods differ in procedures during the extraction. In the DR method the user is asked to rate each attribute on a scale from 0 to 100, whereas in PA the user is asked to distribute a total of 100 points among the attributes. The extra cognitive step of having to keep track of the remaining number of points to distribute in the PA method influences the test-retest reliability, that is, how the decision-maker performs on two separate but identical occasions.

In SMART, the user is asked to identify the least important criterion, which receives for example 10 points, and thereafter the user is asked to rate the remaining criteria relative to the least important one by distributing points. Since no upper limit is specified, the ratings extracted from the same person can differ substantially in the interpretation if the method is applied twice. Consequently, this aspect of the extraction in SMART can affect the internal consistency in the interpretational step of the method. In the SWING method, the decision-maker is asked to consider his or her worst consequence in each criterion and to identify which criterion he or she would prefer most to change from its worst outcome to its best outcome (the swing). This criterion will be given the highest number of points, for example 100, and is excluded from the repeat process. The procedure is then repeated with the remaining criteria. The next criterion with the most important swing will be assigned a number relative to the most important one (thus their points denote their relative importance), and so on. Common to all methods described so far is that the number of judgements required by the user during extraction is a minimum of N, where N is the number of attributes.

In trade-off methods, the criteria are considered in pairs where two hypothetical alternatives are presented to the decision-maker during extraction. These alternatives differ only in the two criteria under consideration. In the first hypothetical alternative the performance of the two criteria is set to their worst and best consequences respectively and in the second alternative the opposite is applied. The decision-maker is asked to choose one of the alternatives, thereby indicating the more important one. Thereafter (s)he is asked to state how much (s)he would be willing to give up on the most important criterion in order to change the other to its best consequence, i.e. state the trade-off (s)he is willing to make for certain changes in outcomes between the criteria. The minimum number of judgements is N−1, but a consistency check requires consideration of all possible combinations of criteria, which would result in N·(N−1) comparisons. Consequently, the extraction component of the trade-off method is operationally more complex and more cognitively demanding in practice due to the large number of pairwise comparisons required. Moreover, there is a tendency to give greater weight to the most important attribute in comparison to methods like DR and SWING.

IMPRECISE WEIGHT ELICITATION

Accurate determinations of attribute weights by using ratio weight procedures are often hard to obtain in practice since assessed weights are subject to response error, and some researchers suggest that attempts to find precise weights may rest on an illusion. Consequently, suggestions on how to use imprecise weights instead have been proposed. In MCDA, there are different approaches to handling more imprecise preferences, mainly along one or more of the following sets of approaches: (1) ordinal statements; (2) classifying outcomes into semantic categories; and (3) interval assessments of magnitudes using lower and upper bounds.

Rank-order methods belong to the first set of approaches. During extraction, decision-makers simply rank the different criteria which are represented by ordinal values. Thereafter, these ordinal values are translated into surrogate (cardinal) weights consistent with the rankings supplied in the interpretational step. The conversion from ordinal to cardinal weights is needed in order to employ the principle of maximising the expected value (or any other numerical decision rule) in the evaluation. Thus, in these methods ratios among weights are determined by the conversion of ranks into ratios. Several proposals on how to convert such rankings to numerical weights exist. However, decision data is seldom purely ordinal. There is often some weak form of cardinality present in the information. A decision-maker may be quite confident that some differences in importance are greater than others, which is ignored in purely ordinal approaches. In some applications, preferential uncertainties and incomplete information are handled by using intervals, where a range of possible values is represented by an interval. Such methods belong to the third set of approaches, and are claimed to put less demands on the decision-maker as well as being suitable for group decision making as individual differences in preferences and judgments can be represented by value intervals.

The different methods for weight elicitation discussed above are summarised in Tables 1 and 2.

APPROACHING ELICITATION PRESCRIPTIVELY

Using a single number to represent an uncertain quantity can confuse a decision-maker's judgements about uncertainties with the desirability of various outcomes. Also, subjects often do not initially reveal consistent preference behaviour in many decision situations or they protect themselves from exposure by obscuring and managing their preferences. Organisations often work with a two-faced perspective and logical approach, where the logical

Table 1. An overview of some of the most prominent weight elicitation methods. N = no. of criteria.

Weight Elicitation Method	EXTRACTION			REPRESENTATION	INTERPRETATION
	Assessment	Input	Min. no. of judgements		
Direct Rating	Cardinal Joint procedure	Precise	N	Point estimates	Normalized criteria weights
Point Allocation	Cardinal Joint procedure	Precise	N	Point estimates	Normalized criteria weights
SMART	Cardinal Joint procedure	Precise	N	Point estimates	Normalized criteria weights
SWING	Cardinal Joint procedure	Precise	N	Point estimates	Normalized criteria weights
Trade-off	Cardinal Pairwise procedure	Precise	$N \cdot (N-1)$ (with consistency check)	Point estimates Relative between pairs of criteria	(Combined) normalized criteria weights
Rank-order methods	Ordinal Joint procedure	Rank-order	N	Comparative statements	Surrogate criteria weights (translated using a conversion method)
AHP	Cardinal Pairwise procedure	Semantic	$N \cdot (N-1)$ (with consistency check)	Semantic estimates Relative between pairs of criteria	(Combined) surrogate criteria weights (translated from semantic to exact numerical)
CROC	Ordinal & Cardinal Joint procedure	Rank-order and imprecise cardinal relation information	N (>N with cardinal input)	Comparative statements + imprecise cardinal relation information	Surrogate (centroid) criteria weights
Interval methods	Normally, a generalized ratio-weight procedure	Interval endpoints (precise)	$2 \cdot$(min. no. of judgements in employed ratio-weight procedure)	Intervals	Interval criteria weights

Table 2. A summary of assessment procedures during the extraction step of some of the most prominent weight elicitation methods.

Weight Elicitation Method	Extraction (assessment procedure)
Direct Rating	Rate each criterion on a 0–100 scale.
Point Allocation	Distribute 100 points among the criteria.
SMART	1) Identify the least important criterion, assign 10 points to it. 2) Rate the remaining criteria relative to the least important one.
SWING	1) Consider all criteria at their worst consequence level. 2) Identify the criterion most important to change from worst to best level, assign 100 points to it. 3) Continue with steps 1 and 2 with the remaining criteria, rate relative to the most important.
Trade-off methods	Judge criteria in pairs. 1) Make a choice between two alternatives, - alt.1: the best consequence level of the first criterion and the worst of the second, - alt.2: the worst consequence level of the first criterion and the best of the second. 2) State how much the decision-maker is willing to give up on the most important criterion in order to change the other one to its best level. 3) Continue with steps 1 and 2 with the remaining criteria.
Rank-order methods	Ordinal statements of criteria importance, i.e. rank all criteria from the most important to the least important.
AHP	Use a systematic pairwise comparison approach in determining preferences. 1) Make a choice between two criteria to determine which is the most important. 2) State how much more important the criterion identified in step 1 is in comparison with the second criterion using a semantic scale to express strength of preference. 3) Continue with steps 1 and 2 with the remaining criteria.
CROC	1) Rank all criteria from the most to the least important. 2) The most important criterion is given 100 points. The decision-maker is asked to express the importance of the least important criterion in relation to the most important. 3) Adjust the distances between the criteria on an analogue visual scale to express the cardinal importance information between the criteria. See Chapter 6 for a presentation of CROC.
Interval methods	Generalized ratio weight procedures which employ interval judgments to represent imprecision during extraction instead of point estimates, as in e.g., interval SMART/SWING.

rationality of a decision has to be legitimised which in turn results in ambiguous preferences. Moreover, in elicitation methods where a risky alternative is compared with a 100% certain outcome, people often overweigh the certain outcome – the so-called certainty effect. In addition, the conditions for procedure invariance are generally not true; people do not have well-defined values and beliefs in many decision situations where decision analysis is used, and choice is instead contingent or context sensitive. People are, furthermore, poor intuitive decision-makers in the sense that judgements are affected by the frame in which information is presented as well as by the context. Decision-makers appear to use only the information explicitly presented in the formulation of a problem, and implicit information that has to be deduced from the display seems to be ignored. The framing (formulation) of the problem strongly affects human reasoning and preferences, even though the objective information remains unchanged.

Over the years, many heuristics and biases have been identified. These can be both motivational (due to overconfidence) and cognitive (due to human thought processes). Studies where methods for elicitation have been compared in practice are often inconsistent (regarding probabilities, concerning preferences, and regarding weights), and there is no general agreement on the nature of the underlying cognitive processes involved in these assessments. Behavioural concerns are highly relevant to (prescriptive) aiding of decision making, especially in identifying where the improvable deficiencies in current practices are, as well as in fitting the design of decision aids to the reality of human abilities. An additional problem in measuring the precision of the method for preference elicitation methods occurs due to the subjective nature of the elicited values. Even though most researchers now agree on the fact that assessed probabilities are subjective in nature, the assessments are intended to represent facts and if experts' assessments disagree, different methods can be used to combine multiple assessments in order to improve the quality of the final estimates. When combining assessments, the main approaches are by mathematical aggregations of individual assessments or by obtaining group consensus. When it comes to preference extraction, it is more difficult to determine that the elicited values correctly represent the preferences held by the decision-maker. This is one reason why elicitation should be an iterative process, where the elicited values may have to be adjusted due to deviations from theoretical expectations or to an increased understanding of the problem and the context by the expert/decision-maker. Coherence in elicited values has to do with how well the values fit together and models of coherence are mainly focused on probability theory, compensating for the fact that it often falls short as a model of subjective probability. Prescriptive analyses must include how to elicit judgements from decision-makers and make sense out of them and is an attempt to narrow the gap between research within the normative and descriptive disciplines while being rooted in both traditions. It is a more practical approach to handling real-life decision problems, still employing a structured model for analysis. In the literature on extraction of the inputs required for decision analysis (probabilities, utilities, weights), there is no consensus regarding:

- the exact nature of the gap between ideal and real behaviour,
- how to avoid the observed extraction complications, or
- how to evaluate whether a method has produced accurate input data.

Reaching consensus on these aspects within the decision analysis community is difficult, but as a guideline, prescriptive research should strive for finding methods that are less cognitively demanding and less sensitive to noisy input within each component. The extraction component is the most error-prone as it concerns the procedural design of the method which could be cognitively demanding during user interaction. Behavioural research has been concentrated on the extraction component of elicitation, most commonly on how different biases occur when people interact with elicitation methods. Within this realm, the interpretational component is mostly discussed during validation as a means for measurement (e.g. illustrating procedure invariance).

One trend in approaches for extracting the required information in a less precise fashion is methods based on visual aids or verbal expressions. For example, the probability wheel is a popular visual method for eliciting probabilities (the user indicates his/her belief in probability on a circle by sizing a pie wedge to match the assessment of that probability). Such methods often use a combined extraction approach, where the user can modify the input both visually and numerically. The representation of visually extracted input is most commonly an exact number, which is then also used in the interpretation. The use of verbal terms during extraction is supposedly more in line with the generally imprecise semantics of people's expressions of preferences and beliefs, but as already mentioned they have been criticised for their vagueness which can cause problems in the interpretational step where the verbal expressions are represented by numbers. Words can have different meanings for different people and people often assign different numerical probabilities to the same verbal expressions.

Another trend in handling preferential uncertainties and incomplete information in a less precise way is by using intervals as representation, where a range of possible values is represented by an interval. Potential benefits of an interval approach include that such representations could facilitate more realistic interpretations of decision-makers' knowledge, beliefs and preferences, since these elements are not stored precisely in human minds. A first analysis of a decision problem can be made using imprecise statements followed by a test whether the input is sufficient for the evaluation of alternatives. If not, the input that needs to be further specified can be identified. Other advantages include that methods based on more approximate preference representations can lead to a more interactive decision support process as the evolution of the decision-maker's priorities can be calculated throughout the process, which in turn could lead to improved decision quality. In addition, such methods are especially suitable for group decision making processes as individual preferences can be represented by a union of the group's judgements. In the latter case, group members can seek consensus by trying to reduce the width of the intervals by compromising their individual judgements if necessary.

Methods for weight elicitation differ regarding the type of information they preserve from the decision-maker's judgements in the extraction component to the interpretation component. The two extremes are to use either exact values or mere ranking during extraction. In the CROC method (see *Chapter 6*), the user supplies both ordinal as well as imprecise cardinal relation information during extraction by providing a ranking of criteria complemented by imprecise preference relation information (using a graphical method). This information is translated into regions of significance in the interpretational step and the resulting weight distribution is obtained by calculations.

There has been interest in these matters for a while, but most important for the practical applicability of MCDA methods is the ease of employment of the method. Simpler tools are often easier to use and therefore more likely to be useful. Moreover, elicitation methods that are more direct are easier and less likely to produce elicitation errors. Some even claim that simpler, fast and frugal methods can produce results that are almost as good as results attributed to those obtained by more extensive analysis. In other words, exactness of results should not be the main aim with decision analysis and that different situations call for different levels of exactness depending on the decision-makers' contextual abilities to provide exact judgments.

DESIGNING ELICITATION METHODS

When designing elicitation methods, there is a need to understand psychological traps within extraction, such as framing and heuristics that produce biased assessments in order to apply measures to lessen their effect in method design. Use of clear terminology is important, such as explaining the meaning of specific terms in the context, thoroughly considering the phrasing of questions, being explicit on whether the required probabilities are single-event probabilities or frequencies (and explaining the difference to people unaware of the difference) etc. In order to reduce the gap between theoretical research and practical needs, there are aspects of the extraction component that need to be considered. It is important to be aware of behavioural aspects, like the heuristics and corresponding biases people use during extraction, in order to reduce such effects, along with how presentation formats affect decision-makers' choices. Moreover, relaxation of the precise statements that are commonly required in the extraction and representation components of elicitation methods could be advantageous. There is a contradiction between the ambiguity of human judgement and the exactness (of elicited values) required by most current decision analysis models. People have problems judging exact values, which poses a problem when the required values are point estimates, and some of the deviations from the traditional decision theoretical expectations could be attributed to this inability. More generally, practical techniques for elicitation are to a great extent a matter of balancing the obtained quality of elicitation with the time available and cognitive effort demand on the users for extracting all the required information. Sensitivity analyses could be used to monitor the consequential variations in the input provided and identify the information most critical for the results, which may need to be considered and specified more thoroughly.

FURTHER READING

Belton, V. and Stewart, T. *Multiple Criteria Decision Analysis: An Integrated Approach*. Boston, Dordrecht and London: Kluwer Academic Publishers. 2002.

French, S. and Rios Insua, D. *Statistical Decision Theory*. New York: Oxford University Press. 2000.

Kahneman, D., Slovic, P. and Tversky, A. *Judgment under Uncertainty: Heuristics and Biases.* Cambridge, UK: Cambridge University Press. 1982.

Keeney, R. and Raiffa, H. *Decisions with Multiple Objectives: Preferences and Value Trade-offs*. New York: John Wiley. 1976.

Lichtenstein, S. and Slovic, P. (Eds.), *The Construction of Preference.* Cambridge, UK: Cambridge University Press. 2006.

Luce, R.D. and Raiffa, H. *Games and Decisions: Introduction and Critical Survey.* New York: John Wiley and Sons. 1957.

von Neumann, J. and Morgenstern, O. *Theory of Games and Economic Behaviour.* 2nd ed. Princeton, NJ: Princeton University Press. 1947.

Shapira, Z. Risk Taking: *A Managerial Perspective.* New York: Russell Sage Foundation. 1995.

Simon, H. *Administrative Behaviour.* 3rd ed. New York: Free Press. 1976.

Tversky, A. and Kahneman, D. Judgment under Uncertainty: Heuristics and Biases. *Science.* 185(4157), pp. 1124–1131. 1974.

6

Cardinal and Rank Ordering of Criteria with Clouds

This chapter is based on Larsson, A., Riabacke, M., Danielson, M. and Ekenberg, L. Cardinal and Rank Ordering of Criteria – Addressing Prescription within Weight Elicitation. *International Journal of Information Technology and Decision Making.* 14(6). pp. 1299–1330. 2014.

Weight elicitation methods in multi-criteria decision analysis (MCDA) are often cognitively demanding, require too much precision and too much time and effort. Some of the issues may be remedied by connecting elicitation methods to an inference engine that facilitates a quick and easy method for decision-makers to use weaker input statements, yet is able to utilise these statements in a method for decision evaluation. In this chapter, we propose a fast and practically useful weight elicitation method, answering to many of the requirements. The method builds on the ideas of rank-order methods, but can also take imprecise cardinal information into account.

With respect to multi-criteria decision analysis methods, multi-attribute value theory (MAVT) and multi-attribute utility theory (MAUT) remain the most used methods in practical cases. Although these two methods are very alike, we can say that they differ in the way that MAUT takes into account the risk attitude of the decision-maker and handles uncertain consequences, and MAVT does not deal with uncertain consequences. Restricting our focus to MAVT, the perceived performance level of the alternatives under each criterion is modelled by means of so-called 'measurable value functions'. The relative importance of each criterion is also assessed and represented by numerical weights. The score of each alternative when taking all criteria into account is then given by aggregating the relative importances and the performance levels. The most common model used for this purpose is the additive model, such that the value $V(a)$ of an alternative a is given by

$$V(a) = \sum_{i=1}^{n} w_i v_i(a),$$

where $v_i(a)$ is the value of a with respect to the i:th criterion, which in turn is assigned the weight w_i. The weights, i.e. the relative importance of the evaluation criteria, describe each criterion's significance in the specific decision context. Central to this chapter is that this information needs to be elicited from the decision-maker(s).

Supporting the process of capturing decision-makers' weights, or 'eliciting' them, remains one of the major obstacles when using MCDA in practice. It is often said that elicitation of weights is cognitively demanding, it is difficult for decision-makers to express weights and the methods proposed are difficult to understand. The elicitation of criteria weights in MAVT/MAUT applications is also often considered the most cognitively demanding step of the MCDA process. Suggestions and attempts to reduce the gap between how elicitation procedures are implemented in current decision analysis applications and practical abilities and needs seem necessary in order to increase the usage of such applications in applied decision making.

A demand for numeric precision is also unrealistic as decision-makers have difficulties judging and expressing such precise input. As a result, good decision methods are not used in practice. Significance information in real-life multi-criteria problems is always more or less imprecise in its nature. People's beliefs are not naturally represented in numerically precise terms in our minds, and some suggest that the attempt of finding precise weights may be an illusion. We will therefore present a way such problems can be circumvented.

Different approaches for eliciting precise criteria weights exist, like direct rating and point allocation methods (see *Chapter 10*). Methods exploiting the trade-offs between criteria have also been suggested, that is, methods where the decision-maker is asked to express what decrease in performance on one criterion can be compensated for with an increase in performance on another criterion. An example is how much money it is worth to obtain a better water quality measured by the presence of a particular indicator bacteria. In practical settings, however, such methods can be too demanding in terms of the need for well-defined scales for all criteria. Cost/benefit analysis (CBA) is one example of this, where each criterion is traded-off against a monetary cost criterion, leading to a need to stipulate such trade-offs precisely.

As a response, approaches that do not require precise statements have been suggested. In such methods, simple rankings or imprecise importance information is used to obtain weights and/ or the values of alternatives under each criterion. Of particular interest here is the use of rankings. Ranking of criteria is assumed to be less difficult and more effort-saving than searching for numerical values. In such methods, the decision-maker is asked to rank the criteria, that is, to supply ordinal information on importance, and thereafter this ranking is converted to numbers. These approaches include rank sum (RS) and rank reciprocal (RR) weights, as well as rank ordered centroid (ROC) weights. Another example is the SMARTER method (SMART Exploiting Ranks), first asking for a criteria ranking in SWING fashion, and then converting the ranking into numerical weights using the ROC method (see *Chapter 10*).

CARDINAL AND RANK ORDERING OF CRITERIA

An advantage with methods based on judgements of non-numerical or approximate importance is that the decision support process can become more interactive, and in turn lead to improved decision quality, as well as being especially suitable for group decision making processes as individual importance judgements can be represented by a union of the group's judgements. An approximate approach can save time and effort since a user can quickly conduct a decision evaluation given an imprecise input and test whether the input is sufficient for ranking of the alternatives at hand.

In the additive model, the weights reflect the relative importance of one criterion to the other criteria. This relative importance is directly related to the value difference between the worst possible performance level of the criterion and its best possible level. Methods not considering this range explicitly in the elicitation process have been criticised for containing an intellectual error.

However, in order to use computer-based methods numbers need to be derived somehow from the user's input, whether the input is in the form of a ranking or in the form of words. Most current methods for converting a ranking into numerical weights – that is, converting rankings to exact surrogate weights, employ automated procedures for the conversion and result in exact numeric weights. Of these approaches, ROC weights have gained most recognition. The assumption that decision-makers are confident in their rankings is also a rather strong assumption. Decision-makers can also be uncertain with respect to the ordering of criteria. This means that it might be difficult to allow for imprecision in both the ordinal and the cardinal weight information.

We would then need elicitation methods that (i) do not require a deeper understanding of decision analysis, (ii) are not too cognitively demanding nor require decision-makers to state more than they are able to, (iii) do not require much time, and (iv) make use of the information the decision-maker is able to supply.

To address these issues, a weight elicitation method called CROC (Cardinal and Rank Ordering of Criteria) has been developed. CROC supports imprecise weights and where ordinal and cardinal information is mixed as appropriate. CROC does not employ constant trade-off in its basic form.

CROC extends the well-known ROC weight method into also handling rank ambiguity and cardinal information. With respect to the formal representation, CROC conforms to interval decision analysis where imprecision is modelled by means of linear constraints (see *Chapter 12*). Thus, the weight w_i for each criterion Gi is a variable bounded by range (interval) constraints $w_i \geq a_i$ and $w_i \leq b_i$ and/or by comparative constraints such as $w_i \geq w_j + e_{ij}$ for real numbers a_i, b_i, e_{ij}. A collection of constraints concerning a group of variables is referred to as a constraint set, which forms the basis for the representation of decision problems in interval decision analysis. As will be seen in the sections below, of concern for the CROC method is the ability to handle comparative constraints. Additionally, the weights are subject to $w_i \geq 0$ by default together with a normalisation constraint $\Sigma w_i = 1$. The CROC method allows for generating consistent constraint sets for criteria weights through the use of an accessible and interactive interface. The method is employed in two real-life cases. CROC consists of two stages, the first one is the extraction stage in which user interaction takes place, and the second stage is the interpretation stage where the extracted information is interpreted into cardinal weight statements.

CROC EXTRACTION STAGE

The underlying idea is that a decision-maker expresses *rankings* of criteria and also *distances* between criteria by placing all criteria on a common slider which can be vertical or horizontal. The cardinal information is then represented in the form of linear constraints for weight variables.

In the following, given N number of criteria, we have a criteria set G = {G_1,..., G_N}. During the procedure, each criterion G_i is associated with a criterion weight variable w_i and a slider position value x_i. The extraction stage is then comprised of the Steps 1–3 below which may be iterated until the user is satisfied.

Step 1. In this step an ordinal ranking of the criteria is asked for. The decision-maker ranks the criteria from most important to least important. This can be done in a Swing weighting fashion (see *Chapter 11*). Assume that G_1 is the most important criterion, followed by G_2 in turn followed by G_3 and so forth, making G_N the least important criterion. When several criteria are considered as being equally important, they are ranked at the same level.

Step 2. In this step, the decision-maker is to assess the maximum difference in importance between the most important criterion and the least important. This is done in weight percentage units. The rationale for this is that a decision-maker has more reliable opinions on these criteria than on those in between, see the design study later in this chapter for a discussion. In practice, the decision-maker is asked to express the 'strength' in his/her opinion of the maximum difference allowed in weight percentage units between the most and the least important criteria.

Step 3. Now we have an importance ranking of all criteria, and also a maximum difference between the most important and the least important. In this step, the decision-maker is allowed to adjust the differences between the criteria by moving them along a slider in a graphical user interface. Initially, all criteria ranked on adjacent levels have the same distance between them on the slider, which is called the default *distance*. In this interface, each criterion is surrounded by a 'cloud', so that when the criteria are moved closer together, the decision-maker expresses ambiguity in the ranking, i.e. their weight values are allowed to overlap.

CROC INTERPRETATION STAGE

Once the extraction stage is done, the distances between the criteria on the slider are interpreted and translated into a format ready for computational decision analysis. For this purpose, CROC uses interval decision analysis with linear inequalities (see *Chapter 12*). First we let x_i denote the position on the slider, so that if a criterion G_i is ranked above G_{i+1} then $x_i > x_{i+1}$.

After the first step of the extraction stage, all differences $x_i - x_{i+1}$ are equal (Figure 1, left, the default distance). Each slider position x_i is normalised to y_i such that $y_i = (x_i - x_L) / (x_H - x_L)$. The transformed default differences then becomes $y_i - y_{i+1} = 1/(N-1)$. When the decision-maker moves the criteria on the slider (Figure 1, right), the new differences after this moving of criteria are then viewed relative to the transformed default differences $1/(N-1)$. After the user has modified the slider positions, the new slider positions x_i' are transformed accordingly to $y_i' = (x_i' - x_L) / (x_H - x_L)$. Based upon this, we can define a factor representing how much each criterion has been 'moved', which is called the movement factor $d_{i,i+1}$ for criterion G_i and G_{i+1}. The movement factor is defined as

$$d_{i,i+1} = (N-1)(y_i' - y_{i+1}')$$

This means that the movement factor is smaller than one if the clouds overlap, and larger than one if they are moved farther apart from each other. If they are not moved, the movement factor is one.

Translating this into linear inequalities, inequalities of the form $w_i \geq w_{i+1}$ for all $i < N-1$ will be used. But the positions of the criteria on the slider together with the clouds provide additional information, and we should also take into account the maximum and minimum difference between the top-ranked and bottom-ranked criterion. To do this, we define two functions expressing the minimum and maximum difference between two weight variables w_i and w_j whenever $1 < i < j < N$. We call these functions the lower and upper constraint functions, f_L and f_U. These functions take a movement factor and provide linear inequalities between the weight variables. For each pair of criteria G_i and G_{i+1}, the movement factor is used to obtain two types of inequalities between pairs of weight variables.

(1) Type 1: $w_i \geq w_{i+1} + f_L(d_{i,i+1})$, the weight w_i of G_i is at least $f_L(d_{i,i+1})$ greater than the weight w_{i+1} of G_{i+1}

(2) Type 2: $w_{i+1} \geq w_i - f_U(d_{i,i+1})$, the weight w_{i+1} of G_{i+1} is at most $f_U(d_{i,i+1})$ smaller than the weight w_i of G_i

Thus, from a visual slider we can pick the slider positions and the movement factors between criteria pairs. Based upon these movement factors we can obtain two inequalities for each criteria pair and represent the visual ranking in an interval decision analysis model. Now, there are some technical issues with respect to deriving the lower and upper constraint functions which we will not discuss in detail in this book; see the suggested reading below for sources providing all the details. For example, in order to preserve *transitivity*, inequality constraints between adjacent criteria alone are insufficient, there need to be inequalities between all criteria pairs G_i and G_j whenever the former is ranked above the latter.

THE DESIGN STUDY BEHIND CROC

The work behind the development of CROC is an iterative participatory study involving decision-makers at a Swedish municipality. This design study included two phases: (1) A test of the initial design of the extraction stage, the ranking and the moving of criteria on a slider; and (2) A comparison of the suggested CROC method with two other commonly employed weight elicitation methods, namely DR (Direct Rating) and SMARTS.

Two decision-makers tested the initial design of the CROC extraction stage, focussing on decision-makers' abilities to indicate importance in some way. The feature of only asking the decision-maker to assess the least and the most important criteria and expressing the difference between them was tested in the first design phase. The two participants were confronted with a car purchase decision and were to provide the relative importance of seven different criteria upon which they were to assess the cars, using MAVT. The participants felt most confident in their statements with respect to the most important and the least important criteria, which promoted the idea of saving effort by only asking decision-makers to assess this difference numerically. They also felt that assessing this difference was easier to do if one of the criteria had points to which they could relate. Therefore, the design of the extraction stage was that the most important criterion was given 100 points, and the decision-maker was asked to assess how many weight percentage units lower the least important criterion is allowed to be.

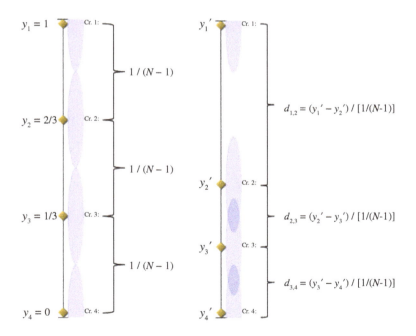

Figure 1. Normalised slider positions with default distances on the left-hand side, and moved criteria on the right-hand side.

Later, five new participants were confronted with the same decision problem with the same cars. However, they were to provide their relative importance information on two occasions, the second occasion one week after the first. On both occasions, weights for the criteria were elicited using CROC, DR and SMARTS, in different orders. The subjects were asked about their opinions with respect to how they perceived the credibility of each method, and how demanding each method was to them. Again, the participants were more confident in their statements with respect to the most important and least important criterion. They were also rather insecure with respect to the ranking order of intermediate criteria. This was demonstrated explicitly since the rankings of these criteria differed between the two occasions, their ranking at the second run was inconsistent with the ranking in the first run!

The result was that all participants preferred SMARTS over DR. They did however perceive the task of giving points to each criterion as quite demanding. Their preferences between SMARTS and CROC varied. However, SMARTS yielded inconsistent results when comparing the two separate occasions. As an example, one participant awarded the most important criterion 50 points in the first occasion, and then 100 points on the second occasion. Another participant altered the points for one criterion from 20 to 90 between occasions. So with respect to the internal consistency, SMARTS was demonstrated to be inferior to the other methods. This can be explained by the so-called 'availability heuristic' – the participants were biased by the available information. CROC showed most consistency when comparing the two occasions. This indicates that with respect to internal consistency, CROC is a more robust method, which is not surprising since it is less sensitive to minor changes in input from the user compared with the other two methods.

CASE STUDIES

The first case concerns a debated decision that the governing politicians in Örebro (a medium-sized municipality in Sweden with around 140,000 inhabitants) faced was how to improve the water quality of Svartån, a river running through the city of Örebro. The problems with Svartån had been debated for long, and the decision was multi-facetted in nature. For several years, there had been unacceptably high amounts of intestinal bacteria in the water, and the different spots for bathing along Svartån had been deemed unsuitable according to European Union regulations. A goal of the decision-makers was to make it possible to swim without health risks in Svartån by the year 2010, but more importantly to reach a solution yielding increased fresh water quality in general. The decision was a multi-criteria, multi-stakeholder problem and primarily involved seven elected politicians as decision-makers.

In Örebro, we tested CROC as part of the MCDA model used to aid the decision making process of the seven politicians.[1] Decomposed scaling, where the weights and the partial value functions are assessed separately, was used. The seven main criteria were identified collectively by the decision-makers and thereafter the weights were elicited individually from the decision-makers on two occasions using the CROC method. The first occasion was early on in the process, right after the identification of the top-level criteria, in order to initiate and motivate the decision-makers' reflections about their own beliefs. The second occasion was later on in the process, when the decision-makers had understood the problem better, the different options, and their own beliefs better. On both occasions, the decision-makers were asked about their perceived effort and views on the criteria. The identification of the seven alternatives under consideration, the sub-criteria and the value assessments (often represented by a value interval) were initially performed by civil servants. The decision-makers thereafter continuously confirmed and/or adjusted these assessments as the work proceeded in workshop settings (lead by facilitators), where the participants were both politicians/decision-makers and civil servant representatives.

In the following example, the extraction section of the CROC method for one of the politicians is illustrated in Figure 2, and the resulting interpretation from CROC is shown in Table 1 (the resulting movement factor matrix) and Table 2 (the resulting constraint function values).

Example. Consider the CROC elicitation stages visualised in Figure 2. In the example, note that 'Ecological sustainability' and 'Water quality' are placed at the same level, that is, they have the same modified competition ranking order, which is two. The same holds for 'Economy/costs' and 'Practicability' which share the ranking order of five. Also, x_L is set to 10 so that $h = (x_H - x_L)/x_H = 0.9$.

Let the set of criteria be indexed according to the following order derived from step 1 of the elicitation stage shown to the left in Figure 2:

G_1: Eco. sustainability
G_2: Water quality
G_3: Nature/wildlife

---

[1] The MCDA model was subsequently evaluated using the DecideIT decision tool (Danielson *et al.*, 2003).

G_4: Economy/costs
G_5: Practicability
G_6: Business impact
G_7: Bathability (clean bathing water at river beaches)

For the untouched distances on the left-hand side in Figure 2, all movement factors in the movement factor matrix are 1. The movement factor matrix resulting from the modified distances to the right is given in Table 1.

Result of steps 1 and 2 on the left-hand side and the final result after step 3 on the right-hand side. Note that the lowest ranked criterion 'Bathability' has an initial position of $x = 10$, meaning that $h = (x_H - x_L)/x_H = 0.9$.

Table 1. Resulting matrix holding movement factors between all criteria (rounded to two decimal places) after the extraction step 3.

	G_1	G_2	G_3	G_4	G_5	G_6	G_7
G_1		0	0.83	1.36	1.36	2.03	2.03
G_2			0.83	1.36	1.36	2.03	2.03
G_3				1.36	1.36	2.03	2.03
G_4					0	2.03	2.03
G_5						2.03	2.03
G_6							1.78
G_7							

These movement factors then yield the following constraint function values shown in the matrix in Table 2. As before, in the matrix the cells above the separating line of cells (i,j) refer to $f_L(d_{i,j})$ and the cells below refer to $f_U(d_{i,j})$. Hence, between non-adjacent criteria G_1 and G_5 we have the following constraints of type 1 and type 2 (see *Chapter 6* for definitions).

(1) Constraint type 1:
$$w_1 \geq w_5 + f_L(d_{1,5}) \rightarrow$$
$$w_1 \geq w_5 + h \cdot (d_{1,5} - 1) / (N - 2) \cdot p(d_{1,5}) \rightarrow$$
$$w_1 \geq w_5 + 0.9(1.36 - 1) / (7 - 2) \cdot 3 \rightarrow$$
$$w_1 \geq w_5 + 0.0216$$

(2) Constraint type 2:
$$w_5 \geq w_1 - f_U(d_{1,5}) \rightarrow$$
$$w_5 \geq w_1 - \min\{1/p(d_{1,2}) + f_L(d_{1,5}), 1\}$$
$$w_5 \geq w_1 - \min\{0.9/2 + f_L(d_{1,5}), 1\} \rightarrow$$
$$w_5 \geq w_1 - \min\{0.4716, 1\} \rightarrow$$
$$w_5 \geq w_1 - 0.4716$$

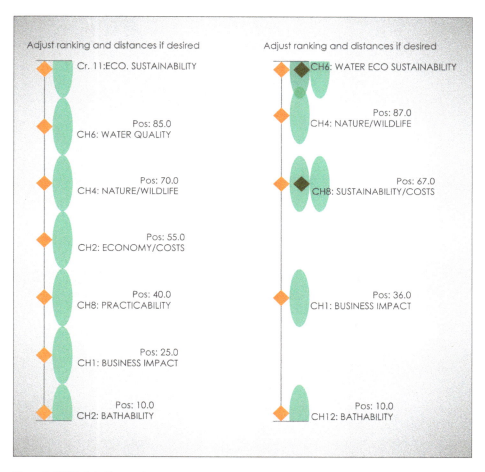

Figure 2. CROC elicitation result.

Table 2. Constraint function value matrix.

	G_1	G_2	G_3	G_4	G_5	G_6	G_7
G_1		-0.225	-0.038	0.022	0.022	0.037	0.037
G_2	0.225		-0.038	0.022	0.022	0.037	0.037
G_3	0.412	0.411		0.022	0.022	0.037	0.037
G_4	0.472	0.472	0.322		-0.09	0.037	0.037
G_5	0.472	0.472	0.322	0.09		0.037	0.037
G_6	0.487	0.487	0.337	0.217	0.217		0.023
G_7	0.487	0.487	0.337	0.217	0.217	0.173	

Note: Numbers rounded to three decimal places, from the slider positions after step 3 shown in Figure 2. For instance, $w_1 \geq w_5 + 0.022$ and $w_5 \geq w_1 - 0.472$

The weights were assigned directly by the politicians, reflecting the differing opinions held by the individual politicians as well as by their political parties. The values were assigned by the politicians after civil servants assessed and compiled the information on the various alternatives under each criterion. The values were then open to discussion until agreements were reached. Agreements did not have to be a specific number (value) for an alternative under a criterion but could be an interval where the width corresponded to the amount of disagreement on the particular alternative under that criterion. The values (or value intervals) were public information while the weights were not (for reasons of integrity on the part of the politicians). In this chapter, only the weight assessments are considered.

For the assessment of criteria, each of the five politicians (members of the Council Board, i.e. the ultimate decision-makers) participating in the process were asked to rank or weigh the criteria regarding two of the urban planning decisions according to their individual preferences. They were each given a total importance mass of 100 to distribute over the criteria. The weights were assessed by the politicians on two occasions, once at the beginning of the process and once close to the end. When all the alternatives had been thoroughly investigated by the civil servants and experts, the results of these investigations, described as factual consequences of each alternative with respect to the criteria, were handed over to the politicians, who were asked to value each alternative under each criterion on a scale from 0 to 10.

In the second case study, the aim was to look at ways to achieve public participation and democratic decision making by combining a multi-criteria decision approach with different forms of discussion and deliberation. The problem formulation faced was the same as the first case (improving the water quality of the city's waterway), but the sample was larger (90 students aged 17–19 living in Örebro), although they were citizens and not the real decision-makers. The promising results of the first case study and the similar setting promoted the employment of the CROC method, since part of the purpose of this study was to find a method suitable for lay people. Participants were to express opinions on choice criteria, individually and remotely within a reasonable amount of time without exerting too much effort, which supported using a method like CROC. The participants were guided to a wiki website, which contained background information about the Svartå problem, MCDA and the necessary steps of the decision making process, the identified criteria, the available alternatives, and links to a discussion forum and a web-based application of the CROC method, where continuous instructions guided the user through each stage.

The CROC elicitation method was applied on two occasions one week apart, where the aim of the intermission was to stimulate increased understanding of the criteria and contemplation of their own views. The subjects were divided into three groups with different discussion instructions for the period in between elicitation occasions, one group discussed the problem in a group led by a teacher, the second group had access to a discussion forum where they could discuss the problem, and the third group had no explicit instructions to discuss the matter, but were not forbidden to. After the second occasion, the participants filled out a questionnaire in order to find out their views on the method, suitability of criteria, whether they changed preferences (and if so, why) and the time expended.

RESULTS AND DISCUSSION

In the first real-life case, all decision-makers found the CROC method easy to understand and use, they could all provide an importance order over the seven main criteria, and they all had a clear understanding of what they considered to be important. They also adjusted the criteria slider positions to indicate the magnitudes of the differences between the criteria. In general the decision-makers found the step to express the maximum difference between the least and most important criterion to be the most difficult, as well as deciding upon the order of the in-between criteria. However, they considered the time required to complete the elicitation exercise as acceptable.

An interesting observation is to compare the extracted information from the decision-makers between the two occasions and how this information is represented and interpreted in the

CROC method. Since the CROC method is graphical and its elicitation design encourages imprecision, it is virtually impossible in practice (other than by chance) to provide exactly the same visual view of criteria preferences on two different occasions. As expected, none of the decision-makers had exactly the same visual view of criteria preferences on both occasions, although most of them had quite similar ordinal input. Two of the politicians had one major change each (a change in priority order of 4 and 5 steps respectively) between the two elicitation occasions due to changed views on criteria after discussions within the group. These changes were sorted out from the analysis. Looking at the remaining changes among the decision-makers, 80% were minor; either a switch in priority between two subsequently ordered criteria or placing two subsequently ordered criteria at the same priority level. Since the decision-makers in these cases seemed to have unchanged views, these types of (minor) change could be attributed to unintended change. When using the preferred representation of the extracted information, statements from both elicitation occasions are represented in the constraint set generated by the interpretation. This fact makes it reasonable to favour this interpretation of the user's interaction with the tool within such contexts, as there seems to be a prominent vagueness even in the ordinal weight information (one step up or down in the priority order of the criteria is perceived as unchanged views) provided by decision-makers. The remaining 20% of changes in priority order between occasions were variations of up to two steps. These could be attributed to either change in view or imprecision of method.

In the second real-life case study employing the CROC method, the participants had not given the problem considerable thought before the first weight elicitation occasion in the way the politicians in Örebro had, yet they were familiar with the problem at hand as it had been debated for a long time within the municipality. On average, the participants found the first step of the CROC method most difficult, whereas setting a scale and adjusting differences were not considered particularly hard. This is in contrast to the politicians in the first case study who found the first step quite easy. However, the politicians had collectively identified the seven criteria themselves, whereas the participants in the second study were given already formulated criteria and may not have shared the politicians' caution about expressing precise statements. The majority of the students found the task of expressing preferences in the CROC method interface easier or much easier than taking a stand on different alternatives. Moreover, 68% of the students stated that they felt very or pretty sure of their preferences.

This was thus also a difference between the two cases, as all the politicians felt quite sure of their preferences on the second elicitation occasion.

Looking at the first case, and how changes in preferences were reflected in ordinal changes between the two elicitation occasions, no change or an increase or decrease of one in rank of a criterion between priority orders was considered unchanged views (minor), changes of two or three rank positions of a criterion between priority orders were considered medium changes, whereas major changes were four to six shifts in rank of a criterion between occasions. Major changes were sorted out from the analysis in accordance with the analysis of the cases, but worth noting is that in the two groups where deliberate discussions were held, we could see a tendency of more dramatic changes (50% more than in the group where no deliberate discussions were held), whereas the number of moderate changes were almost identical between the groups. Considering the remaining changes, 69% constituted minor changes among participants and consequently 31% were medium changes. The fact that the participants were not familiar with the criteria prior to the first elicitation occasion, and that part of this study tested different forms of discussion and deliberation between occasions, could be the reason for more variations in extracted importance judgement information in comparison with the politicians in the first case. In the questionnaire following the two occasions, people explicitly stated that if they changed their views it was a result of an increased understanding of their preferences due to their own thoughts about the criteria, discussions and/or influence from others between occasions. Yet most changes were relatively small, which indicates stability of the method. Moreover, the majority of the participants found the method relatively easy to use and 88% of the participants stated that they completed the elicitation within 10 minutes, which is a positive indication of practical usefulness as the participants were novices at this kind of analysis.

In both real-life case studies, people's preferences between some of the criteria were shown to be somewhat dynamic, more so in the second case study. In the latter, a possible explanation for the larger number of variations could be partly attributed to the fact that the participants had no prior information on the criteria or procedure before the first elicitation occasion.

Looking at extraction, one of the main aims was not to force users to express unrealistic precision, not to require too much cognitive effort of users and not to demand too much of their time. Such aims are quite difficult to validate adequately as they are measured on a subjective (qualitative) basis and some people may find any effort exerted tiresome whereas others are quite tolerant. Yet, from the results of the case studies, the requirements were reasonably fulfilled as the application of the CROC method was manoeuvred without difficulty by the participants, they understood their task and completed the elicitation within a relatively short time.

Looking at interpretation, it is reasonable to say that, although there are many methods for weight elicitation, it is virtually impossible to find a method which always generates the same weights when employed on more than one occasion, even though the decision-maker has unchanged views. The CROC method is less sensitive to noisy input than most methods offered today, as the interpretation section of the method, using the representation and interpretation, handles differences in extracted information so that small variations in user input (most likely unintentional) have no effect, whereas major changes do, which they should as this would imply that the user has changed views.

ADDRESSING PRESCRIPTIVE ISSUES

This chapter presents a weight elicitation method that acknowledges that there might be ambiguity with respect to the ranking of criteria, and accounts for that in computational decision analysis. The CROC method extends rank-order weighting procedures by taking both ordinal information as well as imprecise cardinal relation information of the importance of the attributes into account, without forcing people to state more than they can or want to. The CROC method, utilising visualised rankings translated into linear constraints, seems to be a more prescriptively useful method than most methods offered today. When completing all three user interaction steps during the first stage of the method, the method recognises the fact that there may be uncertainty regarding both the magnitude and ordering of weights and that people can express that some differences in importance can be greater than others.

We conclude that the CROC method addresses prescriptive issues and is a useful way of eliciting criteria weights when the aim is to employ a fast and easy method, not only in comparison with point allocation methods but also in comparison with most traditional methods (in terms of procedural aspects) requiring precision during extraction. The use of a less precise extraction component is more in line with people's natural abilities in expressing views on importance. The CROC method handles minor and major changes well, that is, slight differences (most likely unchanged views) do not have an effect when using the preferred interpretation, whereas major changes do. When moderate changes occur, they could be either intentional or unintentional, but such changes constituted a small part of the total changes in the case studies where the CROC method was employed.

With respect to future research, there is a need for additional empirical testing in real-life cases in order to further evaluate where its employment is most suitable, that is, in what contexts the CROC method is most appropriate as there may be different needs depending on the decision-maker(s), type of problem, number of attributes, and alternatives involved. Further, it is important to equip the method with features supporting unsupervised use and providing a decision-maker with informative feedback from a CROC weighting scheme, such as showing the possible trade-offs between criteria that a certain CROC weighting scheme will result in. Finally, future research also includes the case of multiple decision-makers and/or stakeholders resulting in a set of rankings and the aggregation of CROC weights in such situations.

FURTHER READING

Barron, F. Selecting a Best Multi-attribute Alternative with Partial Information about Attribute Weights. *Acta Psychologica*. 80(1–3), pp. 91–103. 1992.

Barron, F. and Barrett, B. The Efficacy of SMARTER: Simple Multi-attribute Rating Technique Extended to Ranking. *Acta Psychologica*. 93(1–3), pp. 23–36. 1996.

Barron, F. and Barrett, B. Decision Quality Using Ranked Attribute Weights. *Management Science*. 42(11), pp. 1515–1523. 1996.

Edwards, W. and Barron, F. SMARTS and SMARTER: Improved Simple Methods for Multiattribute Utility Measurement. *Organisational Behavior and Human Decision Processes*. 60, pp. 306–325. 1994.

Kilgour, M., Chen, Y. and Himpel, K.W. Multiple Criteria Approaches to Group Decision and Negotiation, in M. Ehrgott, J.R. Figueira and S. Greco (Eds.) *Trends in Multiple Criteria Decision Analysis*. New York: Springer. 2010.

Riabacke, M., Åström, J. and Grönlund, Å. eParticipation Galore? Extending Multi-Criteria Decision Analysis to the Public. *International Journal of Public Information Systems*. 7(2), pp. 79–99. 2011.

7

Attitude Ranking

To avoid costly conflicts within and between stakeholder groups, and to identify which stakeholder groups are advantaged or disadvantaged by different alternatives, it is of great interest for the executive authority to engage the stakeholders in the process, and to elicit their preferences. The use of web-based techniques is one approach which may be used for gathering stakeholder preferences on a larger scale, which can then be examined with decision analytic concepts to inform the decision-makers. A vital step in this approach is to elicit the citizens' opinions or attitudes regarding different potential 'actions': actions that might be turned into a better-defined project.

REPRESENTING CITIZEN OPINIONS

To derive a method suitable for real-life use, we ground our proposed method in a real, large-scale case. We investigate the opinions of citizens with regard to a set of possible future actions planned by the municipality of Upplands Väsby, a short distance to the north of the city of Stockholm. The actions planned are loosely defined, but still elicit opinions from the citizens as to whether they will be affected positively, negatively, or not at all. Of interest for the municipality is to investigate how different combinations, or portfolios, of actions arouse more or less disagreement between the citizens. A portfolio is then a combination of actions, where each action is associated with a disagreement measure and different portfolios are generated by imposing different constraints on the level of disagreement between the citizens. For this purpose, attitudes need to be represented by using a measurable value function, and the questionnaire becomes a front-end for preference elicitation. We propose a questionnaire inspired by attitude surveys which commonly employ different versions of the

This chapter is based on Fasth, T., Larsson, A. and Ekenberg, L. *Online Scalable Preference Elicitation Using Bipolar Cardinal Ranking.* Manuscript.

Likert scale. The questionnaire enables the capture of positive, neutral and negative attitudes through the use of a cardinal ranking dichotomous scale. The responses provided on this scale are then interpreted by means of cardinal ranking methods providing surrogate values and criteria weights. The questionnaire also includes meta-data questions regarding the citizens' demographic variables. These variables can be used in the analysis to investigate how different citizen groups view different decisions, in order to identify clusters of stakeholders from a preference perspective. Beyond cardinally ranking elements, respondents can state if the elements are negative, neutral or positive with regard to fulfilling an overall goal.

We will use a 'two-point scale' which is a scale with two endpoints (poles) and a neutral midpoint; one pole representing negative affect and the other pole representing positive affect. It is assumed that in between these poles lies a neutrality level which represents affect that is neither negative nor positive. Two types of three-point scales are the dichotomous univariate model and the unipolar bivariate model. A dichotomous univariate scale is represented by one single axis divided into two poles, representing negative and positive affect. For instance, the neutrality level on a scale ranging between −1 and 1 is represented by 0 where negative affect is represented by a negative value bounded by −1 and positive affect is represented by a positive value bounded by 1. The other representation, the unipolar bivariate model, is based on two unipolar scales forming a two-axis plane. The horizontal axis represents the positive pole and the vertical axis the negative pole, for instance, a unipolar scale could be bounded between 0 and 1. The method in this chapter utilises the dichotomous univariate model, and extends the CAR method, described in *Chapter 11*, into D-CAR (Dichotomous CAR) by enabling stakeholders to state whether they believe that an alternative is counter-productive, neutral or productive with regard to an overall aim.

The stakeholders' preferences are elicited by a CAR surrogate weight and value approach through the use of a web-based questionnaire, meaning that the users rank both the criteria and the actions and then surrogate weights and values are obtained. In this it is assumed that: (i) all stakeholders are equally important, (ii) the stakeholders' preferences are independently stated, (iii) the stakeholders' preferences are not influenced by other stakeholders, and (iv) that the questionnaire is self-explanatory. The questionnaire consists of a set of focus areas, each consisting of a set of actions. A focus area is an area of improvement, and can be considered as one criterion. The actions under a focus area are the suggested actions that may improve it. For instance, in the area 'Development' possible actions might be 'Build apartments in the city centre' and 'Build apartments by the seashore'.

In our design, each stakeholder's preferences with respect to each action are expressed on this scale. The midpoint (neutral affect) is called the neutrality threshold t, communicating that the actions placed there are not considered to improve the focus area, nor to be counter-productive. This enables us to partition the stakeholders into two groups, one group holding the stakeholders with negative affect and one with the stakeholders with positive affect towards the action, with respect to each focus area.

ASSESSING DISAGREEMENT

Assume that we consider a set of actions $A_1, A_2, ..., A_m$ and that an action A_l is evaluated against a set of mutually preferentially independent criteria $G_1, G_2, ..., G_l$, and this is to be done by each stakeholder $S_1, ..., S_n$. According to decision analysis, this means that each stakeholder is to assess his/her value v_{ik}^j of each action A_l under each criterion G_K together with the weight w_k^j of G_K such that $w_k^j \geq 0$ and $\sum_{k=1}^{l} w_k^j = 1$. Conforming to MAVT, the additive value function (MAVT) in Eq. 1 is then used to obtain the utilitarian value of an action by summing up the weighted values from all stakeholders.

$$V(A_l) = \sum_{j=1}^{n} \sum_{k=1}^{l} w_k^j v_{ik}^j \qquad (1)$$

In order to study disagreement, for each action A_i we form two stakeholder subsets called the con group R_{ik}^- and the pro group R_{ik}^+, such that the stakeholders of R_{ik}^- assign a value of A_i with respect to G_k lower than the neutrality level and that the stakeholders of R_{ik}^+ assign a value at the neutrality level or greater than it, see Eq. 2.

$$R_{ik}^- = \left\{ S_j \in S : v_{ik}^j < t \right\}_{1 \leq j \leq n}$$
$$R_{ik}^+ = \left\{ S_j \in S : v_{ik}^j \geq t \right\}_{1 \leq j \leq n} \qquad (2)$$

Having this information, for each action A_i we create two value ranges for each criterion G_k, one range for each of the two groups. These are labelled as the con-support S_C and pro-support S_P respectively and are given from the minimum and maximum stakeholder 'part-worth value', that is, given a criterion G_k the value of the action under that criterion times the criterion's weight, see (3).

$$S_C = \left[\min_{j|s_j \in R_{ik}^-} \{w_k^j v_{ik}^j\}, \max_{j|s_j \in R_{ik}^-} \{w_k^j v_{ik}^j\} \right]$$

$$S_P = \left[\min_{j|s_j \in R_{ik}^+} \{w_k^j v_{ik}^j\}, \max_{j|s_j \in R_{ik}^+} \{w_k^j v_{ik}^j\} \right]$$

(3)

For each action A_i and criterion G_k we let the average con-index c_{ik} and average pro-index p_{ik} be two quantitative measures of the sets of part-worth utilities in the two stakeholder groups R_{ik}^- and R_{ik}^+. These are defined as

$$c_{ik} = \sum_{j|S_j \in R_{ik}^-} w_k^j v_{ik}^j / |R_{ik}^-|$$

$$p_{ik} = \sum_{j|S_j \in R_{ik}^+} w_k^j v_{ik}^j / |R_{ik}^+|$$

(4)

Thus, the average con- and pro-indices are the arithmetic mean of the part-worth utility for each of the two stakeholder groups. Then $d_{ik} = |c_{ik} - p_{ik}|$, that is, the distance between the pro-index and the con-index indicate an additive level of disagreement with respect to the performance of the action A_i relative to criterion G_k. This level of disagreement is called the additive disagreement index d_{ik} for action A_i under criterion G_k, relative to one set of stakeholders. The total disagreement index for action A_i is denoted with T_i and is the sum of all criterion specific disagreement indexes, such that

$$T_i = \sum_{k|G_k \in G} d_{ik}$$

(5)

To illustrate, assume a set of eight stakeholders who have provided their weight and value statements for action A_1 of criterion G_1 and the weight for G_1 such that

$$w_1^1 v_{11}^1 = -4, w_1^2 v_{11}^2 = -3, w_1^3 v_{11}^3 = -3,$$
$$w_1^4 v_{11}^4 = -2, w_1^5 v_{11}^5 = 1, w_1^6 v_{11}^6 = 2,$$
$$w_1^7 v_{11}^7 = 3, w_1^8 v_{11}^8 = 3$$

Then the con group R_{11}^- and pro-group R_{11}^+ for action A_1 and criterion G_1 are $R_{11}^- = \{S_1, S_2, S_3, S_4\}$ and $R_{11}^+ = \{S_5, S_6, S_7, S_8\}$ with $c_{ii} = -3$ and $p_{ii} = 2.25$. See Figure 1.

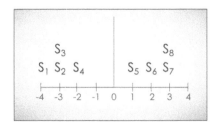

Figure 1. Illustration of two stakeholder groups.

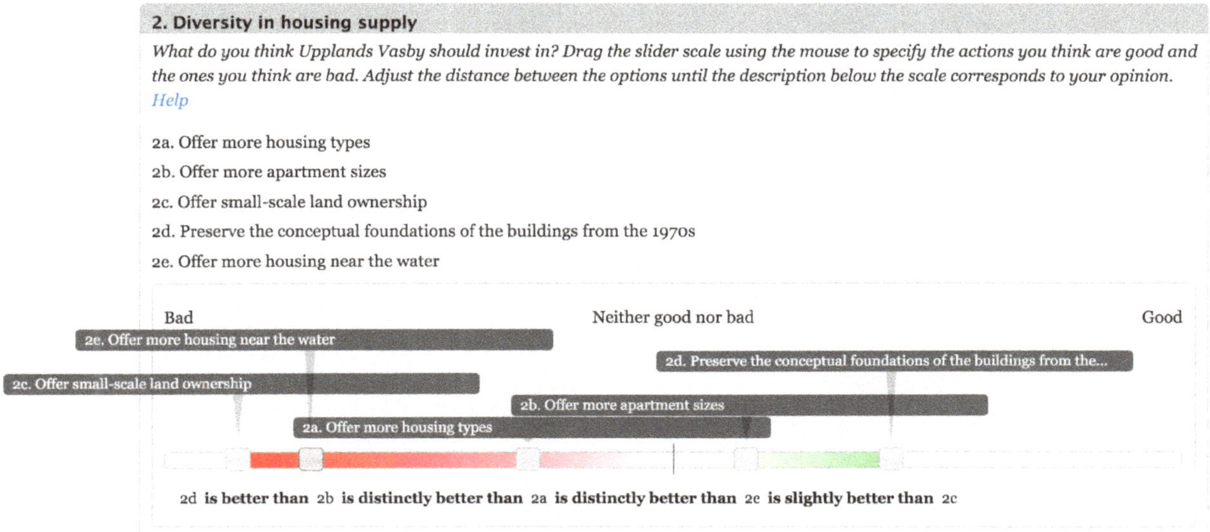

2. Diversity in housing supply

What do you think Upplands Vasby should invest in? Drag the slider scale using the mouse to specify the actions you think are good and the ones you think are bad. Adjust the distance between the options until the description below the scale corresponds to your opinion.
Help

2a. Offer more housing types

2b. Offer more apartment sizes

2c. Offer small-scale land ownership

2d. Preserve the conceptual foundations of the buildings from the 1970s

2e. Offer more housing near the water

Bad	Neither good nor bad	Good

2e. Offer more housing near the water

2d. Preserve the conceptual foundations of the buildings from the...

2c. Offer small-scale land ownership

2b. Offer more apartment sizes

2a. Offer more housing types

2d **is better than** 2b **is distinctly better than** 2a **is distinctly better than** 2e **is slightly better than** 2c

Figure 2. Question 2 from part 1 of the questionnaire.

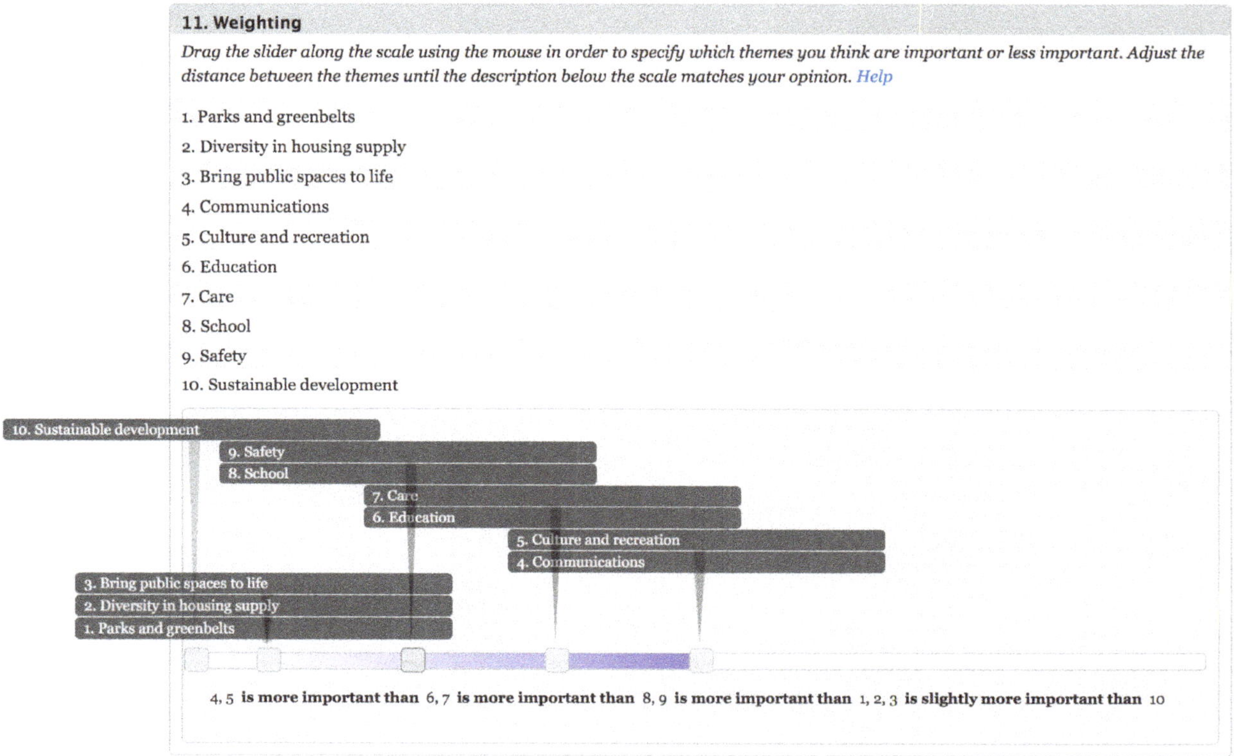

11. Weighting

Drag the slider along the scale using the mouse in order to specify which themes you think are important or less important. Adjust the distance between the themes until the description below the scale matches your opinion. Help

1. Parks and greenbelts

2. Diversity in housing supply

3. Bring public spaces to life

4. Communications

5. Culture and recreation

6. Education

7. Care

8. School

9. Safety

10. Sustainable development

10. Sustainable development

9. Safety

8. School

7. Care

6. Education

5. Culture and recreation

4. Communications

3. Bring public spaces to life

2. Diversity in housing supply

1. Parks and greenbelts

4, 5 **is more important than** 6, 7 **is more important than** 8, 9 **is more important than** 1, 2, 3 **is slightly more important than** 10

Figure 3. The weighting for the focus area.

THE CASE OF UPPLANDS VÄSBY

Given that decision-makers in a municipality want to investigate the opinions of citizens with regard to a set of possible future actions, then it is of interest to investigate if any of the actions could potentially lead to conflicts among the inhabitants. Together with the municipality of Upplands Väsby (UV) we decided to conduct a survey by using a web-based questionnaire. The focus areas and the actions under each focus area were developed in cooperation with the civil servants at UV. The questionnaire was divided into the following four parts:

- Part I consisted of ten questions each representing one 'focus area'. Under each focus area the respondent specified their preferences regarding five actions by using an implementation of D-CAR.
- Part II consisted of the task of weighting each of the ten focus areas using an implementation of CAR.
- Part III consisted of three questions regarding contradictions. The respondent was presented with two contradicting actions, and faced the task of either selecting one of the actions or neither of them.
- Part IV consisted of questions regarding the respondent's background.

An invitation letter was sent out to 10,000 inhabitants. The sample was obtained by conducting a simple random sampling on the sampling frame consisting of 31,408 inhabitants. The letter contained an invitation to participate and a URL to the online questionnaire. In total we received 1034 answers, of which, when asked to identify their gender, 528 answered male, 511 female, 18 did not want to disclose and 3 other/no gender. In this analysis, we focus on the two largest stakeholder groups, male and female. For each stakeholder group (male and female), for each action and criteria, we divide the stakeholders into two sets, the con group and the pro group. For the actions in the e-questionnaire, the respondents drag the handles on the slider. Each handle represents one action. Actions to the left of the midpoint are regarded as bad and actions to the right of the midpoint are considered to be good. Actions placed on the midpoint are considered to be neither good nor bad. The intensity of preference on the underlying absolute scale is represented by the coloured gradient on the slider (red to the left of the midpoint, and green to the right). The strength of preference between pairs of actions is described textually below the slider (Figure 2).

For the weighting of the focus area, the respondents drag the handles on the slider. Each handle represents one focus area. Focus

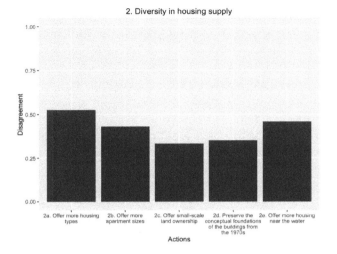

Figure 4. Disagreement within the female and male groups.

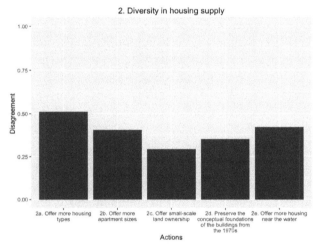

Figure 5. Disagreement within the female group.

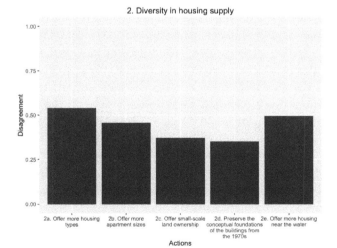

Figure 6. Disagreement within the male group.

areas to the right are considered more important than those to the left. The focus area's importance on the underlying absolute scale is represented by the blue coloured gradient on the slider. The strength of preferences between pairs of focus areas are described textually below the slider (Figure 3).

RESULTS

Without adjusting for different group sizes, we then analyse the levels of disagreement regarding the second focus area 'Diversity in housing supply'. First, the levels of disagreements between the combined female/male group are calculated. Then the female and male groups are analysed separately. Figure 4 shows the disagreement within the combined female/male group, in which the actions with the highest disagreement are 2a, 2b and 2e. Figures 5 and 6 show that this result is not affected when analysing the groups separately

DISCUSSION

Public decision problems involving multiple actions and multiple stakeholders involve complexities beyond those commonly addressed in decision analysis literature, which typically focus on handling uncertainty and/or conflicting objectives. One such complexity to consider is that the decisions affect many stakeholders who may have conflicting opinions regarding the potential actions, which may cause problems of both implementation and communication even though the criteria taken into consideration do represent social welfare criteria. In this chapter, we suggest and utilise a preference elicitation questionnaire where the stakeholders state negative, neutral or positive attitudes towards how different actions on the agenda perform against comprehensible objectives. We show how the so-called Dichotomous Cardinal Ranking (D-CAR) approach can be utilised to elicit stakeholder preferences and enable assessment of whether certain options involve greater degrees of disagreement than others, making them more controversial from a decision-maker perspective.

FURTHER READING

Allen, I.E. and Seaman, C.A. Likert Scales and Data Analyses. *Quality Progress.* 40(7), pp. 64–65. 2007.

Bayley, C. and French, S. Designing a Participatory Process for Stakeholder Involvement in a Societal Decision. *Group Decision and Negotiation.* 17(3), pp. 195–210. 2008.

Grabisch, M., Greco, S. and Pirlot, M. Bipolar and Bivariate Models in Multicriteria Decision Analysis: Descriptive and Constructive Approaches. *International Journal of Intelligent Systems.* 23(9), pp. 930–969. 2008.

Norman, G. Likert Scales, Levels of Measurement and the Laws of Statistics. *Advances in Health Sciences Education.* 15(5), pp. 625–632. 2010.

Pell, G. Use and Misuse of Likert Scales. *Medical Education.* 39(9), pp. 970–970. 2005.

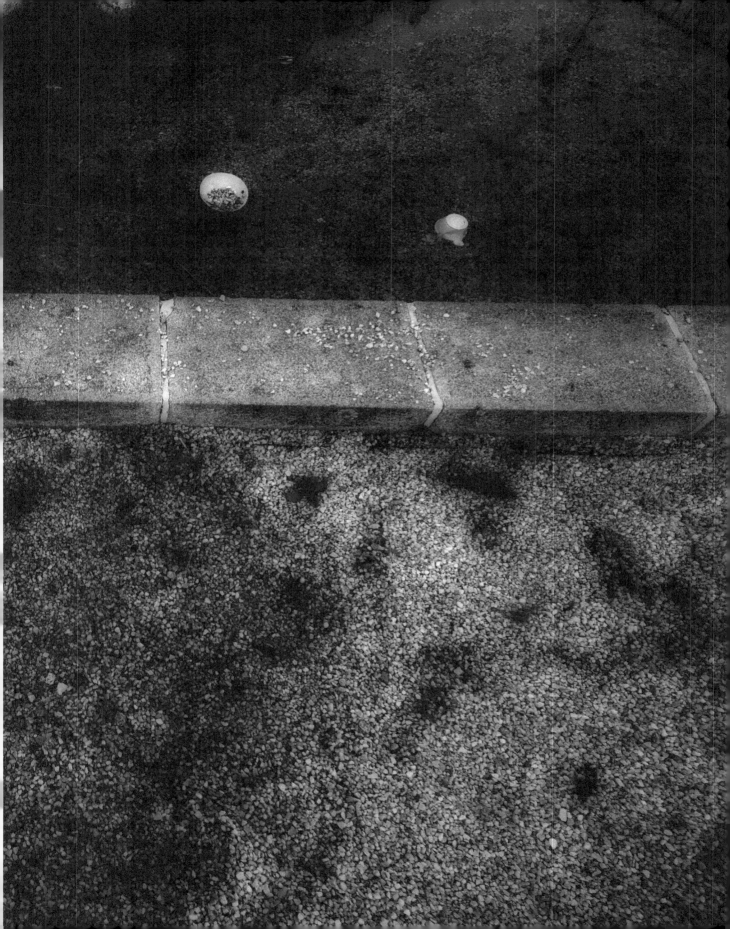

Evaluating ICT and Development

This chapter is based on Kivunike, F., Ekenberg, L., Danielson, M. and Tusubira, F. Towards a Structured Approach for Evaluating the ICT Contribution to Development, *The International Journal on Advances in ICT for Emerging Regions.* 7(1). pp. 1–15. 2014.

The evaluation of the contribution of information and communication technologies (ICT) to development has been challenged from theoretical, ethical and methodological angles. This chapter proposes a model to address some of these challenges that enables systematic evaluation of the contribution of ICT to development. The proposed model is conceptually motivated by Amartya Sen's capability approach – which defines development as freedom – as well as the ICT for development (ICT4D) value chain. Development is a process that involves the provision of opportunities (capabilities) from an ICT resource, as well as actually exploiting the opportunities to realise development benefits. The conversion of resources to opportunities and opportunities to development benefits is facilitated or inhibited by various contextual factors. Development from the capability perspective is both people-centred and multidimensional. This requires consideration of both instrumental effectiveness and intrinsic importance. The proposed evaluation process involves assessing the opportunities to realise benefits as well as the exploitation of them. Five evaluation dimensions concerning social and economic development are proposed, namely: research and education opportunities, healthcare, economic facilities, political freedoms and psychological well-being. ICT4D evaluation indicators are suggested for each dimension and a multi-criteria decision analysis (MCDA) structured evaluation process is proposed to guide the evaluation.

The evaluation of the contribution that ICT investments make to development continues to be an issue of great concern for both researchers and practitioners in ICT related development. The realisation of development benefits from ICT involves complex interactions between the technology, people and the context.

Development is a complex phenomenon, meaning different things to different people. The predominant or most promoted approach to ICT related development evaluation today focuses on the 'D' in ICT4D to tease out the development benefits. Progress has been registered especially in incorporating theoretical approaches such as development theories in the evaluation of the contribution of ICT to development. Given the inherent complexities, these studies/ evaluations are typically micro-based, focusing on individual or community evaluation and are mostly achieved through qualitative in-depth descriptions. These approaches generate a large amount of qualitative data and are not suitable for macro/ meso levels, as they would lead to complex analysis problems. However, there is still limited evidence of approaches seeking to establish the contribution of ICT even at higher macro/meso levels, such as national development goals, or multiple projects such as healthcare delivery, education, universal access and so on.

There is a need for structured approaches to facilitate an objective process for evaluation of the contribution of ICT to development. It is envisaged that the structured approach is intended to streamline the data collection and analysis process to ensure that the method is neither so simplistic that it overlooks essential details nor so elaborate that it inhibits proper reporting. It is believed that such structured approaches support large-scale evaluations which lead to inclusive development rather than selective development for only a few, as is normally reported for specific project evaluations. Moreover, a structured evaluation approach can also facilitate evaluation of a specific initiative at a micro level, for example, the contribution a community ICT facility makes to individuals' overall well-being.

To contribute to a growing field of ICT4D evaluation, this chapter addresses some of these challenges by adopting an interdisciplinary approach to ICT4D evaluation. It adopts an indicator-based approach whose model is based on development and information system models. It then applies multi-criteria decision techniques to facilitate structured data collection, analysis and reporting.

A literature review of the current state of evaluating the ICT contribution follows. A discussion of the underlying conceptual foundations applied in this study as well as the composition and interactions of the proposed model are then presented in the next section. This is followed by a proposition of possible criteria, and an explanation of how a MCDA can be applied to perform the evaluation. The chapter also gives different scenarios in which the evaluation approach could be applied, before concluding with a discussion of limitations and recommendations for future works.

EVALUATING THE CONTRIBUTION OF ICT TO DEVELOPMENT

There is an increase in studies in the area of ICT4D evaluation, with the most prevalent development-based approaches being the capability approach, the sustainability livelihoods approach and others mostly used in international development evaluation such as logical framework and results-based management. The capability approach is being increasingly applied to ICT4D research especially for qualitative evaluation. Studies have recently emerged that apply the approach to the development of ICT4D evaluation indicators. These propose both quantitative and qualitative indicators for ICT infrastructure, uses and capabilities and also suggest other indicators to evaluate the contextual influences on uptake. Partially drawing from the capabilities aspect of the approach, 'sustainable livelihoods' is defined as comprising the capabilities, assets (including both material and social resources) and activities required for a means of living. There is also evidence of substantial use of the sustainable livelihoods approach (SLA) in ICT4D. The SLA framework is applied in development evaluation because it is considered to be flexible and therefore applicable to different contexts, since it considers a wide range of aspects pertinent to the development process. On the other hand, it is criticised for its complexity as it contains a multiplicity of variables that make it more costly and time-consuming to implement, and difficult to form conclusions and generalisations from.

Programme theories include a collection of approaches that aim to show the logic between programme or project activities and expected outcomes. Common to all programme theory approaches is the underlying causal logic model which may be implicit or explicit, depending on the sources of information. The influence of contextual factors on programme results and a mechanistic approach to determining causality are also central in programme theories. It is apparent that any social intervention involves several factors that would contribute to the realisation of the outcome; yet it is complicated to attribute change to specific interventions. The goal, therefore, in programme evaluation is to understand the contribution of specific interventions and not to attribute change to them. This is the basis upon which the evaluation criteria are developed in this chapter. Programme theories have been referred to by a variety of names including theories of change, impact pathways and pathways of change.

Examples of methods that apply programme theories to establish a causal logic model are the theory of change (also contribution analysis), logical framework and results-based management. They are typically formative evaluation approaches that assess project progress against objectives. A more recent application of programme theory in development evaluation is the use of randomised control trials (RCTs) or randomised impact evaluation. Proponents point out that RCTs combat selection bias, which is inherent in several social programmes. While they may not be appropriate for all development problems, they have been applied to various cases, and are only starting to be adopted in ICT4D evaluations.

The majority of the ICT4D evaluation studies cited above apply development approaches to perform in-depth descriptive analysis. As a point of departure and contribution to this body of knowledge, the model suggested in this study illustrates the use of a structured evaluation approach that relies on indicators in the evaluation of the ICT contribution to development.

CONCEPTUAL FOUNDATIONS

Theoretical and conceptual foundations are essential to the realisation of sound evaluation approaches to support ICT evaluations. This facilitates the understanding of how technology interacts with society to achieve development. ICT4D studies fall within an emergent multidisciplinary field now referred to as 'development informatics' that seeks to integrate development theories within information systems, communication studies as well as computer science. This fairly new field resulted from the knowledge that there is more to ICT4D than just diffusion, adoption and use. The need to establish the real benefits of ICT in terms of what they are used for within various contexts called for new approaches. Consequently, there is a need for sound theoretical premises as a basis for research on how ICT is integrated and affects people's everyday lives and businesses as well as national and international development goals. Starting with the ICT4D value chain as a guide, the focus of evaluation in terms of the ICT4D implementation lifecycle in this study is identified. The capability approach is then applied to facilitate the definition and understanding of what development is and how it is realised.

THE ICT4D VALUE CHAIN

The ICT4D value chain model facilitates an understanding of ICT4D evaluation. It is based on the standard input-process-output model, linking resources and processes in order to systematically analyse the stages an ICT initiative traverses over time (see Figure 1). The input, an ICT4D intervention in combination with

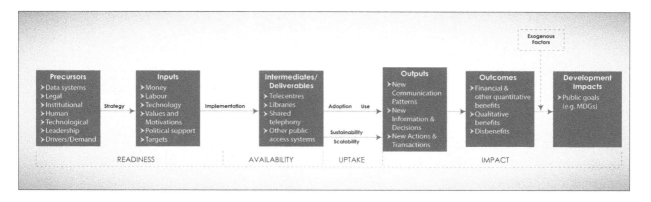

Figure 1. ICT4D value chain.

fulfilled prerequisites such as policies and implementation skills, facilitates the realisation of a deliverable, for example, a telecentre, or an e-library platform. These deliverables, once exploited by the target beneficiaries, result in outputs, which lead to outcomes and ultimately impact. The realisation of outcomes from outputs as well as impact from outcomes is affected by various contextual factors such as skills, institutional barriers and cultural or personal beliefs and so on.

Over the years interest in the domains along the value chain has shifted from readiness, availability and uptake towards development impact. This shift arises from the need for ICT4D initiatives to demonstrate that they actually contribute to social and economic development. However, the challenge in such evaluations is that as, one moves from outputs to impact, evaluation becomes more complex since the focus shifts from the technology to the development goals. As a result outcomes and impact cannot be attributed to a specific initiative since there are other factors or even initiatives that could have affected the outcome. To address this challenge, it is argued in this chapter that, rather than aiming at proving causality, emphasis should be placed on the contribution an initiative has made to social and economic development. This refers to the change in terms of social and economic development resulting from the presence of that intervention, within the boundaries of the contextual factors. Furthermore, focusing on the contribution is appropriate in situations where baseline studies were not performed to facilitate a longitudinal evaluation of the initiatives.

Moreover, the impact concepts – that is, outputs, outcomes and impact as per the value chain – have been variously defined based on the different approaches applied to the design and the evaluation of projects or programmes in international development. Generally, outputs are the immediate results of the programme or initiative. These can either be goods or services: such as workshops held, information produced, or changes in skills. In this study ICT4D *outputs* are the behavioural changes associated with technology use, consisting of the new information and decisions, new communication patterns and new actions and transactions that an ICT enables. Moreover, outputs in telecommunications are similarly defined as information made available and retrievable by computer. Outcomes (purpose), on the other hand, are the effects of outputs; in this study they are the direct benefits in terms of measurable (both quantitative and qualitative) benefits as well as costs associated with the outputs. Finally, *development impact* refers to the contribution of ICT to the broader development goals – impacts are less tangible. They are the long-term effects of the interventions. The output and outcome definitions adopted in this study are similar to the concepts of opportunities and achievements that are discussed in the subsequent section.

The value chain assumes a linear relationship between ICT and development, but this does not adequately represent the process since there are several aspects involved in explaining how and why development would result from an ICT4D initiative. For this reason, and because of the need to define adequately what development is and how it is realised in a given context, there is a need to adopt and integrate a development perspective as discussed in the following section.

THE CAPABILITY APPROACH

A development theory perspective facilitates the definition of what constitutes development. For this purpose, Amartya Sen's so-called capability approach has been adopted since it facilitates a multi-dimensional, people-centred approach to defining what constitutes development. Development, according to Sen, is the expansion of freedoms (capabilities or opportunities) to enable people to lead the lives they value. Development is more than the provision of access to a resource such as ICT: it is about what ICT can enable people to be or do given their contextual aspects. One of the reasons freedom is central to development is for purposes of evaluation. Sen points out that 'assessment of progress has to be done primarily in terms of whether the freedoms that people have are enhanced'. Basically it (1) views development in terms of values, for example, being healthy, being educated or being happy; and (2) evaluates how these have been enhanced by, for example, access to the internet in a given context. The premise of the capability approach is that a vector of a resource is transformed into a capability set within the restriction of conversion (contextual) factors. The capability set consists of functionings – things one can be or do to obtain the life one values. Simply defined, the capability set is the opportunities a development initiative offers. Achieved functionings, on the other hand, are the opportunities one chooses to exploit given one's specific context.

The capability approach also highlights the role human diversity plays in the realisation of development. Diversity mostly results from people's personal as well as external factors. These factors, referred to as conversion (or contextual) factors, determine people's preferences and choices of potential functionings. Conversion factors are classified as personal – individual characteristics such as physical disabilities, motivation, level of education, age, gender and sex; and social factors – the external legalities or societal requirements that may consist of public policies, social or cultural norms and discriminating practices. Another emerging category of social factors here is that of intermediaries, for example, non-government agencies that seek to promote ICT usage. Lastly, environmental aspects focus on location and accessibility of facilities, as well as technical aspects such as quality of service. An individual's capability set comprises both *well-being* – the opportunities available for a better life – and *agency* – one's ability to choose from the available opportunities based on personal values and circumstances. Agency takes into consideration the active involvement of beneficiaries in their development process; that is, whether they choose to exploit the available facilities for the improvement of their lives or not, depending on what they value and the prevailing circumstances.

The following are the multiple evaluation spaces within which policies and initiatives can be evaluated: well-being freedom which focuses on the capabilities or opportunities an initiative fosters; well-being achievement which is the achieved functionings; agency freedom which evaluates the freedom to achieve whatever a person decides he or she should achieve; and finally agency achievement which is the outcomes in terms of one's values, including those of other people and things.

PROPOSED ICT4D EVALUATION MODEL

As suggested by the capability approach, the realisation of development from an initiative is a process that besides the provision of the opportunities (capabilities) also involves the interaction of these capabilities with choice that is influenced by the conversion factors. This highlights two aspects: first, the need to perform a

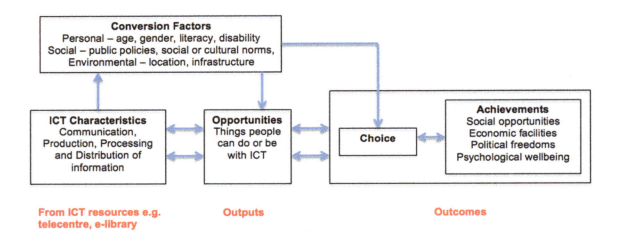

Figure 2. Proposed ICT4D evaluation model.

process analysis from capabilities to achieved functionings; and second, the need to explicitly establish the conversion factors that influence people's choices. Focusing on achieved functioning alone denies one insight into the process that is essential given that development initiatives are highly dependent on context. On the other hand, focusing on capabilities alone offers limited development evaluation, focusing on what the initiative initially can do, and not what it has actually done. Focusing on capabilities alone may also be perceived as techno-centric since evaluation is only performed on the opportunities an initiative can offer and does not investigate whether these were achieved.

Based on the above discussion, the constructs of the proposed evaluation model include ICT characteristics, conversion factors, opportunities (capabilities) and achievements (choice, personal or community goals, and achieved functionings), as shown in Figure 2. The ICT characteristics that a resource enables (communication; production, processing and distribution of information) provide opportunities within the limitations of the personal, social and environmental factors. Achievements are the opportunities one chooses to exploit within the restriction of conversion factors, and choice is also explicitly evaluated as one of the achievements.

Although governments (as well as development partners) can provide opportunities, they cannot decide how people live their lives. It is assumed that if someone's ability to make choices is increased or strengthened, it will enable them to choose to live the life they value. Outputs in relation to these definitions are the opportunities, while outcomes are the achievements. The achievement of certain functionings enables other opportunities: this is shown by the double pointing arrows between outputs and outcomes. For example, sensitisation to the benefits of using the internet empowers individuals to make wise decisions on how to use it.

ICT4D EVALUATION CRITERIA

Sen proposes five instrumental freedoms that enhance people's capabilities: social opportunities, economic facilities, political freedoms, transparency guarantees and protective security. It is argued that the extent to which these are secured is indicative of the level of an individual, household or community development. Since these freedoms are interrelated and supplement each other, they have been condensed to three: social opportunities, economic facilities and political freedoms. A fourth dimension, psychological well-being, is proposed as this evaluates the substantive freedoms such as choice and self-esteem.

Contingent on the nature of the initiative being assessed, all or just some of the dimensions may be applied. It is however imperative that psychological well-being is evaluated for all initiatives since it affects the achievements in other dimensions (e.g. as discussed in relation to choice). The dimensions are defined as follows:

- *Social opportunities*: arrangements society makes available to enable an individual to live a better life. From the capability perspective, this specifically focuses on education and healthcare.
- *Economic facilities*: opportunities that individuals enjoy to utilise resources for the purpose of consumption, production or exchange. This includes aspects such as productivity, employment etc.
- *Political freedoms*: opportunities people have to exercise their political rights e.g. being able to participate in local elections, community development programmes etc.
- *Psychological well-being*: physical, emotional and personal development opportunities. These are mostly a result of using ICT or participating in ICT4D projects. Examples include gaining respect from peers or gaining increased self-esteem. Psychological well-being has both substantive and instrumental value in that it enables people to exploit other opportunities in pursuit of development.

Depending on the nature of the evaluation, a set of criteria (as well as sub-criteria if necessary), such as 'Improvement in research quality and innovations' or 'Improved access to health services', can be defined for each dimension to facilitate an evaluation process. For each dimension, achievements (outcomes) and opportunities (outputs) are proposed. For example, it is presumed that to assess whether an initiative has improved access to formal or non-formal education (outcome/achievement) in the research and education dimension the following opportunities (outputs – what people do) are evaluated:

- Accessing information in relevant online resources, e.g. research journals, online libraries
- Participating in online research collaborations, e.g. through discussion forums
- Producing and publishing research outputs, e.g. journals, patents etc.

These are further granulated to define output and outcome indicators, such as:

- Accessing information in relevant online resources e.g. research journals, online libraries
- Accessing information in relevant online resources e.g. online courses/tutorials, e-learning platform, research journals, online libraries
- Accessing health-related information e.g. websites or short text messaging services that share information on good health practice, immunisation, pandemics etc.

Those indicators measure whether end users exploit the opportunity in terms of quality and usage. Quality seeks to establish whether end users actually value the opportunity, which will determine whether it is exploited.

The indicators proposed in this study are mostly qualitative and do not require precise data specifications. It is envisaged that the qualitative assessment facilitates a structured, approach that provides sufficient information to report the contribution of ICT to development. Elicitation of data for this approach relies on beneficiaries' perceptions, which can be imprecise information about how initiatives have been of benefit to people's well-being. Moreover, the use of structured approaches to evaluate the contribution of ICT to development is also recommended as a replacement for access and usage measures, which offer little as far as defining the actual ICT benefit is concerned.

Given the qualitative nature of the evaluation process, data collection, analysis as well as presentation of results can be supported by the more flexible systems-oriented and modelling techniques such as systems dynamics and MCDA. These facilitate the decomposition of complex decision problems for which quantitative approaches may be difficult or even inappropriate. For instance, the DecideIT platform for handling imprecise and vague information can be adapted for ICT4D evaluation. The approach facilitates multidimensional and multi-stakeholder assessment processes and evaluations, when the handling of uncertainty attributed to incomplete and vague information is necessary. This is a more instrumental alternative to the predominantly descriptive ICT4D evaluation approaches. An illustration of its applicability is presented in *Chapter 19.*

BENEFITS TO THE ICT4D EVALUATION PRACTICE

Recent empirical studies have proved that the proposed evaluation approach can be applied in different assessment scenarios depending on aspects such as the purpose of evaluation, level of analysis and availability of data. Examples include:

- An evaluation of how an initiative or project contributes to one or more development outcomes. In this case the evaluation is of a single initiative aimed at achieving one or more goals. This was demonstrated in the evaluation of the contribution of online learning (the initiative) to students' access to learning (the aim or goal). This study is reported in *Chapter 19*. While the study considered a single goal, the evaluation could be performed for more goals.
- A comparative assessment of the performance of two or more similar projects or initiatives on various social and economic outcomes. The initiatives should be similar in the sense that they aim at achieving the same goal, and can be evaluated according to the same set of criteria (outputs, outcomes and contextual factors). A typical case is the comparative evaluation of the ICT contribution to improved healthcare delivery in rural healthcare facilities in Uganda.
- An ex-ante evaluation of project proposals to establish perceptions of how they will perform on various outcomes and within the different contexts. Depending on the number of project proposals, as well as the target goals, this form of appraisal could take on the format in either scenario (a) or (b) above. For instance, if it is a single project aimed at achieving multiple goals, then scenario (b) would be the most appropriate. On the other hand, if there are multiple projects aimed at achieving one or more goals, then scenario (a) is the preferred option.
- An evaluation of the influence of contextual factors on the development outputs and outcomes of one or more initiatives. This is achievable in various ways. In the first instance, the contextual factors are one of the criteria categories just like the outputs or outcomes in the evaluation model. Alternatively, the influence of the contextual factors on the outputs and outcomes can be explicitly performed especially when the aim is to assess project risks.

Furthermore, the application of such an approach to evaluating the contribution of ICT to development is particularly recommended to supplement access and usage indices that offer little as far as defining the actual benefits is concerned. For example, when the proposed approach is applied for the evaluation of telecommunications and communications policies, ICT resources are assessed in relation to their provision of a range of opportunities rather than quantities. In this way, these evaluations establish how well or badly the policy, such as universal access/service, performs in terms of which of the defined opportunities have been achieved, and those that have not been realised. This provides a rich analysis in comparison with the evaluations of quantities which have been predominant with policy evaluations.

A STRUCTURED EVALUATION MODEL

This chapter proposes a structured model for the evaluation of the contribution of ICT to development. The model is based on the capability approach with aspects drawn from the ICT4D value chain as conceptual framework. One of the major challenges with the capability approach has always been its strongly and profoundly philosophical basis, which complicates attempts at its operationalisation. The work presented here contributes to the operationalisation of the capability approach as well as applying a development perspective to the evaluation of the contribution of ICT to development. However, unlike the existing applications of the approach, this study illustrates the use of indicators in the evaluation. Moreover the proposed approach offers more in comparison with the quantitative evaluations of availability and uptake. It is also multi-dimensional, explicitly considering the instrumental and substantive benefits of ICT, as well as the context in which they should be obtained. It further stresses the need to evaluate psychological well-being alongside the other dimensions, because this is both a means and an end in ensuring development.

The approach is envisaged to benefit ICT4D evaluation efforts for which in-depth descriptive evaluations are not possible due to various constraints related to budget, logistics or insufficiency of data. It may also serve for the comparative evaluation of multiple projects, ex-ante evaluation of development project proposals, and establishing the influence of contextual factors on the realisation of development benefits. To demonstrate its applicability, various empirical studies have been conducted, and a subsection of the proposed criteria was also applied in iMentors, an EU project developing a platform which will enable donors and development partners to review complete or existing projects to provide policy support and assist programme planning and implementation.

A limitation of the model is that it does not explicitly address unintended or negative benefits that are prevalent in any development initiative. In addition, the use of the more flexible systems-oriented and modelling techniques which facilitate the modelling of more qualitative, imprecise information are only in their infancy and would benefit from further studies to test their applicability. The proposed model could also provide a good basis upon which similar evaluations in other fields besides ICT could be built.

FURTHER READING

Heeks, R. Do Information and Communication Technologies (ICTs) Contribute to Development? *Journal of International Development.* 22, pp. 625–640. 2010.

Kivunike, F., Ekenberg, L., Danielson, M. and Tusubira, F. Using a Structured Approach to Evaluate ICT4D: Healthcare Delivery in Uganda. *The Electronic Journal of Information Systems in Developing Countries.* 66(8), pp. 1–16. 2015.

Sen, A. *Development as Freedom.* Oxford: Oxford University Press. 1999.

Senne, F., Barbosa, A. and Cappi, J. ICT in Brazilian Non-profit Organisations: Progressing towards the Development of ICT Indicators. Paper presented at the 12th International Conference on Social Implications of Computers in Developing Countries, Ocho Rios, Jamaica. 2013.

A Mobile Urban Drama as a Model for Interactive Elicitation

This chapter is based on Ernst, M. and Sauter, W. Antigone's Diary – Young Audiences as Co-creators of GPS-guided Radio Drama. *Nordic Theatre Studies*. 27(1). pp. 32–41. 2015.

RATS Theatre in Stockholm is a significant public forum that has revised popular conceptions of the city's suburbs of Husby and Kista. In this chapter we examine *Antigone's Diary*, one of the theatre's projects that has attracted a lot of attention (Figure 1–5) since its premiere in 2011. The drama has been performed over 50 times in Husby; more than half of the performances were arranged for classes of local school children, but teenagers also participated in performances targeted at a more general audience. Some performances were staged as part of Stockholm city council's cultural festival of. Approximately 1,200 people have participated in performances, up to and including the autumn of 2013 (since attendance is not dependent on ticket sales, the total the number of participants can only be estimated).

Having attended many of these performances, it strikes us as observers how closely the audience groups focused on the performance while they walking through the rather dull, uniform housing areas of this suburb. This was true not only of experienced theatre goers, but also the groups of teenagers from the nearby schools who followed the route from scene to scene, focusing on the play through their earphones and regularly responding to the questions posed to them. This connection was made possible through the distinctive way in which this production was devised.

Antigone's Diary, a new play based on the Greek tragedy *Antigone*, was written by Rebecca Forsberg, director of Swedish RATS Theatre. Sophocles' drama is transposed from ancient Greece to a contemporary Stockholm suburb and is staged through its audiences' mobile phones.

RATS Theatre began as a free theatre group in 2008 under the name Kista Teater and has from the start been located in the Stockholm suburbs of Husby and Kista. Ever since its inception, the theatre group has worked in collaboration with the Department of Computer and Systems Sciences (DSV) at Stockholm University, which has provided technical assistance. At the turn of 2012–2013, Kista Teater became RATS Theatre ('Research in Artistic Technologies for Society') and a part of DSV, with the aim of investigating possible encounters between theatre and digital technologies. A major focus of the cooperative work between DSV and RATS Theatre relates to the development of digital technologies enabling new opportunities for audience participation which will promote dialogue and social engagement.

The extent to which participation in a theatrical performance can serve as a test bed for more politically targeted involvement will be discussed in the conclusion of this chapter. First, we will discuss how mobility was used in an immigrant suburb to literally move audiences, and digital communication was employed in ways that transgress the limitations of time and place. After a brief presentation of the dramaturgical concept of this mobile drama we will focus on young audiences' responses to the performance and discuss how their opportunity to be part of the performance created a strong sense of participation. Their response also points towards

Figure 1. R. Forsberg, *Antigone's Diary*. Husby, Stockholm, 2011. Photo by Rebecca Medici.

the democratic appeal of this approach. From the perspective of computer science, the performances by RATS Theatre confirm that participatory digital techniques should be employed in the development of e-government, providing options for citizens to engage in public decision making.

Antigone's Diary works on a number of levels. Sophocles' *Antigone* is and has always been a political play: the confrontation between individual ethics and the power of the state has reverberated across history, not the least in the wake of fallen dictatorships. The play has inspired dramatists to create new versions of and Rebecca Forsberg's adaptation follows upon versions of *Antigone* by such writers as Friedrich Hölderlin, Jean Anouilh and Bertolt Brecht. And while the interplay of morality and power is intriguing, the production of *Antigone's Diary* brings two more aspects into play. One is the local theme, the closeness to the suburb – Husby is not only the setting of the work, but also its focus: it is right there, in their own streets and parks, that the audience finds the traces of *Antigone*. And Husby is in a way elevated by becoming the scene of an eternal conflict which includes both the mobile audience and all the inhabitants of this suburb – all of whom participate in creating the frame of the performance.

THE MOBILE STAGE

As developing digital technologies are increasingly integrated into performing arts productions, unexpected options are opened up for audience encounters. Today's digital innovations offer interactive possibilities whereby spectators are no longer mere recipients of performing arts, but can also examine, modify, and transform productions: the audience becomes part of the artistic expression and co-creator of the finished work. When RATS Theatre invites the audience to participate in its productions, they are not just engaged in the digital staging, but also included to air their own opinions and comments.

During its early years, RATS Theatre had no premises of its own, which gave rise to cooperation with local businesses and the use of temporary locations in the area. Instead of rootlessness being an obstacle, the theatre group saw it as an asset and a mobile existence became their artistic method. Movement prompted by necessity also touches on the basis of the migrant experience. The theatre group lacks a stable location, and its performances require its spectators to move from place to place – in a suburb that is dominated by migrants and their children. While their parents still struggle to make Husby their new home, far away from their original dwellings, the young generation have made this environment their own, though their experience is overshadowed by the traumas of their elders.

The neighbouring suburbs of Kista, where RATS Theatre and DSV are located, and Husby where the performances are staged, are neighbourhoods of strikingly contrasting social conditions. Husby was planned and built in the early 1970s and its first tenants moved in a few years later. Today, of its 12,000 inhabitants 84% were not born in Sweden or are children of immigrant parents. The district is afflicted by high unemployment and low levels of educational achievement. On the square where the performances commence there is a pizzeria, a kebab restaurant, some grocery stores, a dry cleaner and a pharmacy, as well as the public assembly hall.

Kista, located one subway stop before Husby, is known as the Silicon Valley of Sweden. Several of Sweden's leading new technology companies are headquartered here and 25,000 people are employed. Its shopping facilities include a big shopping mall with many international brands on offer.

Back to the teenagers gathered in the square of Husby. *Antigone's Diary* is a GPS-guided audio drama in twelve locations. The performance is designed as an application for smartphones, and audio files are played when the audience approaches predetermined venues. Before listening to the opening scene when Antigone and her friends have raised a sculpture, the young audience was given the information on their phones that Antigone has now disappeared, but her diary has been found. To join the search for her they have to enter their name or an alias into the smartphones.

To orientate themselves on their nomadic journey through the performance the teenage audience follows a map that appears on their phone display and voices and music are played in their earphones as they move on. After each scene the participants are invited to respond by text message to a question posed by Antigone. When they send in their answers participants can read other responses as they walk on to the next location. (After the performance the responses can also be found on the theatre's webpage.) This part of the performance creates a dialogue between the participants and is a significant part of the experience. And since many of the participants are locals, from Husby or neighbouring suburbs, the excursion also provides a new view of their quotidian environment.

When the teenagers leave the square they have a two-minute walk to a nearby schoolyard. The real sound of children playing in

Chorus

The world is full of wonder, but the greatest wonder is man

Antigone

In the centre there is a map, a shopping list of Husby

Everything that one need is here

But they have forgotten to write love

Chorus

The world is full of wonder, but the greatest wonder is man

Antigone

The most marvellous thing is to see Husby from above,
with all the courage that is there,
on the roofs, the trees, the street below.

Kista is the backdrop, is in the background of Husby.

Apartment upon apartment, they become great and tall.

Is Akalla the first or the last station on the blue lifeline?

Quote from Forsberg, R. Antigone's diary. Husby, Stockholm. 2011.

Figure 2. R. Forsberg, *Antigone's Diary*. Husby, Stockholm, 2011. Photo by Rebecca Medici.

Figure 3. R. Forsberg, *Antigone's Diary*. Husby, Stockholm, 2011. Photo by Rebecca Medici.

Figure 4. R. Forsberg, *Antigone's Diary*. Husby, Stockholm, 2011. Photo by Rebecca Medici.

the schoolyard mixes with the voices talking in the headphones. In the play, Creon tells the citizens of Thebes that Antigone's brothers are dead and that he has buried only one of them, Eteocles. Polynieces will remain unburied, to be eaten by dogs and birds. Creon says that whoever defies this order will be condemned to death. Antigone is distraught and her voice in the earphones asks participants: 'When is it permissible to refuse an order?'

In the following scenes the audience follow Antigone as she prepares and caries out her brother's funeral and then is arrested by the police and buried alive. Each location reflects to a greater or lesser degree the scenario played on the headphones. The scene where Antigone buries her brother is played out on a height where tall pine trees cast shadows over a rocky waterfall that is drained and filled with rocks of various sizes. While the park below is lush the rocks and pines express a barren environment. The twelfth and final scene brings the participants back to the square where they started. In their headphones they can hear mass protesters shouting in Arabic, a recording from the turmoil in Cairo's Tahir Square in. And the last question is about what freedom means to each individual participant.

The staging of *Antigone's Diary* focuses on its young audience as the main agent of the performance. The text of Sophocles' classical play has been scrutinised and reworked by RATS Theatre's artistic director Rebecca Forsberg in close collaboration with a group of teenagers from Husby. In particular, the questions asked at the end of each scene have been thoroughly discussed with the young participants, and as a result reflect the pressing concerns for young people: freedom, brother- and sisterhood, anxieties and secrets. At the same time, the responses of the participants, which everybody could read on their mobile telephone's display, added to the dramaturgy of the performance in an unpredictable way. The interactive responses did not change the plot of the play, but they contributed vividly to the involvement of the listeners. The participants had to define the visual expression of each scene, as it was set in Husby, through their audio experience. Although some locations helped this effort of imagination, the individual's experience was challenged more than it would have been by a play performed in a regular theatre. The young audience also had to identify and imagine the characters from their voices and bind together the fragmented plot. They completed the impulses of the performance with their own imaginations, their knowledge of the locations, and the interactions that the text messages prompted.

CHILDHOOD AND ADOLESCENCE IN THEORY

In recent decades, a new paradigm of childhood has emerged which is characterised by the basic concept that a young person's life has to be understood as a social construction. The young audience's behaviour and the way we chose to invite their interactions with new technologies have to be referred to the interdisciplinary field of children's culture. In all cultural expressions, children's participation is permeated by adult values and norms which are continuously debated and redefined. The interest in involving children and young people in adult-produced culture is based upon theoretical foundations in research fields such as childhood sociology and childhood studies. The concept of childhood varies over time and changes according to social, cultural and historical conditions as well as parameters such as gender, class and ethnicity. Children are thus not passive recipients of cultural and social patterns, but are agents who are able to supply, as well as change, the cultural and social life world they share with adults. Norms and ideals about children, childhood and adolescence are apparently in flux. The emergence of new technologies such as computers, social networking, computer games and mobile phones have come to change children and young people's position further. The view of children and young people as competent is particularly prominent in media research. Through their 'natural' proximity to digital media, young people become more interactive, creative, innovative, curious, open-minded, democratic and globally oriented, and challenge generational systems and power relations between children and adults. In the interviews, the young spectators very much confirmed these new insights in childhood studies.

AN IMMERSIVE EXPERIENCE

After each of the surveyed performances, interviews with young participants (who were usually pupils from the nearby schools) were carried out. When talking to the pupils it was obvious that they were committed to the performance and that they took their participation very seriously. They enjoyed it being staged in their mobile phones mainly for the focus on sound, and the freedom of movement. The voices and the music – and the lack of other theatrical devices – invited the pupils to create large parts of the performance in their minds. They had to imagine the appearance of the characters and the fictional places they inhabited. In the interviews it turned out that the making of the character and the fact that they had to walk around made the pupils feel like characters themselves: the teenagers confirmed that they entered a co-creation process during the performance. They also appreciated the fact that they had a lot more freedom to move about at their own pace – in contrast to seeing performances in theatres.

The way the performance is staged gives the pupils a lot of freedom. They could talk during the performance – and it was allowed. Other school experiences can easily have a negative impact, with adults repeatedly correcting pupils' behaviour. Even when the pupils had the freedom to do whatever they liked during *Antigone's Diary*, they turned out to be extremely focused on the performance.

What these young people express in the interviews is no less than a testimony of a deep-felt and honest involvement. Rosemary Klich and Edward Scheer have described this kind of response as immersion. Their conception of immersive involvement means that for the viewer/listener or simply the participant of a multimedia performance the technology of the performance becomes (almost) invisible and instead the beholder enters the fictional or symbolic world of the performance. Such an immersive effect of the performance on school children could not be taken for granted. The Bolter and Grusin's hypermediacy seems to disappear in favour of the immediacy of the encounter.

CONFRONTING ANTIGONE'S QUESTIONS

The audience is involved primarily in two ways in *Antigone's Diary*. They create the performance by combining the elements found in the audio drama, and they experience the surrounding environment; these are primarily individual processes. In addition, the audience has the opportunity to interact with the drama by answering the questions that Antigone asks. This interaction is an optional feature of the performance, but the vast majority of the spectators readily become active participants. The access to other participants' responses enhances a collective process among the audience: they all become part of creating the dramaturgy of the performance.

The analysis of the text messages of the teenagers' responses to Antigone's questions during the performance provides insights into how pupils perceived their role in the performance. The web-based material that is analysed here includes responses from seven school performances. Together, the material consists of 714 text messages from 77 different identities. The youngsters were mostly walking in pairs and thus many more individuals were involved in the responses. The young people who participated in the interviews represented very closely the majority of those who sent text messages. The material also includes messages from audience members who were observed but not interviewed.

When analysing the messages they were divided into different categories. The main category consists of proper answers to the questions and consists of 617 messages or 89.3 % of the total responses that have been analysed. It is not possible to make a detailed presentation of all the answers from the twelve locations. Instead some may serve as examples. After the first scene where Antigone and her friends have a discussion with the guard about the sculpture, Antigone asks the audience, 'What makes you angry?' The responses revealed a variety of thoughts and emotions: both caused by other people and instigated by the teenagers themselves. In some cases it can also be something concrete that makes them angry. In the scene where Creon proclaims that Antigone's brother Polynieces will remain unburied and Antigone decides to defy power, she asks the audience, 'When is it permissible to refuse an order?' From a democratic point of view, the responses to this question are of particular interest. Many of these school children have parents, relatives or neighbours who have escaped from dictatorships very similar to Creon's reign over ancient Thebes. These young citizens are in the process of adopting democratic visions of society and Antigone's situation reflects their own struggle to participate in tomorrow's politics.

Figure 5. R. Forsberg, *Antigone's Diary*, and J. Gustafsson Fürst, Scene 1, *Public Furniture In Public Space*. Husby, Stockholm, 2011. Photo by Rebecca Medici.

Some of the questions were more provocative than others. And there were a few answers that made fun of the questions in various ways. From the point of view of participation, even these answers are interesting: these members of the audience did not wish to take the opportunity of sharing their thoughts, but still wanted to be part of the performance. There was a demonstrable interest in showing their presence. And even amongst the very powerful and personal experiences of pupils observed and interviewed, we could also register differences between the pupils who lived and went to school in or close to Husby, and pupils who lived elsewhere. Those pupils who already had a relation to Husby were very positive about the performance, and most of them answered the questions in an engaged way. The pupils that had not been to Husby before did not participate with the same concentration and were much more likely to make fun of the questions than the local pupils.

ARTISTIC METHODS IN CITIZEN INTERACTION

During the season of the production newscasts were reporting the uprisings in Egypt, Tunisia and Libya. This had a strong influence on the young audience and several individuals explicitly connected the news reports to Antigone's actions and her fate. In this context, the development of e-democracy has had a special focus. Husby, as we have indicated earlier in this chapter, has been considered, not the least in the media's coverage, as a 'problematic' suburb, neglecting the potential and activism of its multi-cultural inhabitants. Indeed, the local population have displayed a degree of scepticism with regard to numerous reforms that have been initiated during recent years, not the least because these are considered to have been imposed on the citizens without significant dialogue in advance. Here *Antigone's Diary* has had an interesting function. It has been able to engage different groups of people and has, to a certain extent, changed the media image of Husby. News images of ethnic males presented as potentially dangerous 'other' have been replaced by attentive young women with headphones, listening to mobile theatre. So it is highly relevant to consider whether such modalities can be used for citizen communication in a broader setting, involving people whose voices are not often heard to any significant extent from a societal perspective. This is particularly interesting since deliberative forms of democracy in which citizens participate more actively in the planning and decision making procedures are generally considered utopian. The prevailing formal processes give disproportional power to people having the means, time and opportunity to participate in decision making and negotiations. Naturally, this situation in effect undermines a reasonable concept of democracy. In trying to understand this field one should probably start by asking what a decision actually is. Viewed abstractly, a decision is merely a concept. Concepts frequently designate a form and define how the form is used. In order to make form accessible in a specific context, it is necessary to study both the form and the context.

After all, this is all a matter of choice. We all seem to have a notion about individuality that we express in choices. And we can hardly choose to refrain from choosing, but an individual's own room for manoeuvre is always limited. A group naturally lends power to a decision that the individual often lacks. How are we to unite our professed individuality with more or less carefully considered concepts of collective choice mechanisms and power structures? Growing populations lead to different types of representations as well as to principles regulating relations, characteristics, agendas and participation. The collective aspect is of particular interest here, since people are not engaged to any significant extent and the actual empowerment, if there is any at all, tends to belong to a very small group, where a large proportion of the citizens are ignored. In this context, it is worth noting that *Antigone's Diary* is all about decision making. While Antigone herself is confronted with personal conflicts – with the ruler Creon, her sister Ismene, her lover Haimon – the performance does not stop at the fictional content. These conflicts are at the same time experienced by a collective of participants. The design of the performance with its interactive possibilities opens up for an immersive experience, which eventually implies access to an augmented reality. In terms of decision making, experiences of augmented reality enhance the insight citizens can gain into questions that concern their physical environment, such as city planning or other far-reaching political strategies. The concerns involved here are many, but everything circulates around how to design public process models and how these can be incorporated in highly complex decision making, encompassing different points of view, different perspectives, multiple objectives, and multiple stakeholders using different methods for appraisals.

How can *Antigone's Diary* contribute to this intricate elicitation, modelling and development of e-democracy? The performance shows how such interaction can be organised and also indicates the conditions under which the interaction can become successful. The creative process that has been invested in *Antigone's Diary* became a crucial prerequisite for the interaction potential of the performance. The clear, intelligible plot enhanced the communication, while in contrast the perceived lack of comprehensibility of the real-life problems at hand is something that forcefully prevents active participation in decision making processes. City planning is a typical example; the ground plans and blueprints are difficult for most people to understand and the terminology used to explain such documents is of such a technical character that only experts tend to understand it. In this situation, a significant proportion of people who are concerned or likely to be affected by the proposed plans are largely excluded from the public discourse. Despite not having a notion of pre-conceptive decision theory, *Antigone's Diary* skilfully demonsrated the importance of place, where city planning can serve as an obvious example. Often the plans are exhibited in the official locations where the authorities are based instead of bringing the exhibition to the population likely to be affected by these changes. The accessibility in terms of the location that is part of the stakeholders' own environment is as essential for city planning as it was for the drama of Antigone. Furthermore, guiding the participants to the exact locations which are the objects of the public discussions creates not only a virtual engagement but becomes the playground for practical involvement. The movement through places, especially in collective groups, enhances the participatory potential. Participation becomes a kind of playful way of engaging with serious issues. In addition, social media allow participants to instantly give expression to their perceptions.

EMOTIONAL IMMERSION AND RATIONAL RESPONSES

For those listening to the voices in their earphones, the interaction with *Antigone's Diary* expands from the physical to the mental. The performance triggers emotional immersion and rational responses. This transformation from nomadic movement to sensory and intellectual engagement is of utmost importance for the experience of participation – not only in a theatrical performance but also in society at large. What we have observed during the performances, in the interviews and the digital messages, are the meandering relations between the physical movements and the freedom these outdoor activities inspired. The youngsters were invited to contribute their own, often very personal, thoughts to a public discussion that they were longing to participate in, but rarely had an opportunity to engage with. The freedom they experienced during the walk provoked at the same time a mobility to their thoughts, reflected in their text messages that liberated them to think along new lines of perception of their own lives in this restricted suburb of their parents. As such, the experience of *Antigone's Diary* becomes a vehicle for democratic involvement and political engagement. The physical movements are transformed into a mobility of mind. The active citizen sees and hears, thinks and reacts and it all starts in one's own environment.

Husby is not a strange place for the majority of the young audiences. The suburb is, just as for the fictional Antigone, their home and the place where they grew up and live their daily lives. Unlike their parents, the teenagers no longer experience this suburb as an alien place. For the young audiences, the performance paves a way for leaving the older generation's traumatic histories, supported by the collective process of sharing their participation with friends and moving along neighbourhood streets with Antigone's classical dilemma in mind. As expressed in their comments, the young pupils realise that they are not only part of an age-old conflict, but that there might be a future that allows them – and which demands of them – to become part of a democratic society: freedom, equality and sisterhood (even more than brotherhood) are no longer only utopian ideals. The responses are not simply replies to Antigone's question. They also reflect the way the audience is invited into the play. Throughout the performance the participants function as co-creators. Although they cannot control the predetermined course of the production and their responses do not affect the structure of the drama, their voices become a supplement of the play's dramaturgy. The audience's answers are not edited by anyone. The teenagers' reactions, thoughts and feelings are displayed exactly as they are sent in by means of text messages. Besides the possibility of individual expression, the technology also creates opportunities for dialogue, discussion and interaction between the young people. *Antigone's Diary* illustrates a number of pertinent points about the issue of community involvement that have implications for the ways in which participation (on both a theoretical and practical level) can be considered by those working with these communities or supposedly representing their 'interests'.

Antigone's Diary ends as it began, in the square. In Ancient Greece the square – the agora – was a central place in the city-state, surrounded by shops and grocery stalls along the façades. It was a gathering place for citizens and at the time of Sophocles even women, servants and slaves went about their business there. The square was the place for debates, news and gossip, and personal deals were as much part of public life as the political speeches that addressed the decision making of the future. Most important then and now is openness in engaging in the questions and problems of society, and equal opportunities to participate in democracy.

FURTHER READING

Bolter, J.D. and Grusin, R. *Remediation – Understanding New Media.* Cambridge, MA: MIT Press. 1998.

Klich, R. and Scheer, E., *Multimedia Performance.* Basingstoke: Palgrave Macmillan. 2012.

Mortensen, C. and Vestergaard, V. Ordet er frit – og dit, in *Det interaktive museum,* K. Drotner, C. Papsø Weber, B. Larsen and A. Warberg Løssing (Eds.), Fredriksberg: Samfundslitteratur, pp. 43–60. 2011.

CALCULATION

During the last 50 years of activity in the field of decision analysis, a multitude of suggestions have emerged for compensating for people's inability to provide precise numbers as decision parameters. In particular, approaches based on sets of probability measures, upper and lower probabilities and interval probabilities have prevailed, as we have seen in earlier chapters. Various authors have also investigated other approaches to imprecise information. Viable approaches include upper and lower previsions, fuzzy logic, and interval logic as well as higher order theories. From a decision theoretical viewpoint, a common denominator of these approaches is a strong focus on representation and a lesser focus on the actual evaluation of problems represented using the respective format. Nevertheless, for a decision theoretical framework to be instrumentally useful, there is a need for efficient algorithms to solve the quite complicated equation systems that these types of models sometimes generate. In some model formulations, other statements such as comparisons between probabilities or between values are also allowed, adding further to the power of expression but also to computational complications. The limited amount of good tools for supporting elicitation of preference information in multi-criteria decision analysis causes practical problems that in our experience can be remedied by allowing more relaxed input statements from decision-makers. This causes the elicitation process to be less cognitively demanding and able to actually make use of the information the decision-maker is able to supply. Utilising this in relation to earlier chapters, we then propose some useful weight elicitation methods for multi-criteria decision making; the easier ones build on the ideas of rank-order methods, but increase the versatility by adding numerically imprecise cardinal information as well.

More precisely, in this section, we discuss various technical aspects of decision making. *Chapter 10* begins with a general overview of the area of multi-criteria decision analysis (MCDA). It discusses important classes of methods that, from a ranking of the criteria, receive an ordering which can be handled in various ways by, for example, converting the resulting ranking into numerical weights, so-called surrogate weights. Various proposals on how to do this exist, including rank sum, rank reciprocal and centroid (ROC) weights, as well as several variations thereof.

Thereafter, *Chapter 11* proposes combined methods for facilitating the elicitation process and shows how this provides a way to use partial information from the strength of preference judgement over weights in assessing weights for multi-attribute utility functions and suggests a method, the CAR method, trying to balance between the need for simplicity and the requirement of accuracy. CAR takes primarily ordinal knowledge into account but, recognising that there is sometimes a quite substantial information loss involved in ordinality, extends a pure ordinal scale approach with the possibility to supply more information. Thus, the main idea is not to suggest a method or tool with a very large or complex expressibility, but rather to present one that should be sufficient in most situations and in particular perform better than some hitherto popular ones from the SMART family as well as AHP.

Chapter 12 presents a unified method for combining probability-based analysis with multi-criteria decision making and discusses a software design of a general multi-criteria approach for modelling of multi-criteria and probabilistic problems in the same tree form, which includes a decision tree evaluation method integrated with a framework for analysing decision situations under risk with a criteria hierarchy. The general method of probabilistic multi-criteria analysis extends the use of additive and multiplicative utility functions for supporting evaluation of imprecise and uncertain facts.

10

Multi-Criteria Decision Making

During the last few decades, decision theory has developed significantly in a multitude of ways, but decision analysis tools are still seldom utilised to aid decision making processes in most organisations, and people rarely perform formal analysis to help with complex problems. The field of decision analysis has developed as a structured approach to formal analysis of decision problems. The field is based on research from several disciplines, in particular organisation theory, business administration, psychology, statistics, computer science, and philohy. Behavioural concerns have not, despite a quite substantial activity within descriptive theories, received sufficient attention and there is still a lack of support for the decision analytic process itself. Over the years, research on the formal properties of decision making has moved from the initial studies of a rational theory of choice based upon single objective decision problems towards pursuing the design of decision support methods for more realistic decision making situations with multiple objectives. After identifying objectives and the available courses of action, the possible consequences are analysed formally on the basis of the provided input data.

THE DECISION ANALYSIS DOMAIN

In classic decision theory the different alternatives are merely objects of choice, and it is assumed that a decision-maker can assign precise numerical values corresponding to the true value of each consequence, as well as precise numerical probabilities even if uncertainty prevails. Thus, the ordering of alternatives is a delicate matter and an equitable mathematical representation is crucial.

There are basically two main areas within decision theory: decisions under risk (probabilistic decisions) and multi-criteria decisions. Despite similarities between the approaches, these two

This chapter is based on Danielson, M. and Ekenberg, L., Rank Ordering Methods for Multi-Criteria Decisions. *Proceedings of 14th Group Decision and Negotiation – GDN 2014*. Springer. 2014.

areas have separate traditions within which they evolve. This is unfortunate, since in real-life decision making problems are often encountered which contain several aspects (criteria) as well as probabilistic consequences, i.e. the outcome of a choice can be more than one possible state. It would be of great benefit if these two approaches could be merged, yielding a generalisation of both multi-criteria decision making and decisions under risk. Further, in attempting to address real-life problems, where uncertainty about data prevails, some kind of representation of imprecise information is important, such as interval-valued functions or fuzzy sets. This chapter will suggest a unification of the probabilistic and multi-criteria approaches to decision making while also attending to the requirement of handling imperfect information.

DECISIONS UNDER RISK

Decisions under risk (probabilistic decisions) are often represented as a tree. This is to simplify the reading of the tree as a sequence of events leading up to final consequences, the end nodes. For an example, consider the tree in Figure 1.

A decision tree consists of a root node, representing a decision, a set of intermediary (event) nodes representing some kind of uncertainty, and consequence nodes representing possible final outcomes. Usually, probability distributions are assigned in the form of weights in the probability nodes as measures of the uncertainties involved. The informal semantics are simply that, given that an alternative A_i is chosen, there is a probability p_{ij} that an event occurs. This event can either be a consequence with a value v_{ijk} assigned to it or another event. Usually, the maximisation of the expected value is used as an evaluation rule. For instance, in Figure 1, the expected value of alternative A_i is:

$$E(A_i) = \sum_{j=1}^{2} p_{ij} \sum_{k=1}^{2} p_{ijk} v_{ijk1}$$

This is a straightforward characterisation of a multi-level probabilistic decision model.

MULTIPLE CRITERIA

There are also several approaches to multi-criteria decision making, the key characteristic being that there is more than one perspective (criterion, aspect) from which to view the alternatives and their consequences. For each perspective, the decision-maker

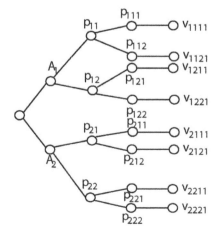

Figure 1. A decision tree for decisions under risk.

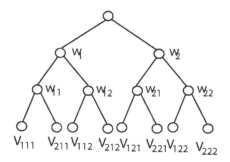

Figure 2. A criteria hierarchy.

must somehow assign values to each consequence on some value scale. One large category of approaches is where the decision criteria can be arranged in hierarchies, see Figure 2. One of the most widespread models in this category is the analytical hierarchy process (AHP) method.

For a criteria hierarchy, on each level the criteria are assigned weights and the alternatives are valued with respect to each sub-criterion. (Flat criteria weight approaches can be seen as a special case – a one-level hierarchy.) As for decision trees, the maximisation of the weighted value is usually employed as an evaluation rule. For instance, in Figure 2, the value of alternative A_i under sub-criterion jk is denoted by v_{ijk}. The weight of criterion j is denoted by w_j. Then the weighted value of alternative A_i is:

$$E(A_i) = \sum_{j=1}^{2} w_j \sum_{k=1}^{2} w_{jk} v_{ijk}$$

Thus, in both probabilistic and multi-criteria approaches, the alternative with the greatest weighted value is suggested to be chosen. This is straightforwardly generalised and multi-criteria decision trees of arbitrary depth can be evaluated by the following expression:

$$E(A_i) = \sum_{i_1=1}^{n_{i_0}} x_{ii_1} \sum_{i_2=1}^{n_{i_1}} x_{ii_1 i_2} \cdots \sum_{i_{m-1}=1}^{n_{i_{m-2}}} x_{ii_1 i_2 \cdots i_{m-2} i_{m-1}} \sum_{i_m=1}^{n_{i_{m-1}}} x_{ii_1 i_2 \cdots i_{m-2} i_{m-1} i_m} x_{ii_1 i_2 \cdots i_{m-2} i_{m-1} i_m} ,$$

One very important practical issue is how to elicit criteria weights (and also values) realistically from actual decision-makers. Considering the judgement uncertainty inherent in all decision situations, elicitation efforts can be grouped into (a) methods handling the outcome of the elicitation by precise numbers as representatives of the information elicited; and (b) methods instead handling the outcome by interval-valued variables. A vast number of methods have been suggested for assessing criteria weights using exact numbers. These range from relatively simple ones, like the commonly used direct rating and point allocation methods, to somewhat more advanced procedures. Generally in these approaches, a precise numerical weight is assigned to each criterion to represent the information extracted from the user. There exist various weighting methods that utilise questioning procedures to elicit weights, such as SMART and Swing weighting. However, the requirement for numeric precision in elicitation is somewhat problematic. For instance, significant information is in practice always more or less imprecise in its nature. People's beliefs are not naturally represented in numerically precise terms in our minds. There are several versions within the SMART family of methods with seemingly small differences that have been shown to have important effects for the actual decision making. For instance, SMART and Swing were later combined into the SMARTS method. In general, trade-off methods appear to be quite reasonable for weight elicitation but can nevertheless be very demanding due to the number of judgements the decision-maker is required to make.

UTILITY AGGREGATION

A variety of approaches for aggregating utility functions have been suggested for evaluations of decision problems involving multiple objectives (criteria). Techniques used in multi-attribute utility theory (MAUT) have been implemented in software packages such as SMART and Expert Choice, the latter being based on the AHP method. However, nearly all of these approaches require numerically precise information when analysing and evaluating decision problems – a requirement that is often considered unrealistic in real-life situations where only imperfect information is available.

Interval approaches have, to some extent, been incorporated to extend decision models for multi-criteria decision making. The tool PRIME is one of the most elaborate approaches to modelling generalised value-tree analysis involving multiple attributes, supporting the imprecision of the input parameters. PRIME features a useful elicitation tour, where the decision-maker makes interval-valued ratio estimates for value differences. In the discrimination of alternatives, PRIME calculates value intervals for each alternative, but does not perform further investigations of the problem when the value intervals are overlapping. Thus, PRIME in its current form is more concerned with the process of elicitation of the input parameters, and to a lesser extent on techniques of evaluation of imprecise data and comparisons between different courses of action. The preference programming method generalises the AHP method in this respect. A related approach is the RICH method. However, both these are limited with respect to expressibility. Software packages that only handle fixed numerical data (i.e. no intervals) do not give rise to complicated algorithms. Thus, from the perspective of software algorithm development, they are not overly complex. The ARIADNE system allows for the usage of imprecise input parameters, but does not discriminate between alternatives when these are evaluated into overlapping intervals. There are also some approaches for combining (one-level) criteria weights with Bayesian reasoning.

IMPRECISION IN ELICITATION

As responses to the difficulties in eliciting precise weights from decision-makers, many approaches have been suggested which are less reliant on high precision on the part of the decision-maker while still aiming at non-interval representations. Ordinal or other imprecise importance (and preference) information could be used for determining criteria weights (and values of alternatives). One approach is to use surrogate weights which are derived from ordinal importance information. In such methods, the decision-maker provides information on the rank order of the criteria – in other words, supplies ordinal information on importance – and thereafter this information is converted into numerical weights consistent with the extracted ordinal information.

In interval-valued approaches to the elicitation problem, incomplete information is handled by allowing the use of intervals. Such approaches also make less demands on the decision-maker and are suitable for group decision making as individual differences in importance weights and judgements can be represented by value intervals (sometimes in combination with orderings). The decision-maker is allowed to enter interval assessments to state imprecision in the judgements. The extracted weight information is represented by constraints for the attributes' weight ratios, which in addition to the weight normalisation constraint determine the feasible region of the weights in the interpretational step.

There are ways of simplifying the elicitation, for example, the idea of assigning qualitative levels to express preference intensities in the MACBETH method, ranking differences using a delta-ROC approach or Simos's method of placing blank cards to express differences. There are also methods such as SMART Swaps with preference programming. Other researchers mix various techniques, as in the GMAA system, which suggests two procedures for weights assessments. The extraction can be based either on trade-offs among the attributes, where decision-makers may provide intervals within which they are indifferent with respect to lotteries and certain consequences, or on directly assigned weight intervals to the respective criteria. The extracted interval values are then automatically computed into an average normalised weight (precise) or a normalised weight interval for each attribute. Such relaxations of precise importance judgements usually seem to provide a more realistic representation of the decision problem and are less demanding for users in this respect. However, there are several computational issues involved that restrict the kind of statements that can be allowed in these representations and often the final alternatives' values have a significant overlap, making the set of non-dominated alternatives too large, which must be handled, for example, by using more elaborated second-order techniques. There are also various approaches to modify some classical, more extreme, decision rules, such as absolute dominance as well as the central value rule. The latter is based on the midpoint of the range of possible performances.

The handling of decision processes could be efficiently assisted by software packages. The SMART method and AHP techniques have been implemented in computer programs. Computer support is even more necessary for methods that are significantly more demanding computationally. In conclusion, there are several approaches to elicitation in MAVT problems and one criterion for categorising the methods is how they handle imprecision in weights (or values).

1. Weights (or values) can only be estimated as fixed numbers.
2. Weights (or values) can be estimated as comparative statements converted into fixed numbers representing the relations between the weights.
3. Weights (or values) can be estimated as comparative statements converted into inequalities between interval-valued variables.
4. Weights (or values) can be estimated as interval statements.

Needless to say, there are advantages and disadvantages with the different methods from these categories. Methods based on categories 1 and 2 yield computationally simpler evaluations because of the weights and values being numbers, while categories 3 and 4 yield systems of constraints in the form of equations and inequalities that need to be solved using optimisation techniques. If the expressive power of the analysis method only permits fixed numbers (category 1), we usually get a limited model that might severely affect the decision quality. If intervals are allowed (categories 3 and 4), imprecision is normally handled by allowing variables, where each y_i is interpreted as an interval such that $w_i \in [y_i - a_i, y_i + b_i]$, where $0 < a_i \leq 1$ and $0 < b_i \leq 1$ are proportional imprecision constants. Similarly, comparative statements are represented as $w_i \geq w_j$.

In another tradition, using only ordinal information from category 2 and not numbers from category 1, comparisons replace intervals as an elicitation instrument handling imprecision and uncertainty. The inherent uncertainty is captured by surrogate weights derived from the strict ordering that a decision-maker has imposed on the importance of a set of criteria in a potential decision situation. However, we might encounter an unnecessary loss of information by using only an ordinal ranking. If, as a remedy, we use both intervals and ordinal information, we are faced with some rather elaborate computational problems. Despite the fact that they can be solved by sufficiently restricting the statements involved, there is still a problem with user acceptance and these methods have turned out to be perceived as too difficult to apply by many decision-makers. Expressive power in the form of intervals and comparative statements leads to complex computations and loss of transparency on the part of the user.

It should also be noted that multi-attribute value theory (MAVT), despite being the main focus in this part of the book, is not the only suggestion for handling multi-criteria decision problems, even if it is one of the most popular approaches today. There are also techniques, such as ELECTRE and PROMETHEE in various versions, where decision-makers are asked to rank information to find outranking relations between alternatives. For the remainder of the book we will, however, focus on MAVT.

SURROGATE WEIGHTS

One important class of methods rank the criteria and receive a *criteria ordering* which can be handled in various ways by, for example, converting the resulting ranking into numerical weights, so-called *surrogate weights*. There are various proposals for how to do this exist, including rank sum, rank reciprocal and centroid (ROC) weights as well as several variations thereof. In this chapter, we analyse the relevance of these methods and to what extent some validation processes are strongly dependent on the simulation assumptions. We also suggest more robust methods as candidates for modelling and analysing multi-criteria decision problems of this kind.

One of the problems in real-life decision making is that numerically precise information is seldom available, and when it comes to providing reasonable weights, there are significant difficulties due to the fact that we do not seem to have the required granulation capacity and we also suffer from other deficiencies. To somewhat facilitate eliciting weights from decision-makers, some of the approaches utilise ordinal or imprecise importance information to determine criteria weights and sometimes values of alternatives. Other approaches use intervals to express the uncertainty inherent in elicitation procedures. However, it is not obvious how to determine the decision quality of a multi-criteria weighting method, but the quality of a candidate method should be assessed in one way or another. One basic idea is to generate surrogate weights as well as 'true' reference weights from some underlying distribution and investigate how well the result of using surrogate numbers matches the result of using the 'true' results. The idea in itself is good, but the methodology is vulnerable since the validation result is heavily dependent on the distribution used for generating the weight vectors. This chapter discusses some important aspects and shortcomings of some popular weight methods as well as the validation techniques for them. We also discuss the relevance and correctness of some common measurements for method validation and conclude with a discussion of more robust methods that might be better candidates.

RANK ORDERING METHODS

In MCDM, different elicitation formalisms have been proposed by which the decision-maker can express preferences. Such a formalism is sometimes based on scoring points, as in point allocation (PA) or direct rating (DR) methods. In PA, the decision-maker is given a point sum, e.g. 100, to distribute among the criteria. Sometimes, it is pictured as putty with the total mass of 100 that is divided and put on the criteria. The more mass, the greater the weight on a criterion. In PA, there are consequently N–1 degrees of freedom (DoF) for N criteria. DR, on the other hand, puts no limit to the number of points to be allocated. The decision-maker allocates as many points as desired to each criterion. The points are subsequently normalised by dividing by the sum of points allocated. Thus, in DR, there are N degrees of freedom for N criteria. Regardless of the elicitation method, the assumption is that all elicitation is made relative to a weight distribution held by the decision-maker. There is also a discussion on weight approximation techniques which includes the suggestions of rank sum (RS) weights and rank reciprocal (RR) weights. They are suggested in the context of maximum discrimination power, and are both alternatives to ratio-based weight schemes. The rank sum is based on the idea that the rank order should be reflected directly in the weight. Assume a simplex S_w generated by $w_1 > w_2 > ... > w_N$, where $\Sigma w_i = 1$ and $0 \leq w_i$. Assign an ordinal number to each item ranked, starting with the highest ranked item as number 1. Denote the ranking number i among N items to rank. Then the RS weight becomes for all $i = 1,...,N$

$$w_i^{RS} = \frac{N + 1 - i}{\sum_{j=1}^{N}(N + 1 - j)} = \frac{2(N + 1 - i)}{N(N + 1)}$$

Another early idea is rank reciprocal (RR) weights. They have a similar origin as the RS weights, but are based on the reciprocals (inverted numbers) of the rank order for each item ranked. These are obtained by assigning an ordinal number to each item ranked, starting with the highest ranked item as number 1. Then denote the ranking number i among N items to rank and the RR weight becomes

$$w_i^{RR} = \frac{1/i}{\sum_{j=1}^{N} \frac{1}{j}}$$

Another weight method is based on vertices of the simplex of the feasible weight space. To use the rank order, the ROC (rank order centroid) weights are calculated. These are the centroid components of the simplex S_w. That is, ROC is a function based on the average of the corners in the polytope defined by the simplex $S_w = w_1 > w_2 > ... > w_N$, $\Sigma w_i = 1$, and $0 \leq w_i$. The weights then become the centroid (mass point) components of S_w. The ROC weights, for the ranking number i among N items to rank, are then given by

$$w_i^{ROC} = 1/N \sum_{j=i}^{N} \frac{1}{j}$$

In this way, it resembles RR more than RS but is, particularly for lower dimensions, more extreme than both in the sense of weight distribution, especially the largest and smallest weights.

A COMBINED METHOD

Of the three methods above, ROC is the candidate that has been considered to be the most promising. However, it has often been argued that ROC weights are perceived to be too steep or discriminative. By that is meant that too great an emphasis is put on the larger weights, that is, on those criteria ranked highest in the ranking order, and similarly too little emphasis on the smaller ones. It is important to note that ROC, RS and RR perform well only for specific assumptions on the assignment of criteria weight preferences by decision-makers.

Since these weight models are in a sense opposites, it interesting to see how extreme behaviours can be reduced. A natural candidate for this could be a linear combination of RS and RR. Since we have no reason to assume anything else, we suggest balancing them equally in an additive combination of the sum and the reciprocal weight function that we will call the SR weight method:

$$w_i^{SR} = \frac{1/i + \dfrac{N+1-i}{N}}{\sum_{j=1}^{N} \left(1/j + \dfrac{N+1-j}{N}\right)}$$

Of course, other combinations of weights would be possible, but the important results of the chapter are obtained using SR and comparing it with other weight functions. For another candidate, the actual mix of the proportions between the methods would affect the results in accordance with its proportions. As will be shown below, all results are sensitive to the underlying assumptions regarding the mindsets of decision-makers. The SR method is representative of a class of methods able to handle varying assumptions on decision-maker behaviour and fine-tuned with respect to the individual in question. It is beyond the scope of this chapter to try to fine-tune a mix of weighting functions. The main results regarding robustness below are obtained using SR and its behaviour in relation to RR, ROC and RS.

GEOMETRIC WEIGHTS

Geometric weights are based on the idea that the rank order should be reflected multiplicatively in the numeric weights. The multiplicative nature of the geometric weight can be motivated by the likewise multiplicative nature of the terms $w_i^X v_i(a)$ that the overall value $V^X(a) = \sum_{i=1}^{m} w_i^X v_i(a)$ consist of. Assign an ordinal number to each item ranked, starting with the highest ranked item as number 1. Denote the ranking number i among N items to rank. Then the geometric sum (GS) weight becomes

$$w_i^{GS}(s) = \frac{s^{i-1}}{\sum_{j=1}^{N} s^{j-1}} \text{ for } 0 < s < 1$$

As usual, a greater weight is assigned to lower ranking numbers. Similar to some other suggested weight methods, GS contains a parameter s.

ASSESSING MODELS FOR SURROGATE WEIGHTS

Simulation studies have become a kind of de facto standard for comparing multi-criteria weights. The underlying assumption of most studies is that there exist weights in the decision-maker's mind which are inaccessible by any elicitation method. We will continue this tradition when determining the efficacy, in this sense, of some ranking approaches below. The modelling assumptions regarding decision-makers above are then inherent in the generation of decision problem vectors by a random generator. Thus, following an $N–1$ DoF model, a vector is generated in which the components sum to 100%, that is, a process with $N–1$ degrees of freedom. Following an N DoF model, a vector is generated keeping components within and subsequently normalising, that is, a process with N degrees of freedom. Other distributions modelling actual decision-makers would of course be possible, and could be elicited in one way or another. However, this is not the main point in the chapter. The important observation is that the validation methods are highly dependent on the model of decision-makers and this produces significant effects on the reliability of the validations. The degree of freedom is consequently only one type of dichotomy, but one actually expressing a meaningful semantics for discriminating cognitive models in this respect.

SIMULATION STUDIES AND THEIR BIASES

Thus, in the simulations described below it is important to realise which background model we utilise. As stated above, when following an $N-1$ DoF model, a vector is generated in which the components sum to 100%. This simulation is based on a homogenous N-variate Dirichlet distribution generator. On the other hand, following an N DoF model, a vector is generated without an initial joint restriction, only keeping components within yielding a process with N degrees of freedom. Subsequently, they are normalised so that their sum is 100%.

We will call the $N-1$ DoF model type of generator an $N-1$-*generator* and the N DoF model type an *N-generator*. Depending on the simulation model used (and consequently the background assumption of how decision-makers assess weights), the results become very different. For instance, ROC weights in N dimensions coincide with the mass point for the vectors of the $N-1$-*generator* over the polytope S_w. Thus, when using $N-1$ DoF generated random vectors, ROC will always outperform all other surrogate weights in a simulation study. This is not a measure of ROC's superiority but of its match to the random generating function. Similarly, since RS weights are very close to the mass point of an N-generator over the polytope S_w, it is likewise not a measure of RS's superiority that it outperforms other surrogate weights when an N DoF simulator is employed. In reality, though, we cannot know whether a specific decision-maker (or decision-makers in general) adhere more to $N-1$ or N DoF representations of their knowledge. Both as individuals and as a group they might use either or be anywhere in between. A, in a reasonable sense, *robust* rank ordering mechanism must employ a surrogate weight function that handles both styles of representation and anything in between. Thus, the evaluation of surrogate weights in this chapter will use both types of generators and combinations thereof to find robust weights.

COMPARING THE METHODS

The idea behind these types of comparisons is to measure the validity of the method by simulating a large set of scenarios utilising surrogate weights and see how well different methods provided results similar to scenarios utilising 'true' weights. Again, note that the notion of a 'true' weight is dependent on the decision-maker model. Some studies assume an N–1 DoF model and base the analysis on a computer simulation consisting of four steps, assuming the problem is modelled as the simplex S_w. The generation procedure for the simulation's random vectors is:

1. For an N-dimensional problem, generate a random weight vector with N components. This is called the TRUE weight vector. Determine the order between the weights in the vector. For each method $X' \in \{\text{ROC,RS,RR,SR,GS}\}$, use the order to generate a weight vector $w^{X'}$.
2. Given M alternatives, generate $M \cdot N$ random values with value v_{ij} belonging to alternative j under criterion i.
3. Let w_i^X be the weight from weighting method X for criterion i. For each method $X \in \{\text{TRUE,ROC,RS,RR,SR,GS}\}$, calculate $V_j^X = \sum_i w_i^X v_{ij}$. Each method produces a preferred alternative, i.e. the one with the highest V_j^X.
4. For each method $X' \in \{\text{ROC,RS,RR,SR,GS}\}$, assess whether X' yielded the same decision (i.e. the same preferred alternative) as TRUE. If so, record a hit.

This is repeated a large number of times (simulation rounds). The hit rate is defined as the number of times a weighting method made the same decision as TRUE. The study also uses two other measures of efficacy: average value loss and average proportion of maximum value range achieved. The two latter measures are strongly correlated to the hit ratio and do not add much insight into method performance. The results of the original study were that ROC outperformed the other two weighting methods which in turn by a wide margin outperformed a method based on equal weights. Of the two other, RR was slightly superior to RS. Since the three methods require equal input from the decision-maker, the conclusion was made that ROC was to be preferred among the surrogate weights. Using an N–1-generator simulation model over the simplex S_w, the results of the Barron and Barrett study can easily be verified. However, note that this distribution favours the ROC method since the centroid of the generated 'true' weights is the same as the vector of the corresponding ROC weights.

It should be noted that most simulation studies to date arrive at the same conclusions regarding ROC, RS and RR. As we have emphasised above, this is not surprising since different simulations using the same assumptions on degrees of freedom and definitions of weighting methods should (except for programming errors) yield the same results. As expected, a study by Roberts and Goodwin, using a more unusual N-generator, came up with a different result where RS performed better than ROC with RR in third place. The random weight distribution in most simulations (in step 1 of the generation procedure above) is generated by an N–1 procedure, thus generating a vector with N–1 DoF. There are however other methods and one can, for example, employ a different distribution generating function where a fixed number, say 100, is given to the most important criterion and the others are uniformly generated as U. As explained above, this N-generator is not the same as N–1-generators based on a Dirichlet distribution and thus their simulation study instead yields the result that RS outperforms ROC with RR in third place. Given an N-generator, RS outperforms ROC and RR with EW far behind. ROC is slightly better than RR. While yielding a different 'best' weighting method, this result is consistent with the other study results considering it is merely a consequence of the choice of DoF in the simulator generator.

SIMULATION RESULTS

The simulations were carried out with a varying number of criteria and alternatives. There were four numbers of criteria $N = \{3, 6, 9, 12\}$ and five numbers of alternatives $M = \{3, 6, 9, 12, 15\}$ creating a total of 20 simulation scenarios. Each scenario was run 10 times, each time with 10,000 trials, yielding a total of 2,000,000 decision situations generated. For this simulation, an N-variate joint Dirichlet distribution was employed to generate the random weight vectors for the N–1 DoF simulations and a standard round-robin normalised random weight generator for the N DoF simulations. Unscaled value vectors were generated uniformly, and no significant differences were observed with other value distributions. The results of the simulations show that ROC is the best method under N–1 DoF, followed by GS, SR, RR and RS in that order. For N DoF, the results are quite different. Now RS is the best, followed by SR, GS, ROC and RR in that order. RR performs so badly that it cannot be seriously considered a candidate for an all-purpose surrogate weight method and is hence discarded from further consideration. Such an all-purpose method must fare well under both degrees of freedom and for any combination thereof. If combinations of both DoF are taken into account, SR and GS perform the best overall, with ROC slightly behind and RS further behind. Since ROC displays the greatest performance drop when changing between DoF, it is deemed less suitable in real-life applications.

ROBUST WEIGHTS

The aim of this study has been to find robust multi-criteria weights that would be able to cover a broad set of decision situations, but at the same time have a reasonably simple semantic regarding how they are generated. In this chapter, we consider decision problems with a varying number of criteria and alternatives and, to summarise the analysis, we look at the average hit rate in percentage over all the pairs (N, M). Considering performance averages, GS and SR are the best candidates when it comes to finding the winning alternative, followed by RS. The other surrogate weights are not in contention. For example, the ROC method relies too heavily on the assumption of decision-makers having an internal decision process with $N-1$ degrees of freedom for a decision problem with N criteria. We have discussed performance above and it can be seen that the GS and SR methods are the most efficient and robust surrogate weights that both perform very well on average and are stable under varying assumptions on the behaviour of the decision-maker. Of the two, GS performs a little bit better but is more complex since it requires a parameter to be selected. As simplicity could be regarded as an additional sign of robustness, we conclude that GS and SR are equally robust and are better choices for surrogate weight functions than the other candidates in the chapter. If one method has to be preferred, it would be SR, which forms the basis for the CAR decision method presented in the next chapter.

FURTHER READING

de Almeida, A.T., Cavalcante, C.A.V., Alencar, M.H., Ferreira, R.J.P., de Almeida-Filho, A.T. and Garcez, T.V. Multicriteria and Multiobjective Models for Risk, Reliability and Maintenance Decision Analysis. Cham: Springer. 2015.

Barron, F. and Barrett, B. The Efficacy of SMARTER: Simple Multi-Attribute Rating Technique Extended to Ranking. *Acta Psychologica.* 93(1–3), pp. 23–36. 1996.

Danielson, M. and Ekenberg, L. Computing Upper and Lower Bounds in Interval Decision Trees, *European Journal of Operational Research.* 181(2), pp. 808–816. 2007.

Roberts, R. and Goodwin, P. Weight Approximations in Multi-attribute Decision Models, *Journal Multi-Criteria Decision Analysis.* 11, pp. 291–303. 2002.

11

Comparing MCDA Methods

This chapter is based on Danielson, M. and Ekenberg, L. The CAR Method for using Preference Strength in Multi-Criteria Decision Making, *Group Decision and Negotiation.* 25(4). pp. 775–797. 2016.

Multi-criteria decision aid (MCDA) methods have been around for quite some time. However, the elicitation of preference information in MCDA processes and the lack of practical means supporting it is still a significant problem in real-life applications of MCDA. There is obviously a need for methods that neither require formal decision analysis knowledge nor impose too great cognitive demands by forcing people to express unrealistic precision or to state more than they are able to. We suggest a method, the Cardinal Ranking (CAR) method, which is more accessible than our earlier approaches in the field while trying to balance between the need for simplicity and the requirement of accuracy. CAR takes primarily ordinal knowledge into account but, still recognising that there is sometimes a quite substantial information loss involved in ordinality, we have conservatively extended a pure ordinal scale approach with the possibility of supplying more information. Thus, the main idea here is not to suggest a method or tool with a very large or complex expressibility, but rather to investigate one that should be sufficient in most situations, and in particular better, at least in some respects, than some hitherto popular ones from the SMART family as well as AHP, which we demonstrate in a set of simulation studies as well as a large end-user study.

THREE CLASSES OF MCDM METHODS

This chapter discusses three classes of value function methods that allow a relaxation of the requirement of precision, but retain simplicity and avoid resorting to interval or mixed approaches. Instead, we will here discuss whether good decision quality can be obtained without significantly increasing either the elicitational or the computational efforts involved, or both, and without making it difficult for a decision-maker to understand the process. To investigate this, we will consider three main classes of methods and compare them. The classes are:

- Proportional scoring methods, here represented by the SMART family,
- Ratio scoring methods, here represented by the widely used AHP method, and
- Cardinal ranking methods, here represented by the CAR method proposed in this chapter.

In the following, if not explicitly stated, we assume a set of criteria $\{G_1,...,G_N\}$ where each criterion G_i corresponds to a weight variable w_i. We also assume additive criteria weights: $\Sigma w_i = 1$, and $0 \leq w_i$ for all $i \leq N$. We will, without loss of generality, simplify the presentation by only investigating problems with a one-level criteria hierarchy and denote the value of an alternative a_j under criterion C_i by v_{ij}.

PROPORTIONAL SCORING

One of the best-known proportional scoring methods is the SMART family. SMART as initially presented was a seven-step procedure for setting up and analysing a decision model. The criteria are then ranked and (for instance) 10 points are assigned to w_N, i.e. the weight of the least important criterion. Then, w_{N-1} to w_1 are given points according to the decision-maker's preferences. This way, the points are representatives of the (somewhat uncertain) weights. The overall value $E(a_j)$ of alternative a_j is then a weighted average of the values v_{ij} associated with a_j:

$$E(a_j) = \sum_{i=1}^{N} w_i v_{ij} \Big/ \sum_{j=1}^{N} w_{ij}.$$

In an additive model, the weights reflect the importance of one criterion relative to the others. Most commonly, the degree of importance of an attribute depends on its spread (the range of the scale of the attribute), what we call the weight/scale-dualism. This is why elicitation methods like the original SMART, which do not consider the spread specifically, have been criticised. As a result, SMART was subsequently amended with the Swing technique (and renamed SMARTS), addressing the weight/scale dualism by changing the weight elicitation procedure. Basically, Swing works like this:

- Select a scale, such as positive integers (or similar)
- Consider the difference between the worst and the best outcomes (the range) within each criterion

- Imagine an alternative (the zero alternative) with all the worst outcomes from each criterion, thus having value 0 (if we have defined 0 as the lowest value)
- For each criterion in turn, consider the improvement (swing) in the zero alternative by having the worst outcome in that criterion replaced by the best one
- Assign numbers (importance) to each criterion in such a way that they correspond to the assessed improvement from having the criterion changed from the worst to the best outcome

As mentioned above, one approach that avoids some of the difficulties associated with the elicitation of exact values is merely to provide an ordinal ranking of the criteria. It is allegedly less demanding on decision-makers and, in a sense, effort-saving. Most current methods for converting ordinal input to cardinal, that is, converting rankings to exact surrogate weights, employ automated procedures for the conversion and these result in exact numeric weights. Another method is the SMARTER (SMART Exploiting Ranks) method to elicit the ordinal information on importance before being converted to numbers and thus the requirements for information input from the decision-maker are relaxed. An initial analysis is carried out where the weights are ordered such as $w_1 > w_2 > ... > w_N$ and then subsequently transformed to numerical weights using ROC weights. SMARTER then continues in the same manner as the ordinary SMART method.

RATIO SCORING

One of the best-known ratio scoring methods is the Analytic Hierarchy Process (AHP). The basic idea in AHP is to evaluate a set of alternatives under a criteria tree by pairwise comparisons. The process requires the same pairwise comparisons regardless of scale type. For each criterion, the decision-maker should first find the ordering of the alternatives from best to worst. Next, he or she should find the strength of the ordering by considering pairwise ratios (pairwise relations) between the alternatives using the integers 1, 3, 5, 7 and 9 to express their relative strengths, indicating that one alternative is equally good as another (strength = 1) or three, five, seven, or nine times as good. It is also allowed to use the even integers 2, 4, 6 and 8 as intermediate values, but using only odd integers is more common.

Much has been written about the AHP method and a detailed treatment of these is beyond the scope of this chapter, but we should nevertheless mention two properties that are particularly problematical. The conversion between scales – between the semantic and the numeric scale – has been questioned, and the employment of verbal terms within elicitation on the whole has been criticised throughout the years as their numerical meaning can differ substantially between different people. There are also particularly troublesome problems with rank reversals that have been known for a long time. Furthermore, the method is cognitively demanding in practice due to the large number of pairwise comparisons required as the number of attributes increases, and there are several variations of AHP. For example, the FARE (Factor Relationship) method is suggested in cases when the number of attributes is large in order to reduce the number of required comparisons between pairs of attributes.

ORDINAL AND CARDINAL RANKING METHODS

As with other multi-attribute value based methods, ranking methods contain one alternative (consequence) value part and one criteria weight part. Since weights are more complicated, we will mainly discuss them in this chapter. Values are handled in a completely analogous but less complex way. There is no need for values to be transformed into surrogate entities since values are not restricted by an upper sum limit.

Rankings are normally easier to provide than precise numbers and for that reason various criteria weight techniques have been developed based on rankings. One idea mentioned above is to derive so-called surrogate weights from elicitation rankings. The resulting ranking is converted into numerical weights and it is important to do this with as small an information loss as possible while still preserving the correctness of the weight assignments. The so-called ROC (rank order centroid) weights are the average of the corners in the polytope defined by the simplex $S_w = w_1 > w_2 > ... > w_N$, $\Sigma w_i = 1$, and $0 \leq w_i$. The weights are then simply represented by the centroid (mass point) of S_w, i.e.

$$w_i = \frac{1}{N} \Sigma_{j=i}^{N} \frac{1}{j}, \text{ for all } i = 1,...,N.$$

For instance, in the case of four criteria and where $w_1 > w_2 > w_3 > w_4$, the centroid weight components become $w_1 = 0.5208$, $w_2 = 0.2708$, $w_3 = 0.1458$, $w_4 = 0.0625$. Despite there being a tendency for the highest ranked criterion to have a strong influence on the result, as has been pointed out, ROC weights nevertheless represent an important idea regarding averaging the weights involved and in the aggregation of values. Of the conversion methods suggested, ROC weights have gained the most recognition among surrogate weights.

However, pure ranking is sometimes problematic. For example, due to the relative robustness of linear decision models regarding weight changes, the use of approximate weights often yields satisfactory decision quality, but the assumption of knowing the ranking with certainty is strong. Thus, although some form of cardinality often exists, information on cardinal importance relation is not taken into account in the transformation of rank orders into weights, thus not making use of available information.

THE DELTA METHOD

Most methods for handling imprecise information try to reduce the constraint sets of feasible values, typically by delimiting the available space by linear constraints, through various elicitation procedures. A major problem in that respect is to find a balance between not forcing the decision-maker to say more than is known in terms of precision, but at the same time obtaining as much information as is required for the alternatives to be discriminated from each other. Furthermore, the model must be computationally meaningful. As an example, the basic idea of the Delta method (relevant for the context in this chapter) is in one way or another to construct polytopes for the feasible weights and the feasible alternative values involved and evaluate decision situations with respect to different decision rules.

To be more precise, the user input statements are collected as linear constraints to the solution sets of the spaces spanned by the weight, and value variables respectively. These constraints may be both range constraints, that is, constraints involving only one variable such as interval boundaries, and comparative constraints involving two variables. For a regular criteria tree like the one in Figure 1 of *Chapter 10*, there is one weight constraint set **W** and one value constraint set **V**. As the criteria model is in the form of a criteria hierarchy tree, the weight constraint set is a union of local node constraint sets, so that $\mathbf{W} = \cup \mathbf{W}_i$, where each $\mathbf{W}_i$ is a local weight constraint set for a criterion node W_i. The value variables and related constraints are assigned to the alternatives of the model. For a decision tree, variables and constraints are assigned to the consequence nodes. These statements constrain the feasible solutions sets.

To aid further in the modelling of the problem, the *orthogonal hull* concept indicates to the decision-maker which parts of the statements are consistent with the information given so far. The decision information can be considered as constraints in the space formed by all decision variables. The (orthogonal) hull is then the projection of the constrained spaces onto each variable axis, and can thus be seen as the meaningful interval boundaries. The same type of input is used for values and weights, although the normalisation constraint $\Sigma \, w_j = 1$ must not be violated. All input into the model is subject to consistency checks performed by the tool.

For each variable, there is also a focal point, which may be viewed as the 'most likely' or 'best representative' value for that variable. Hence, a *focal point* is a unique solution vector whose components for each dimension (variable) lie within the orthogonal hull. Given this, we calculate the *strength* of alternatives as a means for further discriminating the alternatives. The strength δ_{ij} simply denotes the difference in expected value, that is, the expression $\mathbf{E}(A_i) - \mathbf{E}(A_j)$. For multi-criteria models, the expected value for each criterion is aggregated into a weighted sum of expected values for the entire decision problem. By denoting the expected value of an alternative A_i with respect to the kth criterion with $^k\mathbf{E}(A_i)$, this leads to an expression for the weighted strength $\sum_k w_k \big({}^k\mathbf{E}(A_i) - {}^k\mathbf{E}(A_j) \big)$. In its most basic form, (one-level criteria tree) $^k\mathbf{E}(A_i)$ is reduced to $\sum_k w_k \cdot v_{ik} - \sum_l w_l \cdot v_{jl}$ over all criteria and alternative A_i and A_j respectively, such that w_i denotes the weight of the ith criteria, and v_{ij} the value of alternative A_i under criteria j. Hence, in the tool, probabilistic decision trees may be used alone for single-objective decision problems and can also be 'connected' at any time to a criterion leaf-node in the criteria tree as long as the initial alternatives in the probabilistic decision trees map one-to-one onto the alternative set in the multi-criteria tree.

An important feature of the process is the *sensitivity analysis*. This analysis attempts to highlight what information was the most critical for the obtained results and must therefore be subject to careful additional consideration. It also points out which of the assessments are too imprecise to be of any assistance in the discrimination of alternatives and thus should be made more accurate, thereby triggering and facilitating iteration in the process.

The embedded sensitivity analysis, through the concept of *contraction*, is performed by reducing the widths of the intervals (contraction) for the values and weights in the analysis model of the decision problem. The idea is to shrink the orthogonal hull while studying the stability of $\max\{\delta_{ij}\}$ at different contraction levels. The contraction level is indicated as a percentage: for a 100% level of contraction all orthogonal hull intervals have been reduced to their respective focal points. The contraction can be seen as cutting the hull from the extreme points towards the focal point, increasing the lowest permitted degree of belief. When dealing only with interval statements, this is quite simple; it is more complicated when comparative constraints are involved.

As a simple example, consider a decision alternative A_1 with four criteria g_1, g_2, g_3, and g_4, each assigned an interval weight of $w_i \in [0.2, 0.4]$, and interval-valued values $V_1(A_1) \in [10, 30]$, $V_2(A_1) \in [20, 40]$, $V_3(A_1) \in [0, 50]$, and $V_4(A_1) \in [50, 60]$ for each criterion respectively. These interval statements will yield the corresponding orthogonal hulls, and the suggested focal points for the weight variables will be computed to 0.25 and for the value variables to 20, 30, 25 and 55, respectively. This leads to an expected value interval for A_1 of [16, 48], that is, $\max\{\mathbf{W}(A_1)\}$ = 48 and $\min\{\mathbf{W}(A_1)\}$ = 16. Now, at a contraction level of 40%, the widths of the intervals from each orthogonal hull boundary and each focal point will be reduced by 40%. Denoting the weight hull intervals at a contraction level of l by ${}^h w_{il}$, these are obtained through

$$ {}^h w_{il} = [{}^f w_i - (1\text{-}l) \cdot | {}^f w_i - {}^{\min} w_i |, {}^f w_i + (1\text{-}l) \cdot | {}^f w_i - {}^{\max} w_i |] $$

where ${}^f w_i$ is the focal point for the variable w_i, ${}^{\min} w_i$ is the lower bound, and ${}^{\max} w_i$ is the upper bound for the same variable. For values, the same formula applies.

The Delta method and software has been used successfully in numerous applications regarding everything from tactical hydropower management to business risks and applications of participatory democracy. However, a common factor in the applications of the method that has complicated the decision making process is the difficulties real-life decision-makers experience in actually understanding and using the software efficiently, despite various elicitation interfaces and methods developed. Therefore, we have started to investigate how various subsets of the method can be simplified without losing much precision and decision power for general decision situations and can measurably perform well in comparison with the most popular decision methods available at the moment.

VALUE DIFFERENCE RANKING METHODS

Providing ordinal rankings of criteria seems to avoid some of the difficulties associated with the elicitation of exact numbers. It puts fewer demands on decision-makers and is thus, in a sense, effort-saving. Furthermore, there are techniques such as those above for handling ordinal rankings with some success. However, decision-makers might in many cases have more knowledge of the decision situation, even if the information is not precise. For instance, information on cardinal importance relation may implicitly exist, however, it cannot be taken into account in the transformation of an ordinal rank order into weights. This entails that the surrogate weights may not closely reflect what the decision-maker actually means by his/her ranking. Some more fine-grained form of preference strength often exists and this information should reasonably be used when transforming orderings into weights to utilise more of the information the decision-maker is able to supply.

VALUE DIFFERENCE EXPRESSIONS

Assume that there exists an ordinal ranking of N criteria. To make this order into a stronger ranking, information could be given about how much more or less important the criteria are compared with each other. Such stronger rankings also take care of the problem with ordinal methods of handling criteria that are found to be equally important, that is, resisting strict ordinal ranking. One way of introducing expressions of strength into the decision situation is to utilise distance steps on an importance scale. The number of steps corresponds straightforwardly to various strengths that can be derived from, for example, a linguistic analysis. Assume for instance that a decision-maker states something like the following for a set of six criteria:

- Criterion A is more important than criterion B.
- Criterion B is slightly more important than criterion C.
- Criterion C is more important than criterion D.
- Criterion D is equally important as criterion E.
- Criterion E is much more important than criterion F.

This could be displayed as steps on an 'importance ruler'.[1] Here, we classify the strength of preference over weights (difference between weights) in four categories: equally important; slightly more important; more important; and much more important. The first category corresponds to an equivalence relationship between two weights. We assign '0' to this equivalence. The ordering of the other three types of strength of preference over weights (or difference between weights) is by default an ordinal ranking. By following the idea used in ordinal ranking methods reviewed in the previous section, we assign '1', '2' and '3' to 'slightly more important', 'more important' and 'much more important', respectively. Again, as in the ordinal ranking methods reviewed above, the numbers 1, 2 and 3 only represent the ordering over the difference between weights. Thus, it does not try to capture all the potential information contained in the decision situation. However, in the subsequent section, we will demonstrate that it provides a way to use partial information from the strength of preference judgments over weights in assessing weights for multi-attribute utility functions.

[1] Of course, the interpretation of the expressions need not be exactly this, but as a prima facie suggestion for demonstrational purposes it is appropriate. For elicitation procedures, see the next section.

We use $>_i$ to denote the strength (cardinality) of the rankings between criteria, where $>_0$ is the equal ranking '='. Assume that we have a user induced ordering $w_1 >_{i_1} w_2 >_{i_2} \dots >_{i_{n-1}} w_n$. Then we construct a new ordering, containing only the symbols $=$ and $>$, by introducing auxiliary variables x_{ij} and substituting

- $w_k >_0 w_{k+1}$ with $w_k = w_{k+1}$

- $w_k >_1 w_{k+1}$ with $w_k > w_{k+1}$

- $w_k >_2 w_{k+1}$ with $w_k > x_{k_1} > w_{k+1}$ (1)

- ...

- $w_k >_i w_{k+1}$ with $w_k > x_{k_1} > \dots > x_{k_{i-1}} > w_{k+1}$

The substitutions yield new spaces defined by the simplexes generated by the new orderings. In this way, we obtain a computationally meaningful way of representing preference strengths.

To see how the weights work, consider the cardinality expressions as distance steps on an importance scale. The number of steps corresponds straightforwardly to the strength of the cardinalities above such that '$>_i$' means i steps. This can easily be displayed as steps on an importance ruler as suggested in the previous chapter, where the following relationships are displayed on a cardinal (left) and an ordinal (right) importance scale respectively:

- $w_A >_2 w_B$
- $w_B >_1 w_C$
- $w_C >_2 w_D$
- $w_D >_0 w_E$
- $w_E >_3 w_F$

While being more cognitively demanding than ordinal weights, they are still much less demanding than, for example, AHP weight ratios (usually employing nine ratios, i.e. 1/9, 1/7, 1/5, 1/3, 1, 3, 5, 7 and 9) or point scores like SMART (usually employing several integers). In a manner analogous to ordinal ranking, the decision-maker's statements can be converted into weights. For the purposes of value difference ranking, one reasonable candidate for a weight function is a function that is proportional to the distances on the importance scale. To obtain the cardinal ranking weights w_i^{CAR}, proceed as follows:

- Assign an ordinal number to each importance scale position, starting with the most important position as number 1.
- Let the total number of importance scale positions be Q. Each criterion i has the position $p(i) \in \{1,\dots,Q\}$ on this importance

scale, such that for every two criteria c_i and c_j, whenever $c_i >_{si} c_j$, $s_i = |\, p(i) - p(j)\,|$. The position $p(i)$ then denotes the importance as stated by the decision-maker.

- Then the cardinal ranking weights w_i^{CAR} are found by the formula

$$w_i^{CAR} = \frac{{}^{1}\!/_{p(i)} + \dfrac{Q + 1 - p(i)}{Q}}{\sum_{j=1}^{N}\left({}^{1}\!/_{p(j)} + \dfrac{Q + 1 - p(j)}{Q}\right)}.$$

THE CAR METHOD

The CAR method follows a three-step procedure, much in analogy with the two other classes of MCDA methods. First, the values of the alternatives under each criterion are elicited in a way similar to the weights described above:

- For each criterion in turn, rank the alternatives from the worst to the best outcome.
- Enter the strength of the ordering. The strength indicates how strong the separation is between two ordered alternatives. Similar to weights, the strength is expressed in the notation with '$>_i$' symbols.

Second, the weights are elicited with a swing-like procedure in accordance with the discussion above:

1. For each criterion in turn, rank the importance of the criteria from the least to the most important.
2. Enter the strength of the ordering. The strength indicates how strong the separation is between two ordered criteria. The strength is expressed in the notation with '$>_i$' symbols.

Third, a weighted overall value is calculated by multiplying the centroids of the weight simplex with the centroid of the alternative value simplex. Thus, given a set of criteria in a (one-level) criteria hierarchy, $G_1,\ldots,G_n$ and a set of alternatives $a_1,\ldots,a_m$. A general value function U using additive value functions is then

$$U(a_j) = \sum_{i=1}^{n} w_i^{CAR} v_{ij}^{CAR}$$

where w_i^{CAR} is the weight representing the relative importance of attribute G_i, and $w_{ij}^{CAR}: a_j \rightarrow [0,1]$ is the increasing individual value function of a_j under criterion G_i obtained by the above procedure. This expression is subject to the polytopes of weights and values. This means that the feasible values are the ones in the extended polytopes defined by (1) above. Now, we define the value

$$\bar{U}(a_j) = \sum_{i=1}^{n} \bar{w}_i \bar{v}_{ij}$$

for the general value, where $\bar{w}_i$ is the centroid component of criteria weight w_i in the weight simplex and $\bar{v}_{ij}$ is the centroid component of the value of alternative a_j under the criteria G_i in the simplex of values. Since we only consider non-interval valued results, the centroid is the most representative single value of a polytope. This three-step procedure contains a simple workflow that exhibits a large user acceptance, see below.

ASSESSING THE METHODS

Validation within this research field is somewhat difficult, to a large extent due to difficulties regarding elicitation. In this chapter, we look at MCDM methods with less complex requirements (categories 1 and 2 of *Chapter 10*) but with the dual aim of achieving both high efficiency and wide user acceptance. The question of what constitutes a good method is multifaceted, but it seems reasonable that a preferred method should possess some significant qualities to a higher degree than its rivals:

- *Efficiency.* The method should yield the best alternative according to some decision rule in as many situations as possible.
- *Ease of use.* The steps of the method should be perceived as relatively easy to perform.
- *Ease of communication.* It should be comparatively easy to communicate the results to others.
- *Time efficiency.* The amount of time and effort required to complete the decision making task should be reasonably low.
- *Cognitive correctness.* The perceived correctness of the result and transparency of the process should be high.
- *Return rate.* The willingness to use the method again should be high.

We will assess the abovementioned three classes of methods relative to our list of desired properties (qualities). The first quality, efficiency, will be assessed in this section and the others in the next section. The classes will be represented by the methods SMART, AHP and CAR respectively.

Simulation studies have become a de facto standard for comparing multi-criteria weight methods. The underlying assumption of most studies is that there exist a set of 'true' weights in the decision-maker's mind which are inaccessible in their pure form by any elicitation method. We will utilise the same technique for determining the efficacy, in this sense, of the three MCDM methods suggested above. The modelling assumptions regarding decision-makers' mindsets are mirrored in the generation of decision problem vectors by a random generator. In MCDM, different elicitation formalisms have been proposed by which a decision-maker can express preferences. Such formalisms are sometimes based on scoring points, as in point allocation (PA) or direct rating (DR) methods. In PA, the decision-maker is given a point sum, e.g. 100, to distribute among the criteria. Sometimes, it is pictured as putty with the total mass of 100 that is divided and put on the criteria. The more mass, the greater weight on a criterion, and the more important it is. In PA, there is consequently $N-1$ degrees of freedom (DoF) for N criteria. DR, on the other hand, puts no limit on the number of points to be allocated. The decision-maker allocates as many points as desired to each criterion. The points are subsequently normalised by dividing by the sum of points allocated. Thus in DR there are N degrees of freedom for N criteria. Regardless of elicitation method, the assumption is that all elicitation is made relative to a weight distribution held by the decision-maker.

The idea in both cases is to construct a set of unknowable weights that are distributed over the possible weight space. When simulating using DR the generated weights tend to cluster near the centre of the weight space. The first step in randomly generating random weights in the PA case for N attributes is to select $N-1$ random numbers from a uniform distribution on $(0, 1)$ independently, and then rank these numbers. Assume that the ranked numbers are $1 > r_1 > r_2 \ldots > r_{n-1}$ and then let $w_1 = 1-r_1$, $w_n = r_{n-1}$ and $w_i = r_{i+1}-r_i$ for $1 < i \leq N-1$. These weights are uniform on the simplex. The DR approach is then equivalent to generating N uniform variates and setting $w_i = \frac{r_i}{\Sigma r_i}$. For instance, under both approaches, the expected value of w_1 is 1/3 when there are three attributes. However, the resulting distributions of the weights are very different and the weights for DR are clustered in the centre of the weight space and it is much less likely that we observe a large weight on w_1.

SIMULATION STUDIES AND THEIR BIASES

In the simulations described below it is important to be clear which background model we utilise. As discussed above, when following an $N-1$ DoF model, a vector is generated in which the components sum to 100%. This simulation is based on a homogenous N-variate Dirichlet distribution generator. On the other hand, following an N

DoF model, a vector is generated without an initial joint restriction, yielding a process with N degrees of freedom. Depending on the simulation model used (and consequently the background assumption of how decision-makers assess weights), the results become very different. For reasons discussed in the previous chapter, the evaluation of MCDM methods in this chapter will use a combination of both types of generators in order to find the most efficient and robust method.

COMPARING THE METHODS

The idea behind comparing surrogate weights is to measure the validity of the weights by simulating a large set of scenarios utilising surrogate weights and see how well different weights provided results similar to scenarios utilising true weights. The procedure is here extended with the handling of values in order to evaluate MCDM methods. Akin to the procedure in *Chapter 10*, the generation procedure for this simulation's random vectors yield for each method (SMART, AHP and CAR) a hit or miss relative to the underlying, true weight vector. For details, consult *Chapter 10*. This is repeated a large number of times (simulation rounds). The hit rate (or frequency) is defined as the proportion of times an MCDM method made the same decision as TRUE.

SIMULATIONS OF THE CARDINAL SURROGATE WEIGHTS

The simulations were carried out with a varying number of criteria and alternatives. There were four numbers of criteria $N = \{3, 6, 9, 12\}$ and four numbers of alternatives $M = \{3, 6, 9, 12\}$ in the simulation study, creating a total of 16 simulation scenarios. Each scenario was run 10 times, each time with 10,000 trials, yielding a total of 1,600,000 decision situations generated. An N-variate joint Dirichlet distribution was employed to generate the random weight vectors for the $N–1$ DoF simulations and a standard normalised random weight generator for the N DoF simulations. Unscaled value vectors were generated uniformly since no significant differences were observed with other value distributions.

The results of the simulations show that CAR is several per cent better than SMART and AHP. This is a wide margin, much wider than obtained in the comparison between ordinal ranking weights in the previous chapter. While CAR averages 87%, the other two perform at around 81%. The other two methods fare about equal, with SMART being somewhat stronger when fewer alternatives are involved and AHP being somewhat stronger when more alternatives are involved. This is not surprising since a very large amount of information is requested for

AHP's pairwise comparisons when the number of criteria and alternatives increase. The gap up to CAR for both of the other methods is substantial considering the already high hit rate level at which the methods operate.

EMPIRICAL STUDY

While the simulation study clearly points to CAR being theoretically preferable, a useful method must nevertheless be accepted by users in real-life decision situations. To find out how the three methods are perceived in real-life decision making, we made a study involving 100 people each of whom made one large real-life decision. The decisions ranged from selecting the country or area to live in, choosing a university course or buying an apartment to acquiring goods like cars, motorcycles, computers or smartphones. A requirement was that it was an important decision for the individual that he or she would be making in the near future. Furthermore, the report should contain only real facts and data together with the decision made. Each individual was given two to three weeks to complete the task and made the decision using all three methods available and was subsequently asked to reflect on his or her respective traits and characteristics. The methods were assisted by very similar and equally functional computer tools ensuring that all three methods were applied correctly. Adequate help with the methods was available throughout the processes.

Their reports contained decision data and results from all three methods and a comparison between the methods. In particular, the decision-makers ranked the methods on five attributes (qualities): (A) ease of use; (B) communicating the results to others; (C) amount of time and effort required; (D) perceived correctness and transparency; and (E) willingness to use the method again. For each attribute, each decision-maker ranked the methods as 1, 2 or 3 with 1 being the foremost in each attribute, e.g. the easiest to use. Thus, a lower score indicates a more preferred method. Table 1 shows the average position each method obtained for each attribute.

In Table 1, the results of the attribute's ease of use can be seen.

Table 1. Results of ranking attributes of methods.

	A	B	C	D	E
SMART	1.83	1.68	1.76	1.97	2.05
AHP	2.89	2.75	2.72	2.36	2.59
CAR	1.28	1.58	1.53	1.67	1.36

Most respondents found CAR to be the easiest to use. Similarly, the table shows the results for ease of communicating the results to others. In this case, CAR and SMART were almost equal, followed by AHP far behind. In the same manner, the remaining columns show the results for the amount of time and effort required to complete the decision making task (column C), perceived correctness of the result and transparency of the process (column D), and the decision-maker's willingness to use the method again (column E). CAR turned out to be the least time-consuming method, followed by SMART and with AHP far behind. The perceived correctness is in conformity with the simulation results. CAR is the preferred method, followed by SMART and with AHP last. Regarding the willingness to use the method again, CAR clearly outperforms the others. For attributes B, C and D, there were 99 valid responses and for E there were 97 out of 100 respondents. From the table, it can be seen that CAR clearly is the preferred method while AHP is the least preferred in all five attributes. The greatest difference between CAR and the other methods was found in willingness to use the method again, while the smallest was found in communicating the results where SMART was almost equally favoured. These results were not contradicted by the free text parts of the reports. The results of the user study in conjunction with the simulation study indicate the usefulness of the CAR method.

RESULTS OF THE COMPARISONS

There is a need for methods that strike a balance between formal decision analysis and reasonable cognitive demands. We have suggested a method that seems to constitute such a reasonable balance between the need for simplicity and the requirement of accuracy. We also compared this approach (the CAR method) with methods from the popular SMART family as well as AHP. The CAR method takes ordinal knowledge into account, but recognising that there is sometimes quite substantial information loss involved with this, we have conservatively extended a pure ordinal scale approach with the possibility to supply cardinal information as well. We found that the CAR method outperforms the others, both in terms of simulation results as well as in user studies, pointing to CAR as a very competitive candidate to the other hitherto more widespread methods.

Its efficiency was measured by simulation results for various numbers of alternatives and criteria, along the classical lines for assessing surrogate weights. These results show that CAR is superior regarding correctness. We also conducted a real-life user study. We studied 100 individuals who previously were not particularly familiar with MCDA methods, where each individual was given two to three weeks to complete an important decision making task. They made the decision using all three methods available and were subsequently asked to reflect on the methods' respective traits and characteristics. The study clearly showed that the CAR method generally and significantly was ranked in top place for all the criteria above.

In conclusion, the goal was to find a more useful MCDA method with a reasonable elicitation component, which would reduce some of the applicability issues with existing, more elaborate, methods that we and others have developed over the years, but at the same time being able to capture more information than pure ordinal approaches. The CAR method extends rank-order weighting procedures, by taking both ordinal information as well as some cardinal relation information of the importance of the attributes into account. By this, we can sometimes avoid employing methods we and others have previously suggested for handling imprecision in decision situations, and which have turned out to be difficult to understand for normal decision-makers. The suggested method nevertheless gives significantly better simulation results than commonly used competitors, such as SMART and AHP, while still seemingly being reasonably easy to understand. It was perceived not to require too much time nor to be very demanding to apply.

FURTHER READING

Ahn, B.S. and Park, K.S. Comparing Methods for Multiattribute Decision Making with Ordinal Weights, *Computers and Operations Research*. 35(5), pp. 1660–1670. 2008.

Arbel, A. and Vargas, L.G. Preference Simulation and Preference Programming: Robustness Issues in Priority Derivation, *European Journal of Operational Research*. 69, pp. 200–209. 1993.

Barron, F. Selecting a Best Multiattribute Alternative with Partial Information About Attribute Weights. *Acta Psychologica*. 80(1–3), pp. 91–103. 1992.

Bisdorff, R., Dias, L.C., Meyer, P., Mousseau, V. and Pirlot, M. (Eds.), *Evaluation and Decision Models with Multiple Criteria: Case Studies*. Springer. 2015.

Butler, J., Jia, J. and Dyer, J. Simulation Techniques for the Sensitivity Analysis of Multi-Criteria Decision Models. *European Journal of Operational Research*. 103, pp. 531–546. 1997.

Larsson, A., Johansson, J., Ekenberg, L. and Danielson, M. Decision Analysis with Multiple Objectives in a Framework for Evaluating Imprecision. *International Journal of Uncertainty, Fuzziness and Knowledge-Based Systems*. 13(5), pp. 495–509. 2005.

12

Algorithms for Decision Analysis

As seen in the preceding chapters, multi-criteria decision analysis can be a useful tool in rooting out and ranking different alternatives of action. However, many such analyses involve imprecise information, including estimates of utilities, outcome probabilities and criteria weights. This chapter presents the software design of a general multi-criteria approach, allowing the modelling of multi-criteria and probabilistic problems in the same tree form, which includes a decision tree evaluation method integrated with a framework for analysing decision situations under risk with a criteria hierarchy. The general method of probabilistic multi-criteria analysis extends the use of additive and multiplicative utility functions for supporting evaluation of imprecise and uncertain facts. Thus, it relaxes the requirement for precise numerical estimates of utilities, probabilities and weights. The evaluation is done relative to a set of decision rules, generalising the concept of admissibility and computationally handled through the optimisation of aggregated utility functions. The approach required the design and development of computationally intensive algorithms for which there was no template, and for which a pure object-oriented design technique was not optimal. The development was carried out using an object-based approach (object-orientation minus inheritance), a contract based specification, aspect-like management of key code features and a pure imperative programming language.

The task of designing and developing software containing complex algorithms that are not easy to imagine and to specify completely beforehand requires some specific approach regarding choice of design methods. In this chapter, we discuss the development of an algorithmic software library. The moving target nature of advanced algorithm development required techniques and approaches different from more ordinary software development efforts. Developing software containing complex

This chapter is based on Danielson, M. and Ekenberg, L. Software Development of Linear Programming Algorithms for Decision Analysis Applications. *Journal of Communication and Computer.* 8(9). pp. 793–806. 2011.

algorithms differs from everyday software development in some respects. In most software development, the design can be planned in an orderly fashion using experience or extrapolation from previous development projects. In many cases, parts of the code can even be reused or at least patterns of design can be reused. But in designing algorithmic centred software, containing new algorithms or new requirements unknown at the time of specification, what is normally good software design practice cannot always be applied or would not lead to effective development work. For example, while object-oriented design and coding is often good practice, it might become a hindrance when there are no natural objects to discover or structures cannot be manipulated in detail independent of implementation. This chapter describes, as a case study, a software library for decision analysis that was developed for maximal efficiency and minimal footprint over a period of 15 years.

While much of algorithm design is positivist in its nature, the development of user software often adheres to methods closer to design science. Dating back to Simon's work on the sciences of the artificial, design science has drawn more attention in the last decades. Originating from engineering, it emphasises problem-solving methods and explores ideas through innovations by analysis, design, implementation, testing and validation of artefacts. Similar ideas are also evident in the popular CDIO design methods (Conceive, Design, Implement, Operate) found in many engineering schools. Traditional explanatory sciences, either the natural sciences or the more traditional social sciences, are description driven, resulting in theories which are able to explain some observed phenomenon. Design science is more prescriptive in attempting to develop knowledge for the design and implementation of artefacts. This leads to a methodological clash in designing algorithms for decision analytic software, which has to be on the one hand efficient and with a small footprint, and on the other hand adhere to the users' interaction needs when manoeuvring through an interactive software package.

The DMC library package was initially designed using a contract-based specification, an object-based approach (where object-based refers to object-oriented minus inheritance). The use of non-inheriting objects led to a design that could survive requirements changing considerably over time, while at the same time not enough natural code objects were found to allow an efficient implementation using object-oriented programming. Issues of code optimisation and footprint minimisation were handled by using a pure imperative language without object extensions, in this case C. Using conditional compilation and macros, something akin to later-introduced aspect-orientation was used in coding parts particularly involving memory management, logging and exception handling. The size of the library is around 50,000 lines of code, but the main challenge was not the size but the algorithmic complexity and changing requirements and specifications. The code is still alive, more than 15 years after its first release, without requiring a rewrite or architectural redesign.

The purpose of this chapter is to present the software design of a method, integrated into a unified framework, for multi-attribute evaluation under risk generalised to support the use of imperfect information. The work herein originates from earlier work on evaluating probabilistic decision situations involving a finite number of alternatives and consequences. Imprecision is modelled in the form of interval utilities, probabilities and weights, as well as comparisons, derived from convex sets of utility and probability measures. By doing so, the work conforms to classical statistical decision theory, avoiding problems with set membership functions emerging with the use of, for example, fuzzy sets. For computational reasons, we do not include second-order probabilities. We focus on extending the use of the simple additive utility function, often referred to as the weighted sum, and on the multiplicative utility function as defined in MAUT.

THE DELTA METHOD

The method described below is a multi-criteria generalisation of the Delta method but the main results in this chapter are applicable to other decision models as well. Delta is a probabilistic method for analysing decisions containing imperfect information represented as intervals and qualitative statements described in *Chapter 11*. This chapter describes a generalisation of the method to handle a model in which several outcomes can be handled relative to a criteria hierarchy. A main result is that multi-criteria analysis and decisions under risk can be combined in a unified framework. Furthermore, the same computational principles that have earlier been used for evaluating imprecise decision situations under risk can also be applied for evaluating such combined (multi-criteria probabilistic, MCP) problems. Since no such computer tool existed before, the construction of the DMC library package as the computational engine for the software led to the discovery of initially unknown demands and problems.

COMBINING DECISION TREES AND CRITERIA HIERARCHIES

As has been seen above, criteria hierarchies and decision trees are both models of a similar kind and are evaluated using similar rules, as shown in the examples in Figures 1 and 2. Instead of valuing the alternatives directly, using only value functions over the alternatives under each criterion as in multi-criteria analysis, the value of an alternative can be calculated as expected values from decision trees, that is, the valuation of the alternatives can be included in the multi-criteria tree evaluation. In Figure 1, the alternatives' values under weight w_{11} in the criteria hierarchy have been elaborated into entire decision trees, reflecting a deeper analysis of the decision problem. In the figure, the tree's structure is symmetrical. This is, however, not a necessary condition and the respective decision tree parts can be completely different without loss of generality.

The expected value of the alternatives in the combined tree in Figure 1 can now readily be calculated with respect to this structure:

$$E(A_i) = \sum_{j=1}^{2} (w_j \cdot \sum_{k=1}^{2} (w_{jk} \cdot \sum_{m=1}^{2} (p_{im} \cdot \sum_{n=1}^{2} p_{imn} v_{imn1})))$$

The positions of the nodes A_i do not affect this value. It simplifies the forthcoming discussion a bit if we assume that these nodes are on the second level in the tree. In Figure 2, a tree computationally equivalent to that in Figure 1 is shown. The weights have been moved closer to the root, corresponding to rearranging the formula above w.r.t. the sums.

In the next few sections, the criteria-consequence structure is formalised and furthermore, how numerical imprecision and relations can be modelled and evaluated in the new structure is explained.

MCP FRAME

We will let an *MCP frame* represent a combined decision problem. The idea with such a frame is to collect all information necessary for the model in one structure. One of the building blocks of a frame is a graph.

Definition: A *graph* is a structure $\langle V,E \rangle$ where V is a set of nodes and E is a set of node pairs. A *tree* is a connected graph without cycles. A *rooted tree* is a tree with a dedicated node as a root. The root is at *level* 0. The adjacent nodes, except for the nodes at level $i-1$, to a node at level i is at level $i+1$. A node at level i is a leaf if it has no adjacent nodes at level $i+1$. A node at level $i+1$ that is adjacent to a node at level i is a child of the latter. A (sub-)tree is symmetric if all nodes at level i have the same number of adjacent

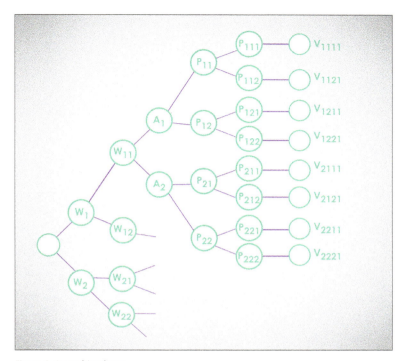

Figure 1. A combined tree.

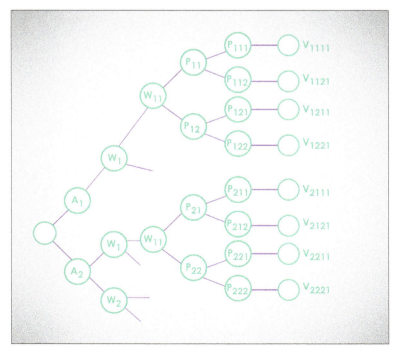

Figure 2. A rearranged tree, equivalent to Figure 1.

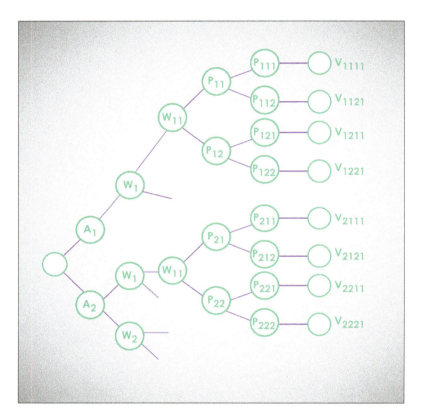

Figure 3. A criteria-consequence tree.

nodes at level i+1. The depth of the tree is max(n | there exists a node at level n).

The general graph is, however, too permissive in representing a combined tree. Hence, we will restrict the possible degrees of freedom in expressing the criteria-consequence tree.

Definition: A criteria-consequence tree $T = \langle C \cup A \cup N \cup \{r\}, E \rangle$ is a tree where:

- r is the root
- A is the set of nodes at level 1
- C is the set of leaves – N is the set of intermediary nodes in the tree except these in A – the tree is symmetric from level 2 until level i, i=2,3,...

A criteria-consequence tree is a way of modelling a criteria hierarchy together with ordinary decision trees in the same structure. In the sequel, we will use the notation that the n children of a node x_i are denoted, $x_{i1}, x_{i2}, \ldots, x_{in}$ and the m children of the node x_{ij} are denoted $x_{ij1}, x_{ij2}, \ldots, x_{ijm}$, etc. The labelling is shown in Figure 3.

The structure is then filled with user statements which can either be range constraints or comparative statements. Given consequences c_i and c_j, denote their values v_i and v_j respectively. Then the user statements can be of the following kinds for real numbers a_1, a_2, b_1, b_2, d_1 and d_2:

- *Range constraints*: v_i is between a_1 and a_2, denoted $v_i \in (a_1, a_2)$ and translated into $v_i > a_1$ and $v_i < a_2$.
- *Comparisons*: v_i is from d_1 to d_2 larger than v_j, denoted $v_i - v_j \in (d_1, d_2)$ and translated into $v_i - v_j > d_1$ and $v_i - v_j < d_2$.

All the value statements in a decision problem share a common structure because they are all made relative to the same MCP frame. Range constraints and comparisons are constraints on the variables, and they are translated into inequalities and collected together in a *value constraint set*. For probability and weight statements, the same is done into a *node constraint set*.

NODE CONSTRAINT SETS

The collection of probability and weight statements in a decision situation is called the *node constraint set*. A constraint set is said to be *consistent* if at least one real number can be assigned to each variable so that all inequalities are simultaneously satisfied.

Consequently, the method deals with classes of functions of which there are infinitely many instantiations, and insists on at least one of them yielding consistent results.

Definition: Given a criteria-consequence tree T, let N be a constraint set in the variables $\{n..._j..._j...\}$. Substitute the intermediary node labels $x..._j..._j...$ with $n..._j..._j...$. N is a *node constraint set* for T if for all sets $\{n..._{i1},...,n..._{im}\}$ of all sub-nodes of nodes $n..._i$ that are not leaves, the statements $n..._{ij} \in (0,1)$ and $\sum_j n..._{ij} = 1, j \in \{1,...,m\}$ are in N.

Thus, a node constraint set relative to a criteria-consequence tree can be seen as characterising a set of discrete probability distributions after a certain level (the *probability constraint set*). In the same way, it can be seen as characterising a set of weight functions before a certain level (the *weight constraint set*). The core of these can be thought of as an attempt to estimate a class of mass functions by estimating the individual discrete function values. The normalisation constraints ($\sum_j x_{ij} = 1$) require the probabilities and weights of sets of exhaustive and mutually exclusive nodes to sum to one. Sometimes, when it is useful to separate probabilities and weights in the presentation below, variables denoting criteria weights will be labelled w_{ij} and variables denoting probabilities will be labelled p_{ij}.

VALUE CONSTRAINT SETS

Requirements similar to those for node variables can be found for value variables. However, no dimension reducing normalisation constraints (variables summing to one) exist for the value variables.

Definition: Given a criteria-consequence tree T, let L be a constraint set in $\{c..._1\}$. Substitute the leaf labels $x..._1$ with $c..._1$. Then L is a *value constraint set* for T.

Similar to probability and weight constraint sets, a value constraint set can be seen as characterising a set of value functions. Finally, all the elements above can be employed to create the MCP frame, which constitutes a complete description of the multi-criteria probabilistic decision situation.

Definition: An *MCP frame* is a structure $\langle T,N,V \rangle$, where T is a criteria-consequence tree, N is a node constraint set and a core set for T and V is a value constraint set and a core set for T.

PROPERTIES OF REPRESENTATION

The probability, value and weight constraint sets are collections of linear inequalities. A minimal requirement for such a system of inequalities to be meaningful is that it is consistent, that is, there must exist some vector of variable assignments that simultaneously satisfies each inequality in the system. In other words, a consistent constraint set is a set where the constraints are not contradictory.

The first step in the evaluation procedure, after the user has asserted the various statements, is to calculate the meaningful (consistent) constraint sets in the sense above. In several dimensions, the solution set is difficult to visualise and a local, that is, dimension-wise, representation is preferred. The local representation of the solution set can be visualised on the individual coordinate axes by orthogonal projections.

Definition: Given a consistent constraint set X in the variables $\{x_i\}$, $^X\max(x_i) =_{def} \sup(a \mid \{x_i > a\} \cup X$ is consistent). Similarly, $^X\min(x_i) =_{def} \inf(a \mid \{x_i < a\} \cup X$ is consistent). Further, given a function f, $^X\text{argmax}(f(x))$ is a solution vector that is a solution to $^X\max(f(x))$, and $^X\text{argmin}(f(x))$ is a solution vector that is a solution to $^X\min(f(x))$.

Note that argmax and argmin need not be unique. The set of orthogonal projections of the solution set is called the *orthogonal hull*. Consequently, this is a concept that in each dimension signals which parts of the intervals are definitely incompatible with the constraint set. Thus, for each variable in a constraint set, it consists of all consistent variable assignments.

Definition: Given a consistent constraint set X in $\{x_i\}_{i \in}$, the set of pairs $\langle ^X\min(x_i), {}^X\max(x_i) \rangle$ is the *orthogonal hull* of the set.

The orthogonal hull is also called upper and lower probabilities if X consists of probabilities, and upper and lower values if X consists of values. The first question is whether the elements in a constraint set are at all compatible with each other. This translates to the problem of whether a constraint set has a solution, that is, if there exists any vector of real numbers that can be assigned to the variables. The second question is to determine the orthogonal hull for the entire tree. In order to calculate the hull, it is necessary to find the pairs $\langle ^X\min(x_i), {}^X\max(x_i) \rangle$, that is, to find minima and maxima for all variables in the constraint set. If the constraint set is consistent, the orthogonal hull can be calculated. Checking consistency and finding all maxima and minima can be carried out at the same time in only one step by the following procedure.

ORTHOGONAL HULL PROCEDURE

The most fundamental component in determining the hull is a way of calculating the consistency in a base. Since the base consists of a linear system of interval equations, the natural design candidate for an algorithm is linear programming.

The area of linear programming (LP) deals with the maximising (or minimising) of a linear function with a large number of likewise linear constraints in the form of weak inequalities. Research efforts in the field are mainly focused on developing efficient representations and algorithms for finding local and global optima. The LP problem is the following optimising problem:

$$\max f(\mathbf{x})$$
$$\text{when } \mathbf{Ax} \geq \mathbf{b}$$
$$\text{and } \mathbf{x} \geq \mathbf{0},$$

where $f(\mathbf{x})$ is a linear expression of the type $c_1x_1 + c_2x_2 + \dots + c_nx_n$, $\mathbf{Ax} \geq \mathbf{b}$ is a matrix equation with rows $a_{11}x_1 + a_{12}x_2 + \dots + a_{1n}x_n \geq b_1$ through $a_{m1}x_1 + a_{m2}x_2 + \dots + a_{mn}x_n \geq b_m$, and $\mathbf{x} \geq \mathbf{0}$ are the non-negativity constraints $x_i \geq 0$ for each variable. Amongst all feasible points, the solution to $f(\mathbf{x})$ is sought that has the highest numerical value, that is, the best solution vector $\mathbf{x}$ the components of which are all non-negative and satisfy all constraints. In the same way, a minimum can be searched for by negating all terms in the $f(\mathbf{x})$ expression.

A base is consistent if any solution can be found to the set of interval equations. Let there be m interval equations in the base. By introducing new variables $y_1, \dots, y_k$, with $k = 2 \cdot m$, to the consistency problem, it can be reformulated as

$$\min (y_1 + \dots + y_k)$$
$$\text{when } \mathbf{Ax} \geq \mathbf{b}$$
$$\text{and } \mathbf{x} \geq \mathbf{0}, \mathbf{y} \geq \mathbf{0},$$

where each interval equation $a_{i1}x_1 + a_{i2}x_2 + \dots + a_{in}x_n \in$ is transformed into the two equations $a_{i1}x_1 + a_{i2}x_2 + \dots + a_{in}x_n - y_j \geq b_i$ and $a_{i1}x_1 + a_{i2}x_2 + \dots + a_{in}x_n + y_1 \leq d_i$. If the obtained minimum of $y_1 + \dots + y_k$ has the value zero, then a solution has been found that does not contain any y_i. Removing the y_is, the resulting solution vector $\mathbf{x}$ is indeed a feasible solution, that is, the base is proven to be consistent. If the minimum of $y_1 + \dots + y_k$ is positive, then it is certain that the optimal values of the y_is are larger than zero, that is, at least one of the y_is is necessary to keep the base consistent. Since the y_is were added to the base, the problem itself has no solution. Hence, the base is inconsistent.

According to the definition, in order to calculate the orthogonal hull, it is necessary to find the hull intervals. First a consistent point is found by employing the procedure above. A search then begins from that point for the minimum and maximum of each variable in turn by taking their respective slack or surplus variable as the objective function. For convexity reasons, the entire interval between those extreme points is feasible, and thus the orthogonal hull has been calculated. The algorithm for finding the orthogonal hull relies on the ability to solve a sequence of small LP (SSLP) problems rapidly. This was not obvious from the outset, and a design not permitting substantial changes in structure and call sequences would have failed.

THE SIMPLEX METHOD

From the early 1950s onwards, the very general nature of the LP problem formulation rapidly led to the solution of an increasing number of ever larger problems in industry and government. With the growth of computing in general, the area of LP soon gained momentum. The Simplex algorithm is one of the earliest solution methods, and was originally suggested by Danzig. At first, it was not much more than a clever way to manipulate matrices in order to manoeuvre from one corner to another of a feasible polytope in such a way that the objective function never decreases. Today it has become an entire sub-field within applied mathematics. The current research focus is on solving larger and larger problems, involving thousands of equations and tens of thousands of variables.

Problems still remain with the Simplex method. A theoretical problem is that it belongs to the class of exponential algorithms. Examples can be designed to reveal this deficiency. Because of this, other non-linear approaches to LP problems were suggested many years ago, notably Khachian's ellipsoid method from 1979 and the Karmarkar algorithm from 1984. The proposed advantages of these non-linear approaches only reveal themselves in very large or contrived problems. It is evident that most of the research focuses on solving large LP (LLP) problems within reasonable time. As was pointed out above, the problem here is to find solutions to a sequence of small problems in a very short time to allow for interactive use. None of the non-linear methods, nor much of the current research in Simplex, is therefore of any great use for the DMC library package. In this chapter, some (fairly trivial) extensions to the standard Simplex algorithm are discussed to show how a search for a fast algorithm for SSLP problems evolves. While they are obvious and well-known techniques for LLP, their appropriateness for SSLP remained to be tried. Many other techniques were tried and discarded because they apply to specially structured or very large problems, and many were related to numerical properties of very large matrices. The descriptions of the extensions given here are intended to be intuitive for the purpose of conveying the experimental nature of the software development of the DMC package.

REVISED SIMPLEX

In each Simplex step one basic solution is replaced by another by means of matrix operations on the coefficient matrix **A** and the right-hand side **b**. If the size of **A** is $m \neq n$, then a Simplex solution to an LP problem can most often be found in $3m/2$ steps, each step including a pivot operation consisting of a large number of multiplications and divisions. Most LLP problems have a structure where $m \ll n$, and only a minor fraction of the columns will ever be pivoted on. Because of this, it seems to be a waste of processing time to update all columns in every step. Using matrix algebra, it can easily be shown that the column to pivot on in each step can be constructed from the original data instead of from the data in the previous step. All potential transformations are held in a matrix, and the total amount of processing of columns is now proportional to m instead of to n, but an overhead penalty is incurred for keeping track of the dormant columns. If $m \ll n$, as in the LLP problems of mainstream Simplex research, then this is a very large improvement. However, in the SSLP case, $m \approx n$. Both methods iterate the same number of steps, but since a large fraction of the columns will be used actively, the overhead introduced in the revised method makes it less attractive than the standard method for SSLP purposes. Experiments with the revised formulation of the method required substantial changes to the fundamental structure of the software design.

UPPER AND LOWER BOUNDS

In many LP problems, a considerable number of the constraint equations have only one variable, reflecting a modelling situation where there are many constraints on single variables, in some cases on most of the variables involved. This means that were there a formulation of Simplex where these constraints could be handled in an efficient way, the computational effort for solving the problem could be greatly reduced. This is due to the fact mentioned earlier that the effort expended on solving an LP problem is roughly proportional to $3m/2$, where m is the number of constraints. Since constraints on single variables are still matrix rows, they account for a fair amount of the computational processing of such problems. While bounds were an obvious inclusion in the library, its implementation was not as straightforward, including trade-offs between speed and accessibility, leading to architectural changes in the software.

GENERALISED UPPER BOUNDS

There is an appropriate generalisation of the upper bound handling in the previous paragraph. Some LLP problems have a structure where many constraints are of a form $\sum x_i = b$ for non-trivial index sets. There is a close relationship with the probability base where the normalisation equation is $\sum p_{ij} = 1$ for each alternative. The theory of generalised upper bounds (GUBs) is a matrix method based on factorising the base into parts with different properties. The new parts are then less complicated to solve. Suppose the coefficient matrix has m rows of which m_2 are of the generalised form above. The GUB technique is then reported to become faster than ordinary revised Simplex when $m_2 \approx 0.3 \cdot m$ and ten times faster when $m_2 \approx 0.8 \cdot m$. While this is a remarkable speed increase for LLP GUB problems, there is in our problem formulation only one such equation per alternative in the probability base, and that falls below the trade-off point.

IMPLICIT IDENTITY MATRIX

The implicit identity matrix technique is a simple observation of how the Simplex algorithm works. In any matrix description of the standard Simplex, it is readily seen that the basic variables (i.e., those with non-zero values assigned) form an identity sub-matrix within the coefficient matrix. Since this is an invariant fact during the entire Simplex execution, that part of the matrix might as well be replaced with index values in a vector. The problems considered here are not very large, and so the trade-off should be balanced between program code for treating special cases and savings in memory space and numerical operations. The outcome depends on the hardware architecture of the executing machine. Thus, the development method should also consider taking varying execution environments into account.

SPARSE MATRIX ENCODING

For LLP problems, the matrices often become very large. An ordinary LLP problem might have 10^3 rows and 10^4 variables and this would result in 10^7 matrix elements, most of which contain zero values. Obviously, this is unfeasible to handle. By observing that only a small fraction of the elements in each row are non-zero, the Simplex algorithm can be modified to work with a one-dimensional structure representing only the non-zero elements of the coefficient matrix. All elements not found in the structure are zero by definition. Extra program code is required to handle this, but the processing overhead is small compared with the savings in memory and increase in speed achieved for LLP problems. Unfortunately, SSLP problems do not gain that much from sparse matrix techniques, since each matrix is rather small. They are not as sparse as LLP matrices and the program overhead makes the approach less interesting. There is, however, one circumstance that is important. If the architectural speed of floating point (FP) operations is much slower than testing integer and pointer vectors, then sparse matrices can be interesting, thus again calling for a design catering for hardware architectural differences.

SENSITIVITY TESTS

An important part of the Simplex theory is the provision of very convenient means to do sensitivity analysis without reworking the problem, but rather by reasoning about small differences in the input data. There are standard reasoning patterns for carrying out sensitivity analysis of the attained optimal solution. In this way it is possible to vary the coefficients of the objective function or the right-hand side to see within which ranges the respective coefficients can vary while still keeping the same solution as optimal (even though its value may change). Unfortunately this does not map very well onto the consistency problem. To see this, notice that the proposed algorithm arrives at a solution to the problem:

$$\min (y_1 + \ldots + y_k)$$
$$\text{when } \mathbf{Ax} \geq \mathbf{b}$$
$$\text{and } \mathbf{x} \geq \mathbf{0}, \mathbf{y} \geq \mathbf{0},$$

and inquire whether this minimal value is zero or not. Usually, there are many combinations of basic variables that achieve this, because there are many possible feasible basic solutions. The Simplex sensitivity analyses focus on properties of the obtained basic configuration, while here any solution (of the often many) with the desired property is accepted. Thus, Simplex sensitivity reasoning is very different from sensitivity analyses in the decision algorithmic software. Instead, the sensitivity analysis takes place on a higher level, partly using the concept of consistency, and relying on the extended specification above. As the sensitivity analyses options evolved over time, they became something very different than specified from the outset, leading to substantial changes in the library structure.

In short, established LLP techniques were not effective in guiding the development of the library. The developments above led subsequently to a different algorithm for finding the hull. The original software architecture had to cope with substantial changes. For example, to find $\langle {}^X\min(x_i), {}^X\max(x_i)\rangle_1$ for all variables x_i with indices of the index set I, we could reformulate it into the optimisation problem

$$^{X'}\max \sum_i (x_i^+ - x_i^-)$$

where each x_i is represented by the two variables x_i^+ and x_i^-. The constraint set X' is then derived from X in the following way (for any inequality operator ⋈):

Range constraints: An inequality $x_i ⋈ k$ is transformed into
a) $x_i^+ ⋈ k$ and **b)** $x_i^- ⋈ k$.
Normalisation constraints: An equality $\sum_{i\in I}(x_i) = k$ is transformed into
$\forall i \in$ I: **a)** $x_i^+ + \sum_{j\neq i}(x_j^-) \leq k$ and **b)** $\sum_{j\neq i}(x_j^+) + x_i^- \geq k$.

The solution vector $(x_1^-,\ldots,x_n^-,x_1^+,\ldots,x_n^+) = {}^{X'}\text{argmax} \sum_i(x_i^+ - x_i^-)$ will then contain the upper and lower bounds such that for each x_i the pairs $\langle x_i^-, x_i^+\rangle$ are the orthogonal hull components. For convexity reasons, the entire interval between those extremal points is feasible. The procedure works regardless of the tree shape and for all tree levels concurrently. Now, it is easy to display to the decision-maker which statements are incompatible or which parts of intervals are not compatible with the rest of the statements.

EVALUATIONS

The primary evaluation rule of the criteria-consequence tree is based on a generalised expected value. Since neither probabilities nor values are fixed numbers, the evaluation of the expected value yields multi-linear objective functions.

$$\text{GEV}(A_i) = \sum_{i_1=1}^{n_{i_0}} x_{ii_1} \sum_{i_2=1}^{n_{i_1}} x_{ii_1 i_2} \cdots \sum_{i_{m-1}=1}^{n_{i_{m-2}}} x_{ii_1 i_2 \cdots i_{m-2} i_{m-1}} \sum_{i_m=1}^{n_{i_{m-1}}} x_{ii_1 i_2 \cdots i_{m-2} i_{m-1} i_m} x_{ii_1 i_2 \cdots i_{m-2} i_{m-1} i_m 1}$$

where $x_{\ldots i_j \ldots}$ denote criteria weights and probabilities and $x_{\ldots i_j \ldots 1}$ denote values.

Maximisation of such non-linear expressions subject to linear constraints (the node and value constraint sets) are computationally demanding problems to solve for an interactive tool in the general case, using techniques from the area of non-linear programming. There are discussions about computational procedures to reduce non-linear problems to systems with linear objective functions, solvable with ordinary linear programming methods. These procedures are also SSLP problems.

A natural way to handle the inherent imprecision is to consider values near the boundaries of the intervals as being less reliable than more central ones. If the strength is evaluated on a sequence of ever-smaller sub-bases, then a good appreciation of the strength's dependency on boundary values can be obtained. This is taken into account by cutting off the dominated regions indirectly. This is called *cutting the bases*, and the amount of cutting is indicated as a percentage, which can range from 0% to 100%. This can be seen as the x-axis in Figure 4, which shows progressively larger cuts. For a 100% cut, the bases are transformed into single points (focal points), and the evaluation becomes the calculation of the ordinary expected value. It is possible to regard the hull cut as an automated kind of sensitivity analysis. Since the belief in peripheral values is somewhat less, the interpretation of the cut is to zoom in on more believable values that are more centrally located. Or conversely, to zoom out from the focal points, adding uncertainty as the zooming out progresses (leftwards in the figure). Thus, this kind of contraction along the x-axis is a sensitivity analysis procedure, in which all intervals are compressed in a controlled way towards the focal point of the multi-dimensional space that all consequences span. For each variable, there is also a *focal point*, which may be viewed as the 'most likely' or 'best representative' value for that variable. Hence, a focal point is a unique solution vector whose components for each dimension (variable) lie within the orthogonal hull. Given this, we calculate the strength of alternatives as a means for further discriminating the alternatives.

The strength δ_{ij} denotes the difference in expected value between two scenarios (alternatives) A_i and A_j, that is, the expression $GEV(A_i)-GEV(A_j)$. For multi-criteria models, the expected value for each criterion is aggregated into a weighted sum of expected values for the entire decision problem. In the evaluation, the alternatives are pair-wise compared and a ranking is induced. The differences in expected value between the alternatives are utilised as an evaluation rule by letting The strengths of each alternative compared with all the others can then be compared using the tool. This results in graphs showing the maximum strengths of the alternatives. More formally, for comparing alternatives A_i and A_j, the upper line is $\max(\delta_{ij})$ and the lower is $-\min(\delta_{ij})$, that is, the lower line is reversed to facilitate an easier comparison. Thus, one can see from which cut level an alternative dominates another. As the cut progresses, one of the alternatives eventually dominates strongly, that is, there are no variable assignments yielding $\max(\delta_{ij}) > 0$.

In the evaluation result in Figure 4, the x-axis shows the base cut in per cent, which is a sensitivity analysis zooming in on

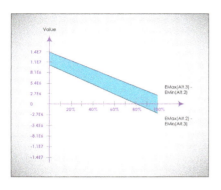

Figure 4. Sensitivity analysis by contraction.

central parts of the intervals. The y-axis shows the difference in strength.[1] The results in the figure should be interpreted as the uppermost alternative being the most preferred one.

Using cut levels as in Figure 4, it can be seen that δ_{23} is strictly less than 0 at cut level 80%. This means that in a quite substantial volume around the focal point, Alt. 3 is definitely better than Alt. 2 and consequently, that there is no possibility for the converse to hold. Thus, the above ranking is fairly stable under this kind of sensitivity analysis.

DESIGN DISCUSSION

One solution to the architectural problem is a configuration program. Such a program would on its own measure the interesting speeds of instructions and set source code aspect parameters accordingly. The source code would then automatically be recompiled prior to execution on a new platform. In this way, the source code becomes independent of the actual target machine. This independence relies on the source code containing all appropriate techniques as inclusion options for the configuration program to choose from. Such inclusions would be simpler to manage using aspect-structured code than object-oriented code.

This is not to argue that object-orientation is less usable in general for research in algorithms. But the point here is that code objects are not always the primary code structure choice, especially not when the outcome of the code exercise is largely unknown at the outset. The concept of aspect-oriented software design was not around when this project commenced. The concept deals with architectural crosscutting concerns such as, inter alia, memory management, code optimisation, and real-time behaviour. The DMC package was designed using an object-based overall design approach but implemented using coding techniques more closely related to what later became known as aspect-oriented techniques. Since there were no aspect tools available at the time, it was coded in C using configuration parameters and macros in addition to a revision control system in order to control the implementational aspects of the package. The development of the library was not at the start a software design study, which is why its account is a case study and not a controlled experiment.

A UNIFIED FRAMEWORK

We have presented a computationally meaningful framework for a unification of probabilistic and multi-criteria approaches to decision making while also attending to the requirement of handling imperfect information. In this framework, a decision

[1] The scales are from the lowest value to the highest value on the y-axes.

problem can be seen as different decision trees under a criteria hierarchy. These trees can then be combined to a general tree modelling the various values, criteria and probabilities involved, that is, all those concepts can be modelled in a common structure. For increasing the usefulness of the approach, the framework allows for imprecise information in all input data. This means that a decision-maker does not need to enter precise information when such is not available. Furthermore, and most important, the criteria weights as well as the relations are allowed to be qualitative. Procedures for evaluating this unified framework are discussed. While the method is used throughout the chapter, all important aspects are applicable to other formalisms as well.

The algorithms for finding the orthogonal hull are optimisation algorithms, but of a slightly different nature than ordinary optimisation problems. In ordinary optimisation, the task is often to find a local optimum (sometimes a global one) for a problem with many variables, possibly millions. This is often done in batch mode, that is, the real-time (or interactive) requirements are low. But in this case, the design is required to solve many (hundreds) of optimisation problems in fractions of a second, the speed requirement being that the user should not experience any delay in response. For this to be possible, a network of result caches had to be devised. While the exact design of the caches is not important, it is interesting to note that these kinds of requirements are not easily anticipated before the orthogonal hull procedure was produced. Thus, the overall software design depends on algorithms whose specifications are not known from the outset and whose development cannot be foreseen since there are no originals or templates to start with.

In summary, the library package continues to evolve more than 15 years after its first release without requiring a rewrite or architectural redesign. Part of its longevity, despite complexity and changing requirements and specifications, is due to the following set of principles:

- an object-based approach,
- a contract-based specification,
- aspect-orientation-like management of key code features, and
- a pure imperative programming language,

resulting in reasonable development control without introducing overheads in the form of overspecification, slow execution or too large a footprint.

FURTHER READING

Danielson, M. and Ekenberg, L. A Framework for Analyzing Decisions under Risk, *European Journal of Operational Research.* 104(3), pp. 474–484. 1998.

Danielson, M. and Ekenberg, L. Computing Upper and Lower Bounds in Interval Decision Trees, *European Journal of Operational Research.* 181(2), pp. 808–816. 2007.

Danielson, M., Ekenberg, L. and Larsson, A. Distribution of Belief in Decision Trees, *International Journal of Approximate Reasoning.* 46(2), pp. 387–407. 2007.

Ekenberg, L., Boman, M., Linneroth-Bayer, J. General Risk Constraints, *Journal of Risk Research.* 4(1), pp. 31–47. 2001.

Ekenberg, L., Danielson, M., Larsson A. and Sundgren, D. Second-Order Risk Constraints in Decision Analysis, *Axioms.* 3, pp. 31–45. 2014.

Ekenberg, L., Thorbiörnson J. and Baidya, T. Value Differences using Second Order Distributions, *International Journal of Approximate Reasoning.* 38(1), pp. 81–97. 2005.

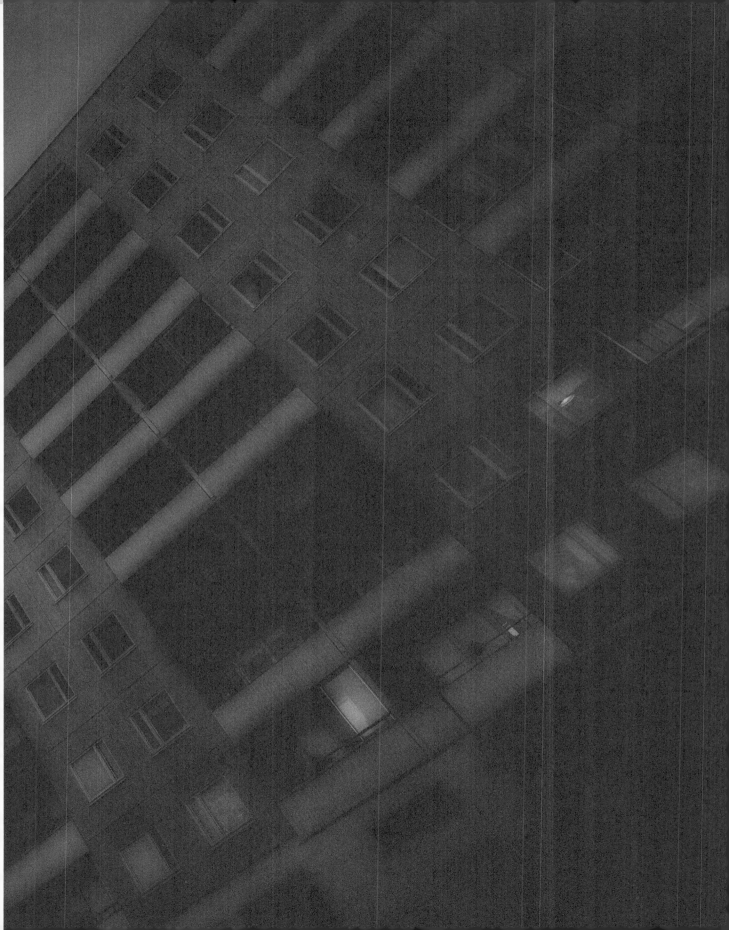

APPLICATIONS

Decision analysis without applications makes no sense and this section details some real-life applications of the theoretical constructs previously described.

Chapters 13 and *14* introduce a framework for multiple criteria decision making for flood risk management. To date, most models assessing flood impacts and coping strategies have focused on economic impacts and neglected environmental and social considerations. The stakeholders include, among others, the public in both high-risk and low-risk areas, insurance companies and the government. With an understanding of the preferences of the stakeholder groups, decision analysis can be a useful tool in establishing and ranking different policy alternatives. The design of a public-private flood insurance system is a multi-stakeholder policy problem, but involves handling extensive imprecise information, including estimates of the stakeholders' utilities, outcome probabilities, and importance.

This section of the book explores a general approach to analysing decision situations under risk involving multiple stakeholders. We develop and test an ex-ante framework for flood damage assessment, which includes a flood simulation model, a decision tool, and suggested policy strategies. Environmental and social criteria are introduced into the framework, and soft evaluations are performed in order to demonstrate the usability of the framework. The Bac Hung Hai polder in northern Vietnam serves as one of the case studies, in *Chapter 13*. In *Chapter 14* a similar approach is employed to assess options for designing a public-private insurance and reinsurance system in the case of the Tisza river in Hungary. The general method of probabilistic, multi-stakeholder analysis extends the use of utility functions for supporting evaluation of imprecise and uncertain data.

Chapter 15 presents another case study arising from the need for and estimated utility of a structured analysis – for the Roşia Montană gold exploitation project. This has been a contentious issue in Romanian public life for the last 15 years and there is a multitude of conflicting information and opinions on the benefits and risks involved. This chapter provides a comprehensive decision analysis of the Roşia Montană project, drawing upon more than 100 historical documents, both official and informal, representing the views of a wide variety of stakeholders. These were analysed with a multi-criteria tree including the relevant perspectives under which the four most commonly discussed alternatives were analysed. The result can be translated into a valuable recommendation for the mining company and the political decision-makers. If these stakeholders want to see the Roşia Montană project continue, and for it to be accepted by civil society, the key challenges will be to increase the transparency of the process and improve its credibility and legal underpinnings; if these requirements cannot be met, the decision-makers will need to pay attention to the alternatives for sustainable development in the area.

In *Chapter 16* we take the municipality of Upplands Väsby in Stockholm County as an example to illustrate the challenges and a possible alternative to the more regular processes in municipal planning, starting from a simple-to-use multi-criteria model that has gained acceptance and explaining how it can be extended utilising the methods described earlier.

In *Chapter 17* we develop a tool that addresses inequalities and provides users with the means to change the rules of the system in favour of certain behaviours. Based on democratic meeting practices, inequalities are measured and made visible to users of the system, and change dynamically as actions are taken. In *Chapter 18*, we include this functionality in a wiki-type participatory tool providing users with integrated and easy-to-use means for structuring and analysing discussion.

Chapter 19 employs the ICT evaluation model described in *Chapter 9* on a case study of e-learning at Makarere University in Uganda. Finally, *Chapter 20* reports on the ongoing work of elicitation and analysis of multi-layered and multi-actor realities in the movement towards a low carbon society by 2050 in Sweden's Stockholm-Mälar region.

13

A Model for Flood Risk Management: Bac Hung Hai

This chapter is based on Hansson, K.E., Danielson, M., Ekenberg, L. and Buurman, J. Handling Multiple Criteria in Flood Risk Management, in *Integrated Catastrophe Risk Modelling: Supporting Policy Processes*. Eds. Amendola, A., Ermolieva, T. Linnerooth-Bayer, J. and Mechler, R. Springer. 2013.

Rivers are vital for survival: for food, for watering livestock and for irrigating crops; changes in the behaviour of the rivers can have catastrophic effects downstream. And water resources in a region are usually highly dependent on the water management policies of neighbouring countries – all of which makes planning in disaster management highly complex. Catastrophic floods are a major contributor to human and environmental misery, accounting for over half of the fatalities and a third of all the damage from all natural catastrophes worldwide.

It is clear that an integrated water resource management approach is necessary to direct action in the best interests of society and the environment. One improvement in recent years has been the development models capable of handling and evaluating multiple criteria as well as multiple stakeholders: a framework called Simulation and Evaluation with Multiple Perspectives and Agents Integrated (SEMPAI) has been developed for this purpose. SEMPAI can manage multiple stakeholders, multiple policy strategies as well as inputs from environmental, financial and social disciplines, combining simulations with a decision analysis tool. Moreover, the framework is designed to handle the specific situations of developing countries where it is vital to incorporate environmental knowledge and multi-faceted river usage. Inhabitants know the river system and its behaviour. They are often dependent on it for everyday tasks such as transportation, gathering food, washing clothes and watering crops and cattle. Therefore, a flood management strategy designed for a developed country may not be suitable in the developing countries which are particularly vulnerable to financial and environmental changes and disease outbreaks.

We use the framework to study risks in one of the largest deltas in Vietnam, the Red River Delta, which is at high risk of flooding. Lives and property are threatened by annual flood events, and extreme floods impose a substantial burden on its communities. The delta exhibits all the characteristics of a region in stress: low-lying land, dense and increasing population, increasing numbers of floods. The 225,000 ha Bac Hung Hai polder serves as the pilot area for our analysis. Most of the polder consists of agricultural land with elevations ranging from 0 to 10 metres, with the highest elevation in the northwest and the lowest in the southeast.

THE FRAMEWORK

The World Meteorological Organisation (WMO) identifies the goals and benefits of cooperation in transboundary river basins, including peace and security, and support for sustainable, environmentally sound management of the water resources. Often a single measure of value is used for the consequences of a decision – typically in financial terms. However, very often more criteria are relevant in policy formulations and decisions.

In this study we took a broader scope and utilised MCDA methodologies on a decision model based on flood simulations that were automatically transferred to one of the DecideIT tools. The simulation model generated probabilistic loss estimations and also linked different subsystems based on weather, economic and hydrological data. The pilot study involved 11,200 persons (out of the total population in the Bac Hung Hai polder of 2.8 million), all of whom are at risk to flood. Micro-level data was provided by experts on site, including property and land use data, as well as other data of choice.

Each geographical location was identified as a vector cell in the simulation model. Additional vectors were also introduced and connected to each other via identification numbers, such as different kinds of land use, soil type, crop data and other information. A transboundary perspective was introduced in the model, making it possible to investigate, for instance, the effects of structural mitigation changes upstream. Stakeholders such as insurers, governments, NGOs and property owners were included, and these were also interconnected via, for instance, insurance contracts or reimbursements after a flood.

Structural measures identified in the model by location. Each location also held attributes such as certain strengths based on material and maintenance, over time. If a flood of a certain strength takes place, a breach, overtopping or seepage may occur and several cells are affected in different manners.

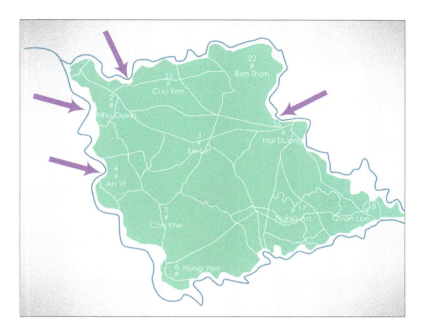

Figure 1. Bac Hun Hai Polder, failure locations, scale 1:200 000.

For instance, a property located in a flooded area may be damaged and its value reduced. Flood data based on historical records was introduced, and simulated in the model using a Monte Carlo (MC) technique. The decision-makers could set up the simulation, choosing the length of the simulation and the nature of the occurrences. In this case, the simulation was set to several different types of floods at different locations along the river, for a 10-year period and at 10,000 time points. Time intervals were changed, providing the decision-makers with data on both long-term and short-term perspectives.

Nine different flood scenarios were implemented. Four scenarios are described as levee failure due to seepage at four different locations in the polder (see Figure 1), four are described as overtopping, and the ninth one represents no event in a particular year. Data on flood probabilities and flood damages were gathered on location, and statistics were retrieved from local authorities.

LOCATIONS AND PROBABILITIES
1. Song Hong, Red River, protected by 64–80 km levees. Probability for overtopping is 4.7% and for levee breach 2.6%.
2. Song Hong 2, Red River, 80–120 km levees. Probability for overtopping is 4.2% and for levee breach 31%.
3. Sound Duong, Duong River, 0–45 km of levees. Probability for overtopping is 0.5% and for levee breach 0.1%.

4. Song Thai Binh, at the Thai Binh River, 0–15 km levees. Probability for overtopping is 4.3%, and for levee breach 44%.

In the study, the simulations were repeated 10,000 times over 10-year periods. Floods were simulated using the Monte Carlo simulation technique, once each year per type of flood.[1] (We restricted the number of floods to one flood per location per year.) This gave us, for a 10-year period, more than $12 \cdot 10^{18}$ possible outcomes $((3^4)^{10})$.

CRITERIA

The three types of default criteria in the decision evaluation model were economic, social/health, and environmental. The following criteria hierarchy of different types of consequences was identified:

1. pollution of drinking water;
2. destruction of mangrove forests; and
3. river pollution.

The criterion social/health aspects includes four different types of consequences:

1. stress on families;
2. increase in water-borne diseases (including mosquito related diseases);
3. historic/religious buildings destroyed; and
4. snakebites.

These criteria are soft and thus more difficult to value, but they can be assigned a preference order. For each unique event and for each location, each group of stakeholders can rank criteria and assign a weight (or a weight interval) if desired. There are numerous factors that can be incorporated into a project.

- After a flood, contaminated *drinking water* is often a problem when sewerage systems are breached and flooded, leading to illnesses such as cholera or dysentery.
- Additionally, stagnant water after a flood (e.g. puddles, water-filled divots) can increase *diseases spread by mosquitoes*, such as malaria and dengue fever, and in some cases different forms of encephalitis. It should be noted that mosquito-borne disease transmission is related to the number of infected mosquitoes able to transmit disease and not to the total number of biting mosquitoes present in a population. (For instance, following a 2002 flood in Mozambique there was an increase of malaria of 1.5 to 2 times.) It should also be noted that increased transmission of mosquito-borne diseases usually occurs several weeks after a flood (and not during the flood).

[1] A flood event is calculated as the probability of a failure of the flood protection measures (using the probabilities for each type of event and for each location) conditional on a 100-year flood occurring. That is, the events of levee breach and overtopping may only occur if a 100-year flood event has struck at a specific location.

- Social protection and sickness allowance is often non-existent in developing countries – families and neighbours rely on each other and if a member of a family falls ill this can be devastating to the household's economy.
- During a flood family members may be separated and the Red Cross works actively to trace *missing people* after disasters. To minimise the risk of such family tragedies, it is important for people living in high-risk areas to be educated regarding suitable escape routes and meeting points.
- Industries along riversides may cause serious disruption to the environment by *polluting the river* if exposed to flooding. Run-off from floods can bring contaminated water into the river, poisoning the fish and affecting the health and livelihoods of poor people dependent on the river.. Such an incident occurred in the Tisza River in 2000, when a flood carried cyanide and heavy metals not only into the river causing fish and microbes to be poisoned, but also into wetland and flood plains along the river causing pollution and harming otters and birds. In more tropical regions, flood run-off can destroy coral, and the nutrients create an algae bloom producing ciguatoxin (toxic bacteria). People ingest the bacteria by eating contaminated fish (conventional cooking does not destroy ciguatoxin bacteria in fish).
- *Snakebites* may cause deaths and injury after a flood. Like humans, snakes seek shelter from the water in trees, houses, and on roof tops. Stressed snakes competing for space bite anything that comes close to them.
- *River mangrove forests* are vital for many reasons. They provide habitats and breeding areas for wildlife such as fish and shrimps. Mangroves protect river banks and coastal regions from erosion, and they reduce the impact of floods. Mangrove forests can be seen as both natural protection and as a consequence of flooding.
- *Historical buildings, ancient monuments and churches* are important to preserve. They serve as symbols for the history, religion and heritage of a nation, region or village. Moreover, for the inhabitants in small villages, religious buildings often serve as meeting halls, and if hazard maps and escape routes are produced, this is often the place where they are kept, accessible to all villagers. Furthermore, cultural and historical buildings can attract tourism and therefore be economically beneficial.

These criteria are implemented as decision trees for the evaluation procedure, together with the strategies. One tree was created per criteria, stakeholder and strategy.

STRATEGIES

Several strategies are implemented in the simulation model. For this study, we consider only the financial aspects (reimbursement or compensation after a disaster) and the generic types of mitigation measures (structural and non-structural), which are drawn from an earlier case and further elaborated to fit the needs of developing countries.

- *Strategy 1*: Low government compensation in combination with structural measures.
- *Strategy 2*: The same settings as in strategy 1, but with considerably more funds to non-structural, pre-mitigation measures (education and warning systems which reduce lives lost and damage).
- *Strategy 3*: The use of a catastrophe fund for compensation and maintenance, where tax revenue is pooled.

Note that the settings used were for discussion purposes and did not necessarily reflect the views of the authors. The purpose was to demonstrate the general applicability of the framework. During this study, we elaborated with several settings on the ranking of the criteria.

The decision tool automatically created decision trees using the data provided by the simulation model. The decision analytical module selected for the framework was based on the Delta method and implemented in DecideIT. We took account of a multitude of weights at the same time (in the form of weight intervals) and explored how they affect the outcome. The results from the simulations were analysed and classes of weighted mean losses were calculated. This analysis also incorporated sensitivity analyses of the various costs and probabilities involved. Weights were set to correspond to the preferences of the stakeholder or aggregated group of stakeholders concerning the choice of strategy. Moreover, adding different criteria gave an additional dimension to disaster management.

Using this approach weights were added to both criteria and stakeholders, and it was possible to rank each consequence if desired. That is, the possibility existed for the stakeholder to specify which specific outcome is more preferable than another, making soft evaluations possible. In this study, each tree created in the decision module consisted of three alternatives representing the different strategies. Each tree represented one criterion that was implemented in the model: economic, social/health, or environmental.

In the economic/financial criterion tree, the alternatives led directly to the consequences, that is, taking into consideration all possible outcomes per each time period during the simulation. The other criteria trees were created by the project members, not by the simulation tool, since they contained soft data. Here, each alternative consisted of events before leading on to the possible criteria consequences. To illustrate the complexity, see Figure 2 where layers of trees are shown.

EXPERIMENTS

To construct the criteria trees, the actual flood events that occur in the simulation round were used to create event nodes (see E10 in Figure 3 for an example of an event node). Thus, the occurrence of each specific flood for each year was saved in a matrix, and each unique sequence per time period was sorted out. In this study, 23 unique outcomes were generated and it should be noted that the order of occurrences is taken into consideration. Thus, for instance, if two levee breaches occurred at the same location within a time period, it affected events in the simulation, such as borrowing, damage rate, reparation costs, etc. The propositions of stakeholders were represented in a tree under each criterion. Each such tree contained all strategies and their consequences. This was modelled for all stakeholders and all criteria in a layered master model with multiple layers of decision trees used to evaluate the problem. Based on real probability data concerning each flood, the event node probability was calculated accordingly as

$$p(F1) \cdot (1 - p(F1))^9 \cdot p(F2) \cdot (1 - p(F2))^9 \cdot 45 \qquad (1)$$

In Equation (1), the probability of two floods occurring within a time period is calculated. F1 corresponds to a specific flood probability, for instance, levee breach at location 1. The probability for each flood concerns one single year and not the accumulated risk. In the equation, one type of flood F1 has occurred during a 10-year period as well as one type of flood F2. Since this concerns an entire 10-year time period, we multiply it by the binominal coefficient

$$\binom{n}{k},$$

where *n* corresponds to the number of possible outcomes and *k* corresponds to the number of floods. However, since in this case the order of the floods is important, we have taken this into consideration. Hence, there are 45 different alternative placements. The same method is used to calculate the probability of an event node when three floods have occurred within a time period of 10 years (see Equation 2).

$$p(F1) \cdot (1 - p(F1))^9 \cdot p(F2) \cdot (1 - p(F2))^9 \cdot p(F3) \cdot (1 - p(F3))^9 \cdot 120 \qquad (2)$$

We can see in Figure 3 how policy makers can assign probabilities and values to the different consequences within a criterion.

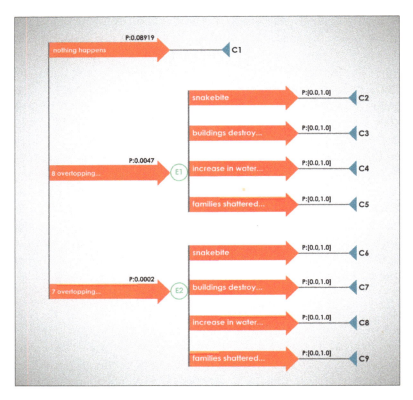

Figure 2. Government environmental criteria tree.

Above, we assumed that the economic criterion is the prominent rank for the government, followed by the social and the environmental criteria in no specific order. The insurer was given the same ranking, with a larger interval between financial and other criteria. The NGOs were given the opposite settings where the social and the environmental criteria were ranked higher than the financial. For the individuals, the financial criterion was ranked the highest followed closely by the social criterion and finally the environmental. In the modelling below, all criteria were ranked equally.

In Figures 4 and 5 all stakeholders and all criteria are equally weighted. A Pareto optimal solution with no restrictions shows that Strategy 3 is the preferred choice. The difference between Strategies 1 and 2 is small and needs further study to be conclusive. Both are inferior to Strategy 3. However, Strategy 3 does not contain direct non-structural mitigation measures affecting the environmental and social criteria, but maintenance spending is enough to decrease the probabilities for failure. No further donations or aid are given. No funds are provided for warning measures or education.

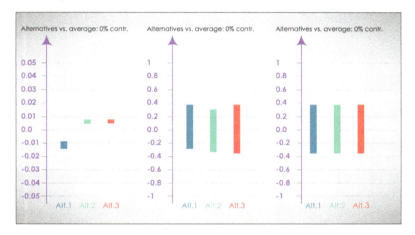

Figure 3. Separate criteria: Economic criterion (left), environmental criterion (middle), and social/health criterion (right).

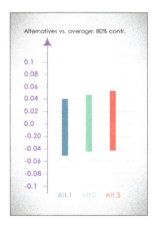

Figure 4. Aggregated criteria: all criteria and stakeholders are equally weighted.

Note that the described setup can also include stakeholder rankings. This is a sensitive matter and should be handled with care when modelling. Nevertheless, when the results of the possible strategies are equal, it might be meaningful to investigate the effects of an explicit stakeholder ranking. The experiments indicated that modelling efforts are essential when analysing new policy options for mitigating and financing the risk of a hazard. In order to estimate and cope with losses, policy makers often make use of computational models when evaluating flood scenarios and other disasters. The benefits of this framework can be summarised as follows:

- Simulation, decision analysis evaluations are integrated into the same framework for iterative assessment of different strategies.
- Predefined parameters to start a policy simulation and evaluation session.
- Handle both micro and macro levels in the same model.
- Handle short- and long-time horizons in the same model.
- Includes several perspectives, (criteria), not only financial.
- Includes several stakeholders' views and preferences.
- Enables a transboundary perspective.

Results from these case studies and stakeholder interviews show that it is useful to add a multi-criteria perspective to flood management decisions to account for differing views and preferences. Furthermore, such a framework enables stakeholder participation in consequence analyses as well as in formulating more elaborated criteria weights. However, it would be beneficial to introduce some additional aspects, such as a transboundary perspective and short-term efforts in combination with long-term strategies.

Using this framework may help governments and decision-makers to identify their own multiple hazard risks as well as to identify activities which can be implemented before the next flood event. It can expose the risks, benefits and drawbacks from these different activities. It can highlight the most important aspects to consider when implementing, for instance, a structural measure or insurance in a region at risk. It can include damage assessments for social, environmental and financial aspects. It can also reveal unfair actions, from both the micro and the macro perspective. Furthermore, the framework holds information on measurable variables which can be used in the evaluation of a flood coping strategy.

FURTHER READING

Conference Report of the Second Workshop on Transboundary Flood Risk Management Geneva, 19–20 March 2015.

Hamza, M. (Ed.), *World Disasters Report*, International Federation of Red Cross and Red Crescent Societies. 2015.

Kundzewicz, Z.W., Kanae, S., Seneviratne, S.I., Handmer, J., Nicholls, N., Peduzzi, P. *et al.*, Flood Risk and Climate Change: Global and Regional Perspectives. *Hydrological Sciences Journal.* 59(1), pp. 1–28. 2014.

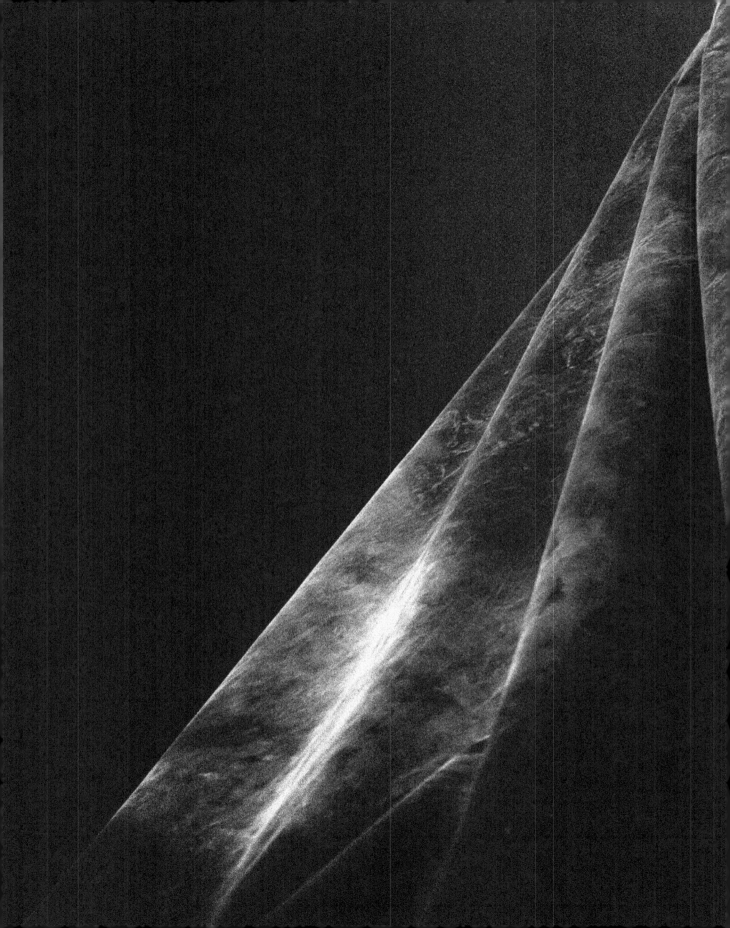

14

A Model for Flood Risk Management: Tisza

The selection of a reasonable policy strategy in order to manage losses from disasters is a complex task, and the design of a public-private flood insurance system is a multi-stakeholder policy problem. Numerous dependencies between different variables affect the outcome of the strategy and there are many contextual aspects to consider. The stakeholders include the public in high-risk and low-risk areas, insurance companies, and the government. The primary purpose of this chapter is to demonstrate a methodological approach for disaster risk management for the Tisza region in north-eastern Hungary, where financial losses from floods are severe and the costs of compensation to victims, and mitigation strategies, are increasing.

This chapter focuses on the decision analysis component of this issue. The background data for the analyses was provided by the Hungarian Academy of Sciences, complemented by interviews with different stakeholders in the region, and by a simulation model for investigating the effects of imposing different policy options for a flood risk management programme in the region. We focus on the application of a decision analytic approach applied to multi-stakeholder policy problems such as the Tisza case, but some background details are necessary to understand the context that follows.

In the case of Tisza, the information involved is severely uncertain. This makes it necessary to base the evaluations on a structured decision analytic method dealing with uncertainty by allowing value intervals to represent incomplete information, about alternative consequences as well as decision-makers' preferences. In the contentious Tisza situation every decision steps had to be accepted and understood by all stakeholders.

This chapter is based on Danielson, M. and Ekenberg, L., A Risk-based Decision Analytic Approach to Assessing Multi-Stakeholder Policy Problems, in *Integrated Catastrophe Risk Modelling: Supporting Policy Processes*. Eds. Amendola, A., Ermolieva, T., Linnerooth-Bayer, J. and Mechler, R. pp. 231–248. Dordrecht and New York: Springer. 2013.

FORMULATION OF THE POLICY PROBLEM

Two stochastic variables are used to represent flood uncertainties in the background simulations. The variable Magnitude represents, for each simulation year, whether there is a 100-year flood, a 150-year flood, a 1000-year flood, or no flood. The probabilities for these events are 1/100, 1/150, 1/1000 and 1–(1/100+1/150+1/1000) respectively. The other variable Failure represents whether the flood causes failure of a levee at one or none of three critical locations. For each of the nine failure scenarios, the inundated land area as well as the water level is calculated. The vulnerability of inundated land is considered, regarding, among other things, soil type, land-use pattern, elevation and property value. For each simulated year, when a flood failure has occurred, the financial consequences for the different stakeholders are collected. Only structural losses are considered here and these are estimated by a loss function, which considers initial property value and vulnerability as well as level and duration of inundating water.

The stakeholders represented in the flood model are the municipalities, insurance companies, individual property owners, and central government. At the end of each simulated year, the financial situations of all agents are updated. If there was a failure, the property values are reduced for the affected cells. Premiums are paid annually, but individual property owners can normally choose whether to buy insurance or not. This choice affects the outcome both for the individuals and for the insurance company. The financial consequences also depend on the current flood management strategy, that is, the level of compensation from the government and the insurance companies. The indicators of the simulations are:

- *Governmental load*: Compensation from government (in addition to subsidies and contribution to a re-insurance fund).
- *Balance for the insurance companies*: Income in the form of premiums for flood insurance, minus the compensation paid to property owners.
- *Balance for entire pilot basin*: Compensation from government in addition to compensation from insurance companies minus property damage and premiums. The individual balances are aggregated for the entire pilot basin (all municipalities).
- *Balance for individual property owners*: Compensation from government in addition to compensation from insurance companies minus property damage and premiums.
- *Balance per municipality*: Compensation from government in addition to compensation from insurance companies minus property damage and premiums. The individual balances are aggregated per municipality.

We have four basic scenarios, with the assumptions for the first scenario as follows:

- No post-disaster government compensation to private flood victims
  - Private insurance system
  - Private, non-mandatory policies
  - Natural disaster (flood, standing water, earthquake etc.) insurance can be purchased separately or bundled with property insurance policies
  - Insurance can cover up to 100% of the damage
  - Risk-based premiums for natural disasters
- Government subsidies for poor persons to purchase natural disaster insurance (can reach 100%)
- Government acts as re-insurer of last resort. Government re-insurance fund financed by tax revenues

This is a private insurance alternative with some government subsidies. Private insurance is used with government subsidies for the poor and the government re-insuring.

In the second scenario, the government compensates flood failure victims. Private insurance with government subsidies for the poor are used and the government re-insures:

- Government compensation to private flood victims for 50% of their losses
  - Private insurance system
  - Private, non-mandatory policies
  - Natural disaster (flood, standing water, earthquake etc.) insurance can be purchased separately or bundled with property insurance policies
  - Can reach 50% of the damage
  - No risk-based pricing for natural disasters (cross subsidies within system)
- Government subsidies for poor persons to purchase natural disaster insurance (can reach 100%)
- Government acts as re-insurer of last resort. Government re-insurance fund financed by tax revenues
- Contribution to prevention fund by insurance companies

In the third scenario the government compensates flood failure victims, but does not re-insure:

- Government compensation to private flood victims for 50% of their losses – contingent upon the purchase of natural disaster insurance
- Private insurance system
  - Private, non-mandatory policies

- Natural disaster (flood, standing water, earthquake etc.) insurance can be purchased separately or bundled with property insurance policies
- Covers 50% of the damage
- No risk-based pricing for natural disasters (cross subsidies within system)
- Government subsidies for poor persons to purchase natural disaster insurance (100%)
- No government reinsurance-fund
- Contribution to prevention fund by insurance companies

In the fourth scenario, the responsibility is partly shifted from government to the individual property owner. It includes mandatory public insurance for natural disasters with government subsidies for the poor:

- Public insurance system administered by private insurance companies
- Public, mandatory policies
- Only for natural disasters (flood, standing water, earthquake etc.)
- Can reach 100% of the damage
- No risk-based pricing (cross subsidies within system)
- Government subsidies for poor persons to purchase natural disaster insurance (can reach 100%)
- Government establishes catastrophe fund to compensate natural disaster victims and to assume all risks (risk of diverting catastrophe fund)

ANALYSING THE POLICY SCENARIOS

DecideIT[1] was employed for the evaluations and the values from the Tisza investigations were entered into the tool from simulations. The final outcomes are divided into the three stakeholder categories: government, insurance companies, and municipalities. Figures 1 and 2 show a simplification of the tree used for the analyses.

The primary evaluation rule for the stakeholder trees is based on the generalised expected values of the scenarios, taking all probabilities, values, and (in the final analysis) criteria weights into account. In the evaluations, the alternatives are pair-wise compared and a ranking is induced. Figure 3 shows the result of asserting government as the most important stakeholder. The importance weights were set accordingly and the probabilities and costs were provided from the simulations. Note that no explicit numerical weights had to be supplied. The x-axis shows the base cut in per cent (see below for a discussion on the concept, which is

[1] DecideIT uses the Delta method, see *Chapters 11* and *12* for a description of the method.

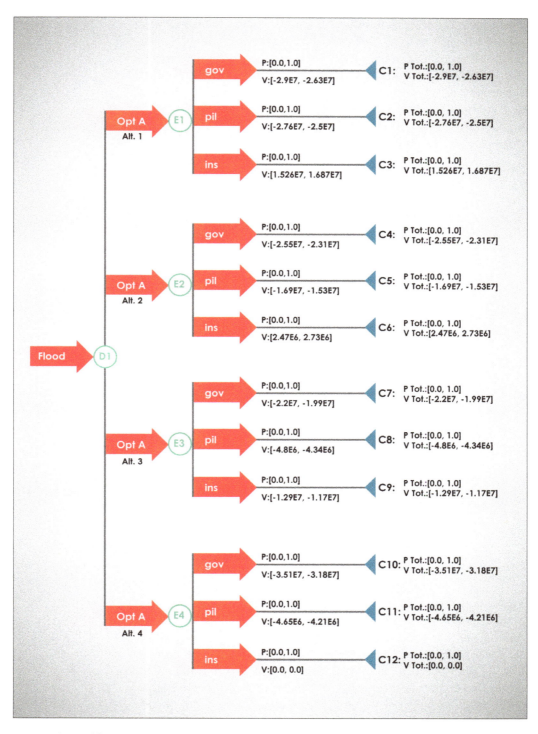

Figure 1. The simplified decision tree.

a sensitivity analysis zooming in on central parts of the intervals). The y-axis shows the difference in strength. The results in Figure 3 should be interpreted as the uppermost alternative being the most preferred one. Thus, in the figure, the ranking of the alternatives is (from most to least preferred): Alt. 3 (Refined Alt. 2), Alt. 2 (Mixed Insurance), Alt. 1 (Individualistic), and Alt. 4 (Public). This means that the likelihood that Alt. 3 is the preferred alternative is much higher than the opposite, so this should be chosen if no other information is available.

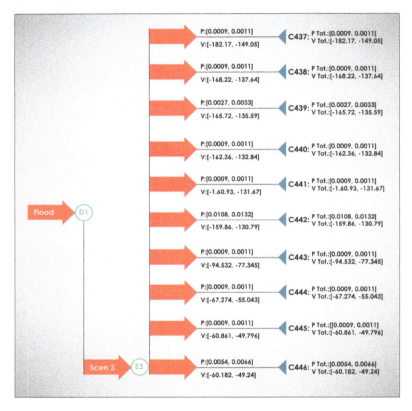

Figure 2. Small part of the decision tree as viewed in the tool.

Figure 3 shows that Alt. 3 is definitely better than Alt. 2 etc. and consequently that there is no possibility for the converse to hold. Thus, the above ranking is fairly stable under this kind of sensitivity analysis. More formally, for comparing alternatives A_i and A_j, the upper line is $\max(\delta_{ij})$ and the lower is $-\min(\delta_{ij})$, that is, the lower line is reversed to facilitate an easier comparison. Thus, one can see from which cut level an alternative dominates another. As the cut progresses, one of the alternatives eventually dominates strongly; that is, there are no variable assignments

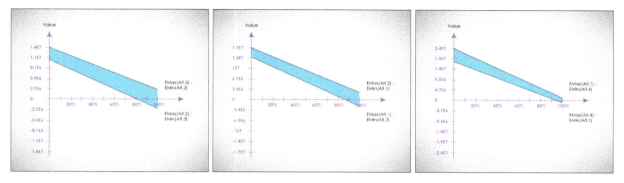

Figure 3. Comparison of alternatives when government is considered to be the most important category.

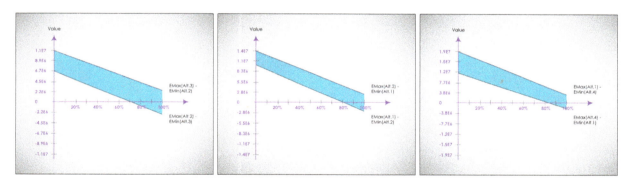

Figure 4. Comparison of alternatives when the weight of government is much greater than the weight of municipalities.

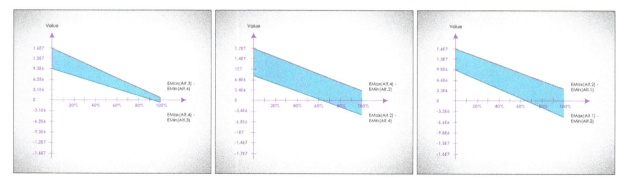

Figure 5. Comparison of alternatives when municipalities is considered to be the most important category.

yielding $\max(\delta_{ij}) > 0$. Similarly, Figure 4 shows the analysis when the difference between the weight of the government and the weight of the municipalities is greater than 30% of the total criteria weight. That is, the government is perceived to be of even greater importance. As in the previous analysis, both these weights are greater than the weight of the insurance companies. It can be seen from the figure that the preference order is still the same as above, but that the relative differences between these have increased. The x-axis shows the cut in per cent ranging from 0 to 100. The y-axis is the expected value difference δ_{ij} for the pairs. Using the same kind of analysis as above, it can be seen from Figure 4 that the ranking of the alternatives this time is the same.

Figure 5 shows the result of asserting the municipalities as being the most important stakeholders (i.e. w(Mun) > w(Ins) and w(Mun) > w(Gov)). The ranking of the alternatives is (from most to least preferred): Alt. 3, Alt. 4, Alt. 2, Alt. 1.

FINALISING THE RESULTS

If it is also assumed that the government and the municipalities are considered as more important than the insurance companies (i.e. w(Mun) > w(Ins) and w(Gov) > w(Ins)), then the result would be that the final alternative from a large stakeholder workshop is the preferred one. Now, one might argue that Alt. 4 ought to be slightly modified to fit the perspective of the insurance companies better also. In this way, information from the analyses can be fed back into the decision process, yielding modified alternatives that in the end would be more acceptable to a majority of the stakeholders. Importantly, it is not necessary to assign explicit weights to the stakeholders (which could be difficult or even controversial) to obtain this result. It is sufficient to give general and comparatively weak preferences and still obtain confidence in the result. The final alternative from the stakeholder workshop seems to be the most preferred alternative given that we do not rank the government and the municipalities against each other, but assert that both of them are more important than the insurance companies. Note that the insurance industry is not neglected in the settings; it can still have a reasonably high importance weight.

Needless to say, the issues involve several non-mathematical aspects, not least political, and it is up to the political process to make the final decision with information based on results from the method proposed.

FURTHER READING

Brouwers, L., Danielson, M., Ekenberg, L. and Hansson, K.E. Multi-Criteria Decision-Making of Policy Strategies with Public-Private Re-Insurance Systems. *Risk Decision and Policy*. 9(1), pp. 23–45. 2004.

Danielson, M., Ekenberg, L., Johansson J., and Larsson, A. The DecideIT Tool, in Bernard, J-M., Seidenfeld, T. and Zaffalon, M. (Eds.), *Proceedings of ISIPTA '03*, pp. 204–217. Carleton Scientific. 2003.

Larsson, A., Johansson, J., Ekenberg, L. and Danielson, M. Decision Analysis with Multiple Objectives in a Framework for Evaluating Imprecision. *International Journal of Uncertainty, Fuzziness and Knowledge-Based Systems*. 13(5), pp. 495–509. 2005.

15

Roşia Montană Gold Exploitation

The lack of a participatory approach or transparent, structured analysis of the Roşia Montană gold exploitation project has led to serious tension within Romanian public life over the last 15 years. There is a vast amount of conflicting information and differing opinions on the benefits and risks involved, and a final decision has yet to be made by government officials. This chapter provides a comprehensive decision analysis of the mining project, based on the examination of over 100 historical documents relating to the project, produced by a wide range of stakeholders and representing the official and the less formal documentation of the case. These were analysed by designing a multi-criteria tree including the relevant perspectives by which the four alternatives most commonly discussed were analysed.

The result of the analysis can be used as a valuable policy recommendation for the mining company and for the political decision-makers. If these stakeholders want the project to be accepted by civil society, and to continue, the key challenge is to increase the transparency of the process and improve its credibility and legal legitimacy; if these requirements cannot be met, the decision-makers will need to focus on the alternatives for sustainable development available in the area.

The Roşia Montană mining project is one of the most controversial investment plans in post-communist Romania, proposed to the Romanian authorities by Roşia Montană Gold Corporation (RMGC), a joint venture between Gabriel Resources Ltd, which owns 81% of its shares, and the state mining company Compania Naţională a Cuprului, Aurului şi Fierului 'MINVEST' S.A. Deva which holds the remaining 19%. Ever since 1999, when the company was granted the exclusive rights for exploring and exploiting the gold and silver mineral deposits in the Roşia Montană

This chapter is based on Mihai, A., Marincea, A. and Ekenberg, L., An MCDM Analysis of the Roşia Montană Gold Mining Project, *Sustainability*. 2015(7). pp. 7261–7288. 2015.

commune in the Apuseni Mountains (Figure 1), more than 15 years of negotiations, debates and evaluations of the development project have passed without leading to a resolution on whether or not the exploitation could develop. The exploitation solution proposed by the company, involving what could become the largest European open-pit mining and cyanide leaching operation, has stirred strong reactions in the public sphere and led to conflicting information and competing discourses among citizens, journalists, artists, political representatives, civil society actors and corporate officials. Although the high political stakes in the clash between corporate interests and public opinion can partly explain the delays in making a final decision, the complexity of the available data poses serious challenges in the deliberation and decision making process.

Despite the social, economic, environmental and cultural implications of this case, as well as its constant presence on the public and political agendas, we could not find any structured analyses or weighing of the data on the RMGC project or on the alternatives for development suggested by some actors. We therefore propose multi-criteria decision analysis (MCDA) as the most appropriate methodology for a participatory and transparent assessment of the available alternatives of development for the Roşia Montană area, to serve the decision-makers both in the present case and in similar current or future decision processes dealing with complex data.

In the current case, the need for and estimated utility of decision analysis is twofold. Firstly, it can systematise the data supplied by stakeholders on the potential risks and benefits posed by a project, and model the problem so as to make it more feasible for decision-makers to weigh the pros and cons under all relevant criteria. Secondly, a structured decision model can evaluate and propose improvements to the lengthy deliberations in agenda-setting and policy-making that were stirred up by the investment plan.

The Roşia Montană project spans a timeframe in which Romania has been going through a sinuous process of democratisation and Europeanisation, from a transition period post-1989 and its accession to the European Union in 2007. The shortcomings of a developing democratic system are evident in the way subsequent governments have handled a mining project proposal which impacts directly on a local community, and has implications for various policy areas, as well as on the citizens at large. Moreover, the tension between economic development and environmental sustainability proves to be difficult to mediate, leading to antagonistic discourses, social divisions and decision blockages. More structured and participatory decision models are urgently needed.

Figure 1. Open-cast mine from the Roşia Montană area. Photo by Love Ekenberg.

Firstly we will analyse the decision process and context in this case, from the perspective of democratic deliberation. Further on, we will discuss the gathering and analysis of data, the formulation of the decision problem according to the elicited criteria and the chosen MCDA method. Lastly, we present our results with a sensitivity analysis of various scenarios and different weights assigned according to the priorities of stakeholders (as identified in the publicly available documentation and statements).

DELIBERATION IN THE LONG-TERM DECISION CONTEXT

The first step in our decision analysis was to conceptualise the decision problem faced by policy-makers in this case. Our research question, informed by the most recent debates on the topic, was to see which would be the wisest decision for Roşia Montană, the implicit goal being to ensure, in a democratic manner and following principles of good governance, a regional sustainable development for a former mining village.

After the fall of communism, the state was confronted with a typical deindustrialisation period which led to significantly lower production in several industries, including mining. High unemployment rates had social and economic impacts in the mountain areas where state mining activities had ceased. Moreover, cleaning the toxic waste following decades of state-run mining activities was far from being a priority for governmental funds; soil and surface water streams still bearing heavy metals and acid compounds drained from old mine galleries, including those in Roşia Montană.

Creating sustainable regional development is a relatively recent goal on the Romanian public and political agenda, which partly arises from the progressive assimilation of European Union and civil society environmental concerns. One of the EU directives Romania had to comply with after its accession in 2007 concerned the rehabilitation and minimisation of waste and toxic tailings resulting from state activities in the extractive industries. Weighing the environmental implications in public planning decisions was also among the EU directives guiding the governmental steps in the pre-accession phase.

But before actually discussing the need for a sustainable development in the Roşia Montană area, there was a long period of time in which government policy-making was focused primarily on economic development and attracting foreign capital. Investments in resource exploitation were seen as goals in themselves and were fully embraced, under conditions often detrimental to the state. In this context, the Romanian government expressed interest in promoting the exploration and exploitation of the mineral resources within the Roşia Montană perimeter, as it was stated in the 1999 licence agreement with the joint venture that came to be known as RMGC. From that moment on, the debates on the Roşia Montană case have largely focused on whether or not the specific RMGC mining proposal should be implemented, without it being evaluated against other mining development projects. No alternate exploitation project was put on the table by the Romanian government or other private companies, nor was there any background feasibility study of the deposits made by the state before granting the licence to RMGC. At the time, a faulty public bid made it impossible for other companies to express interest in exploring the deposits and thus RMGC is the licence holder up to 2018, and the only company with the right to conduct exploration and exploitation activities within the perimeter.

Even if the licence did not guarantee the subsequent approval of the exploitation plans proposed by the company, it obviously limited the demand for or offers of other exploitation solutions for the mineral deposits. From the standpoint of good governance, the lack of competitive bidding for the exploitation rights as well as the process of introducing a specific investment plan to the public agenda before formulating the needs of the area, raised serious problems in the deliberation process. The RMGC exploitation project was not only the most commonly discussed proposal, it was also the one defining the framework of deliberation for many years. The antagonistic discourse – the pros and cons of the RMGC mining project – prevailed in most of the discussion arenas, from parliamentary debates, opinion or research articles, to forums and social media comments, making it difficult for other solutions to be properly analysed and understood.

In time, a number of possible deal-breakers signalled by the local community and civil society, as well as by some governmental representatives coming primarily from the Ministry of Environment, opened the conversation to suggestions for alternative ways of developing the village which might not include mining, at least not until other technological solutions could be offered.

The main issues which have blocked the RMGC project up to the present are the environmental risks and failed negotiations with a number of families from Roşia Montană who have refused to relocate. Discussions concerning modification of the current mining law in order to allow mining developers to relocate locals by expropriating their real estate have been on the table, but this has been severely criticised by public opinion and civil society.

In this context, the need for a sustainable development in the area has penetrated the public discourse, allowing for other options to be considered. This has led to several proposals relating to tourist development of the area, to the exclusion of open-pit mining activities. However, the RMGC project is still the main pillar of the deliberative process within the Romanian public sphere, thus in the following section we will briefly describe the exploitation plans submitted by the licence holder to the public authorities.

UNDERSTANDING THE RMGC EXPLOITATION PROJECT

Over the long-term deliberations the process of communicating the project to the public has been defective. A number of issues have led to citizens' increased mistrust, and suspicions of corruption and vested interests. The first issue is the lack of public access to essential agreements and permits granted to the company. These included the actual licence and its additional contracts describing the exact parameters for exploitation, which were withheld from public scrutiny until they surfaced through journalistic investigations in 2013. Romanian legislation concerning mineral resources is rather vague on defining what data should be classified for reasons of national security and for how long; however, the argument of national security becomes invalid when another party other than the state has access to the data, and here a private company did. A lack of transparency characterised the negotiations between the state and the company, as well as the processes by which they were granted the permits required to conduct explorations and development in the area.

The second relevant aspect concerning the faulty public communication of the project is that most of the data contributing to the information process was supplied on the one hand by the company, and by civil society, research institutes and journalists on the other. Aside from political statements, government officials and local authorities made few, if any, efforts to provide more balanced explanations of the extensive documentation provided by the company – data which was impossible for non-specialist readers to properly understand and assess. For exemplification purposes, we will provide a very short description of the main aspects of the exploitation plans submitted by RMGC and the communication strategy employed by the company, followed by the political statements and parliamentary debates on the project and the citizen responses.

RMGC conducted feasibility studies and published thousands of pages of Environmental Impact Assessment (EIA) on its website, as well as on the website of the Ministry of Environment. Their documentation covers extensive economic, environmental, cultural and social evaluations of the current situation in Roşia Montană and the improvements expected to follow from the gold exploitation project. It includes detailed descriptions of the chosen technological process and a step-by-step description of the project development.

The proposal for exploitation consisted of processing 20 million tons of minerals annually in four open pits from the massifs of Cetate, Cârnic, Jig-Vaidoaia and Orlea, with 'average contents of 1.46 g/t Au and 6.9 g/t Ag, representing 10.1 million ounces (314 t) Au and 47.6 million ounces (1480 t) Ag—in situ metals'. The technological process would involve blasting the pits, cyanide leaching of the ore in a processing plant, and releasing the neutralised sodium cyanide into a tailings management facility, behind a rock dam. The area licensed for the company measured 2388 ha, of which 1346 ha were destined for exploitation and 300 ha for the tailings management facility and dam. The exploitation would require the relocation and displacement of houses, churches, cemeteries and 960 families from three villages (Roşia Montană, Corna and Gura Cornei), and the destruction of four massifs and natural landscapes. The project was set to last approximately 20 years from construction through operation to closing phase.

The company proposed a plan for the displacement and relocation of the locals, and held private discussions between its representatives and the local families affected, some of which accepted the offers to sell their properties to the investor. After a series of renegotiations of unprofitable conditions stipulated in the initial licence agreement, the government estimated a direct benefit of nearly US$ 5.2 billion, including gold and silver royalties, in dividends for the Romanian state as a shareholder, from income tax, and social contributions for employees.

According to their statements, Gabriel Resources Ltd have made, between 1997 and 2013, investments of US$550 million in Roşia Montană. The major areas of investment focused on: geological research, cultural heritage research and preservation measures (US$28 million), displacing sites (US$50 million), property acquisition (US$105 million), taxes and fees (US$50 million), plus mining equipment, technical studies and general and administrative costs. However, no official documentation was submitted to support its budgetary statements, and the media released further accounts showing millions of dollars spent by the company on lobbying, PR and advertising.

Naturally, most of the technological process, including the concentration of cyanide used for leaching and drained in the tailings management facility, the water treatment station, the tailings dam design and stability, and many other operations proposed by RMGC, cannot be understood or evaluated by the majority of citizens or politicians. The opportunities for employment and economic benefits have been at the forefront of the communication strategy conducted by the company, and taken up by its supporters, including some of the local villagers, various media outlets and some public officials. The project has been promoted by the company through institutional lobbying and extensive media campaigns for its potential economic, social and cultural benefits for the local community and for the Romanian state. All the studies conducted by RMGC or its contracted experts are available for consultation on their website, along with infographics, maps and summaries of the project. The Ministry of Environment has also put the EIA reports on its own website, thereby acting as a passive mediator between the company and citizens, the latter being able to send in their inquiries on the data via the Ministry website. All 5600 inquiries received lengthy answers only from the company, the answers becoming annexes of the EIA.

The documentation issued by RMGC that we examined includes the reports available on its website, as well as hearings in front of a Parliamentary Special Committee. In order to have a better understanding of the project and its impact on the area of eventual exploitation, we visited Roşia Montană and met with the spokesperson of the company, Cătălin Hosu, who presented the sites in detail and explained the technological processes involved in the project. The conversation confirmed some of RMGC's official pronouncements, including investments made in the preservation of cultural heritage and in a pilot project filtering acid water, but it failed to answer questions regarding the lack of financial guarantees,[1] the risks associated with setting the tailings management facility in Corna Valley, the inherent risks associated with cyanide leaching (even if considered the best-available technology) and possible solutions proposed by the company for dealing with families who refuse to relocate.

DODGING POLITICS AND PARLIAMENTARY DEBATES

Throughout the years, there has been no consensus on the future of the project within a single party. Well-known public officials supporting the mining project through actions and statements in ministries or in parliament come from all major parties which have been part of the ruling coalitions for the past 15 years. Similarly, opponents have ranged from ministers of Environment and Justice to parliamentary representatives, regardless of their political affiliation. This is also evident in the presidential elections throughout the timeframe under discussion, in which the Roşia

[1] Mandatory requirement, according to EU Directive 26/21/EC, art. 25.

Montană project was always an issue. In the 2009 presidential elections, the socialist-democrat candidate declared that, as long as the project threatened the environment and the principles of sustainable development, he would oppose it. As presidential candidate and president in office Traian Băsescu avoided making statements on the project, stating that he preferred to leave the decision in the hands of experts. However, regarding the exploitation of resources, he did state his position: in principle, it should be done, but without irremediably jeopardising archaeological sites and the environment. Examining the electoral agendas of the 2014 presidential candidates, the six highest-profile candidates appear to have been divided when it came to the Roşia Montană project: two of them were neutral, one was for the development of the project and three tended to opposition to the project.[2] There is obviously still no consensus on what decision should be made, and there are high political risks attached to assuming any definitive position.

The first public attempt to assess the risks and benefits of the submitted project was in 2003, when a Parliamentary Special Committee was appointed to 'formulate a unitary viewpoint concerning the economic, social, cultural and environmental aspects implied by the project'. Two months later, the Committee published a report that reinforced the economic benefits for the Romanian state, estimated at US$583 million, and assured the wider public that no breaches of legislation were observed in the licence agreement or in the activity of the company up to that point.

In 2009, the Ministry of Economy included the project on the agenda of the newly formed government, announcing its intent to accelerate the project's development. The Ministries of Culture and Environment declared that, given the lack of financial guarantees and of more extensive research, they would not issue the necessary permits. In 2011, conflicting opinions emerged: while the prime minister believed that the agreements made between the Romanian state and the company were not in the best interests of the state, the president maintained that the project could proceed after a renegotiation of the state benefits, and that the government should have the courage to take on the responsibility of giving it a green light. Opposition parties launched their visions for sustainable development, which included mandatory measures for the Roşia Montană case: declassifying the agreements, independent cost-benefit analyses, identifying the most appropriate technology for the exploitation, taking into consideration the European Parliament

[2] According to the data gathered by Median Research Centre for the application, TestVot Presidential Elections 2014.

anti-cyanide resolution, respecting the villagers' right to property, and assessing the alternatives for the region's development. No such assessments of alternatives were published.

In 2012, the newly appointed prime minister outlined three conditions for moving forward with the project: environmental safety guarantees, renegotiating the state's shares in RMGC and putting an end to the lobbying influencing the political decision. The Ministry of Economy announced to the local community that the project was set to start and that a favourable decision would be made by the end of the year. Alongside the parliamentary elections, the county of Alba organised a referendum asking the citizens of 35 villages and towns whether they agreed with the company project or not. The result was 62% voting in favour of the project and 35% against, but the referendum failed to be validated due to low turnout, with only 43% of citizens with a right to vote casting a ballot.

In 2013, there was a turning point in the decisional process, when an acceleration inclining to meet the needs of the investing company was clearly discernable at governmental level. Following a legislative proposal for a new mining bill and renegotiation of the initial agreement between the Romanian government and the investors, by which the state's share was raised from 19% to 25%, and the royalties from 4% to 6%, previously withheld documentation was made public. A number of relevant documents were made accessible either on the ministries' websites, or through journalistic investigations, making possible a more extensive analysis of the pro and con arguments, considering the socio-economic, environmental and cultural implications both of giving a green light to the project and of rejecting it.

The draft mining bill aimed, among other things, to redefine mining exploitation proposals as special public interest projects, aligning them, for instance, to infrastructure development projects. This classification would allow for forced expropriations and compensation, thus solving one of the blockages faced by RMGC. The draft bill stipulations were met with heavy resistance by the civil society and citizens at large, leading to mass street protests. As a result of these, for the first time since granting the licence rights to RMGC, an ongoing parliamentary Special Committee was appointed to hear the stakeholders' views and to gather all relevant data leading to advisory conclusions to be used in the decisional process. Following these hearings, the Committee issued a final report and the draft bill was rejected in parliament. The final report issued by the Special Committee in November 2013 includes arguments in support of and opposing the project, stated by the main issuers of reports, laws and permits for the Roşia Montană project, serving as a good starting point for a MCDA that takes into consideration the points of view of different stakeholders. The Committee recommended the rejection of the bill (which took place in parliament the following month), as well as the following: (1) fair partnership conditions between the majority shareholder and the Romanian state-owned company, respecting compulsory community norms and the principles of sustainable development in the areas where the project would be put into execution; (2) real improvement and greater economic benefits after the renegotiations of the initial agreement; (3) a careful re-examination of alternative scenarios on mining exploitation royalty and contribution rate-setting; (4) a thorough investigation of the legality of actions within the project; (5) broader legislation on gold and silver alloy mining projects needed to be debated by parliament so as to enable mining development in Romania and investments.

The final decision on the development of the exploitation project by the investing company in Roşia Montană, as well as on weighing it against other development alternatives for the mono-industrial area, belongs to the Romanian government, through the Ministry of Environment, Waters and Forests, the Ministry of Economy and the Ministry of Culture. Also, given that the Romanian parliament has been discussing the need for an updated mining law based on the current needs and objectives of the mining sector, the negotiations and decisional process in the case of Roşia Montană will serve as a test bed for future exploitations. This is particularly relevant since the National Agency for Mineral Resources announced future auctions for other areas containing gold and silver deposits: the manner in which the decision is taken in the Roşia Montană case could become a precedent for future negotiations and developments in other mining projects in Romania.

A DIVIDED LOCAL COMMUNITY

The residents of the towns and villages that would be impacted by the RMGC project have been extensively informed on the potential benefits and risks of the exploitation by RMGC employees and local authorities, television commercials, talk-shows and political debates. Town halls have held several meetings on the project proposal, inviting representatives of the company and villagers in order to facilitate both negotiations and debates on the future of their communities. The neutrality and transparency of local authorities has been questioned by some of the community members and civil society actors, in particular when the company was granted authorisations for General and Zonal Urban Plans, through which Roşia Montană became a mono-industrial area. The legal implications of this long-term designation were that, until 2015 and within the perimeter destined for use by RMGC, no other public or private economic activities were to be allowed.

The most credible source available eliciting local inhabitants=s' viewpoints on the project development is an independent sociological study coordinated by Mihai Pascaru and conducted by a team of researchers from the '1 Decembrie 1918' University in Alba-Iulia, based on a long-term series of interviews and surveys performed in the areas which would be impacted by the Roşia Montană project, namely the towns of Abrud and Câmpeni, and Bistra, Bucium, Ciuruleasa, Lupşa, Mogoş and Roşia Montană villages. According to the 2007 surveys, 63% of the respondents had former miners in their families and had positive expectations for the project. In further research, the standard of living in the areas was perceived in 2009 to be rather poor or very poor, as most of the respondents declared a monthly income of 300 to 900 RON (between US$100 and US$300 at the time), while 16% of the villagers in Roşia Montană had a daily income of less than US$2, deriving largely from social security benefits. Another study was conducted in the area in 2011, looking at the degree of confidence the community had in the revival of surface exploitation mining. Almost two thirds of the respondents had little or very little confidence in the investors, while one third stated that they had strong confidence in the company. The highest degree of confidence in the company was manifested among the villagers from Roşia Montană (53% of the respondents living there), as some of them were already employed by the company. Some respondents drew attention to the fact that while the people who work for the company have a better standard of living than before, those not employed in the mining project, who were making a living out of agriculture, wood processing, farm animals or tourism, will be severely affected by the project. The jobs that would be created if the project is implemented are the main reasons for the high expectations of the locals. Other expectations for the development of the area include potential solutions such as the reopening of underground mines or long-term surface mining, creating strategies for increasing the tourism in the area, as well as investing in dairies and other types of farming.

The inhabitants of Corna village, which will be the closest to the tailings pond designed within the project, were asked how they feel about the pond being situated in the Corna cut-off. In the 2003 survey, 9% of the respondents said they agreed with the initiative with no regrets about it; 28% declared they agreed with it, but were sad about it; and 30% stated they disagreed with the proposal. Moreover, 31% of the respondents believed that the mining project would have a positive impact on the area, while 49% believed the contrary. Asked about whether they see any other alternatives besides the RMGC project for the future of the area, 47% of the respondents believed there are other alternatives, while 32% believed the project was the only option. In 2013 a series of interviews were conducted with families who have agreed to relocate from Roşia Montană and Corna to the nearby city of Alba-Iulia, where RMGC had built a new neighbourhood from scratch. The questions aimed to extract people's views of the perceived advantages and disadvantages of their decision to accept the company's relocation offer. The main advantages stated by the respondents included better access to public services such as health, education and social assistance, better infrastructure such as a sewage system, running water and street lighting, and better chances of employment. The perceived disadvantages were higher living expenses in contrast with the low salaries they would earn in Alba-Iulia, the perception and fear of being marginalised, as well as homesickness.

GRASSROOTS ENVIRONMENTAL JUSTICE MOVEMENT

As we have seen above, locals reactions to the project proposal were divided, with some of the Roşia Montană villagers accepting the RMGC offer to relocate and sell their land to the company. The villagers and property owners who refused to leave their houses and radically opposed the RMGC exploitation plans formed an NGO in 2002, Alburnus Maior, which would become a leading voice against gold cyanidation, a defender of the right to property and conservation of the natural landscape in the area, as well as a watchdog of the legality of permits issued by local or national institutions to the company. The NGO was at the forefront of the 'Save Roşia Montană' environmental campaign, which has involved a significant number of national and international NGOs, research institutes, universities, artists and journalists in disseminating information on the potential risks of the project both locally and nationally.

The strategy of action and communication employed by Alburnus Maior was developed with the help of former journalist and current environmental activist Stéphanie Roth, whose expertise in political ecology and legislation on mining issues informed the 'Save Roşia Montană' campaign. The main lines of action were twofold: firstly, the families would be able to defend their rights formally and to contest authorisations if irregularities were detected. Secondly, to counter the dominant, investor-focused discourse, a counter-discourse was framed around the dangers posed by cyanide exploitations. The campaign logo of a leaf, half green and half red, became widely recognised and used by all the opposing actors. The other side of the story was starting to take shape. Since 2004, Alburnus Maior has organised a multi-art activist festival in Roşia

Montană called *FânFest*, which became one of the main vehicles for creating national awareness and disseminating the risks posed by the RMGC project. At the same time, the success of the festival was used as an argument for the potential development of Roşia Montană through tourism, lobbying for introducing this alternative on the public agenda. Artists and some journalists have joined the public debates held at FânFest, and helped in further disseminating information about the environmental and cultural risks to the wider public, engaging their audiences in activist theatre plays, concerts and civil society debates. In more recent years, their online presence has helped in disseminating infographics, maps and many other do-it-yourself materials to be used in the campaign against the exploitation, highlighting data that would have otherwise been difficult to select out of the entire documentation

During our visit to Roşia Montană in September 2014, we talked to a representative of Alburnus Maior in order to see if there were any scenarios in which the project would become acceptable, from their point of view; none of the solutions provided by RMGC suited the interests of the NGO members. Irreconcilable aspects included expropriations, the relocation of the cemetery, as well as the interference with the cultural heritage, the threat posed to the buildings by use of explosives, and the cyanide tailings. Aside from Alburnus Maior and many other NGOs supporting their campaign, individuals and teams of researchers from national institutes and universities have also analysed the documentation submitted by RMGC, publishing cost-benefit analyses, evaluations of specific aspects from the Environmental Impact Assessment, reports on the historical cultural heritage from Roşia Montană and many more. The Romanian Academy, the National Institute of Geology and the Bucharest University of Economic Studies are among the opponents of the RMGC project. During the 2013 protests a Facebook community page Uniţi Salvăm gathered over 50,000 members, and shared a wide array of reasons why people opposed the project, as well as slogans and street posters. These depicted concerns over corporate and political greed, media failure and bias in informing the public, corruption, cyanide pollution of soil and water, sacrificing mountains and landscapes, selling of natural and mineral resources to foreigners, responsibility to future generations, bending legislation to suit corporate purposes, and abusive expropriations.

Although it was suggested several times, no national referendum was conducted on the issue and the available opinion polls ask inconsistent questions and fail to clarify whether the public supports the RMGC exploitation project or not: three polls conducted in 2013 concluded that a majority of respondents expect authorities to promote the project (Sociopol), that natural resources should be exploited in general (INSCOP), but also specifically oppose the RMGC project in Roşia Montană (CURS). On a larger scale, there is no structured input on citizen preferences. In time, they have been exposed to the stakeholders' discourses, but they lacked the means of participating in the decision making process. The Chamber of Deputies website features a page dedicated to the project, where a few documents issued by RMGC, as well as by independent experts and institutions are made available, along with a forum for discussion. While users express their views on the project, no interaction between them and a representative from the official host of the forum takes place. The opinions stated on the forum regarding the project are divided, however the most commonly mentioned alternative is tourism.

POSSIBLE ALTERNATIVES FOR DEVELOPMENT

The options for Roşia Montană covered by most of the publicly available data were, as we have seen, developing the RMGC mining project, according to the 1999 exploitation licence and further EIA documentation, or leaving the area as it is, without proposing any other development strategy. The latter option is known as the zero alternative, a non-action alternative that was assessed from a series of documents, including: the EIA, a report of the Hungarian Ministry of Environment and Waters, following the Convention on Environmental Impact Assessment in a Transboundary Context, a study from the Romanian Academy, the 2013 parliamentary Special Committee's Report and other expert studies. An updated version of the RMGC project was also included in our analysis, as it includes the most recent provisions after renegotiations with the Romanian government in 2013. As mentioned above, the changes aimed at increasing the state company's participation in the joint venture and raising the royalty benefits from 4% to 6%. The new agreement also featured a series of mandatory environmental guarantees.

A fourth alternative was considered in our analysis, which was promoted by Alburnus Maior and other civil society actors, research institutes and citizen suggestions. The Chamber of Deputies forum includes a thread designed for discussing alternatives other than the RMGC project for the development of the area. Tourism development in Roşia Montană was the most often mentioned variant.

It was on this forum that we learned of the existence of an extensive study conducted from 2004 to 2006 by the National

Institute of Research and Development in Tourism on sustainable development through tourism in former mining areas. The institute is responsible for elaborating strategies and impact studies for tourism development throughout Romania, with many of their reports leading to regional development strategies financed by the Ministry of Tourism. According to its main investigator, Georgeta Maiorescu, whom we met in September 2014, the model of development for the areas in the Apuseni Mountains affected by mining closures was presented to the local authorities in Roşia Montană, as well as to the Ministry of Tourism, but no follow-ups have taken place. The five-volume report is only accessible in the National Institute of Research and Development in Tourism archives, even though it provides a baseline analysis of the tourist potential of the area, coupled with in-depth estimations and strategies for public and private investment plans that would be profitable on the long term.

Given the available data and the stakeholders' proposals over the years, as well as the current public agenda of creating regional sustainable development, our multi-criteria decision model weighed the four most commonly discussed alternatives for Roşia Montană:

- *Alternative 1 (Alt.1).* The updated project with the provisions from the 2013 Agreement between RMGC and the Romanian government
- *Alternative 2 (Alt.2).* The zero alternative, which implies that the mining project would be dropped, but nothing else would be done instead in Roşia Montană
- *Alternative 3 (Alt.3).* The project in its initial form, with the provisions from the 1999 Exploitation Licence and its additional agreements
- *Alternative 4 (Alt.4).* The alternative of tourism development in the Roşia Montană area

METHODOLOGY

Unsupported decision processes, like the current ones in the Roşia Montană case, are usually problematical regarding elements such as political or economic agendas and the lack of agency of the decision-makers. There have been several attempts in other contexts to solve this to some extent by introducing, for example, computer-based methods for risk and decision analysis, but these have generally had limited success, often due to unrealistic assumptions on the part of decision-makers.

As in so many other cases, a multitude of MCDA methods have been applied to mining applications from various perspectives. These have covered MCDA techniques for everything from maintaining or improving internal mining processes to MCDA methods for balancing various factors similar to our approach. As usual, there are various advantages and disadvantages with these methods, but generally they primarily utilise techniques for asserting precise information, often making them quite inadequate for practical purposes. If the expressive power of the analysis method permits fixed numbers only, we normally have severe elicitation problems that might affect the decision quality.

Here we have chosen to model the decision problem into more detail than is normally done, and utilised a flexible method putting fewer constraints on the decision-makers while allowing for imprecise statements regarding the background information. Imprecision is handled by allowing intervals and comparative statements, while still making this computationally tractable. The main model utilised in this study tries to relax some of these requirements by accepting a larger set of user statements and possibilities to aggregate information. It has also been extended to a participatory model more recently, further enhanced by studying how groups of political decision-makers desire to express values and priorities. The model takes imprecise cardinal relation information of the importance of the attribute ranges into account, and interprets the criteria significance input as regions of significance, using the DecideIT software (based on the Delta method described in *Chapters 11* and *12*) in order to decide which among different decision alternatives is more suitable when considering factors like the stakeholders involved or the values and weights of different criteria.

To get the input to this model, the first step of the analysis consisted in background research of over 100 main official, formal and less formal documents covering the case and produced by a wide range of stakeholders. These documents vary in terms of type and source, from official reports and legislative acts to press coverage and social media, issued by public institutions, RMGC or civil society at large. The corpus was selected so as to cover all the important stakeholders and their points of view regarding the project, in a balanced way. In the selection of the documents, an important criterion was their credibility; we tried to identify with priority those documents that expressed the official position of the different stakeholders involved, as well as documents that are supported by research. In order to facilitate the handling of this large corpus of texts, the NVivo software for qualitative content analysis was used. The documentation process resembled that of a traditional content analysis, following the main identified categories of arguments, namely economic, environmental, social and cultural, to which we later added issues of credibility, considering that arguments concerning the transparency, legality and credibility of the entire development of the Roşia Montană project have played a significant role in the unfolding of the events, especially during the last few years.

Each of these branches was split into multiple sub-problems derived from the arguments brought up by the different stakeholders regarding the possible consequences of the exploitation project, as well as of the other identified alternatives for the area, thus resulting in the most commonly discussed criteria and subcriteria making up our multi-criteria decision tree:

Economic
- Profit/gains for national economy
  - Total profit for economy
  - Royalties from gold and silver mining
  - Profit from state participation
  - Taxes
  - Foreign investments
  - Financial benefits from the conservation of cultural heritage
- Costs for national economy
  - Loss of gold by foreign exploitation
  - Problems in future mining of other natural deposits in the area
  - Costs for the rehabilitation of the ecosystem after the exploitation in case of environmental accidents
  - Costs for cleaning the historical pollution in the area
  - Other environment costs (natural resources versus energy consumption)
  - Other financial risks
- Profit/gains for local community
  - Jobs, training
  - Increased standard of living / Economic growth
- Costs for local community
  - Long-term costs of mono-industrial economy (unemployment, re-qualification of workers, low investments in the region)
  - Costs for other business owners and employees in the area (e.g. tourism, wood processing, agriculture etc.)

Environmental
- Impact on water, air and soil
  - Surface waters – local
  - Surface waters – transboundary
  - Underground waters

- – Air quality
- – Soil quality
- Impact on biodiversity
  - – Habitat
  - – Plant species
  - – Wildlife
  - – Forests
  - – Meadows
  - – Rare metals
- Impact on natural landscape preservation
  - – Attractiveness
  - – Environmental rehabilitation measures
- Environmental financial guarantees
- Regional sustainable development
- Hazard risks

Cultural
- Archaeological discharges and accidental discoveries
- Measures to protect and preserve cultural heritage (other than historic buildings)
- Protection and restoration of historic buildings
- The research and development programme undertaken by RMGC
- Other cultural effects

Social
- Social impact on the community
- Relocations and resettlements
- Safety of locals (health, social and physical safety)

Credibility
- Credibility
- Legality
- Transparency

For each subcriterion, we looked for data and opinions among stakeholders and expert documentation on all four alternatives. The information was used in the process of assigning values to the alternatives and weights to the criteria. While ensuring balance and plurality of stakeholders and perspectives, both negative and positive evaluations for every criterion were identified. Since the background research revealed that the documentation involves mainly projections and scenarios based on rather imprecise or uncertain information, which is often conflicting depending on the source, we used an interval-based method to estimate the values of the criteria, complemented by qualitative estimates (relations between the criteria). We generally used a [−1, 1] interval. The following informal semantics can give an idea of what is aimed for:

- [−1, 0] most probably negative consequences (or best case none), but the intensity is unknown
- [0, 1] most probably positive consequences (or no consequences), but the intensity is unknown
- 0 neutral
- −1 negative (e.g. environmental costs such as the high amount of energy and other natural resources consumed for the project are a certain negative impact)
- 1 positive, which was never used, taking into consideration that it would also imply a relative consensus among experts
- [−1, 1] where experts are almost equally divided and it is difficult to say whether the consequence would be good or bad; or where we do not have enough reliable data for such predictions.

The process of assigning values, weights and relations is based on the previous systematic documentation, where we tried to cover most of the data available from a broad range of sources covering the topic. The selection of the documentation was made on the principle of balanced representation, our goal being to cover the arguments of all stakeholders involved in a fair manner and not to make assumptions that were not directly supported by data. In addition, we assigned different weights to the criteria and defined equivalence relations between the four alternatives for each criterion (better than, equal and approximately equal to, worse than).

EVALUATION AND ANALYSIS OF ALTERNATIVES

The following scenarios were devised according to nine different prioritisations given to the main criteria defined above. While the subcriteria weights and relations came from the consulted data, we have chosen to refrain from assessing the importance of environmental, economic, social, cultural or credibility issues ourselves, since in the Romanian public debates there were competing discourses in the political statements, as well as the civil society and local community. Some consider the environmental aspects much more important than any other, while others prioritise the economic aspects including jobs above anything else. Consequently, we have considered nine different prioritisations, which led to separate weighing choices of the main criteria: (1) all criteria have equal weights; (2) environmental and economic issues are more important than all others; (3) solving and, thus, excluding the credibility problems; (4) prioritising the Romanian state economic interests; (5) prioritising the social, cultural, environmental and credibility criteria, as demanded by the civil society and local opponents; (6) giving a higher importance to environmental issues, according to environmental sustainability and transboundary interests; (7) prioritising the socio-economic impact on the local community; (8) prioritising principles of transparency and good governance; and (9) using the prioritisation stipulated in the 2013 draft mining bill. We have selected for discussion only the scenarios which lead to slight or clear changes in the hierarchy of alternatives, resulting after assigning weights to the main criteria in our decision tree in DecideIT.

Scenario 1. If we give all stakeholders' views and interests equal importance, and refrain from weighting discriminately on account of the expert knowledge available for each category, visibility in the public sphere, local versus national agendas, or types of capital at stake, we consider that all main criteria – economic, environmental, social, cultural and credibility – have equal weights. Our evaluation thus relies on the constraints used for each subcriterion and the qualitative relations thereof. Consequently, by using these settings, the expected value of the four alternatives is visible in Figures 1–3. The expected value graph is a representation of an aggregation of the weighted sum for all criteria. The upper and lower graph lines are the minimum and maximum expected values along the horizontal axis, from 0% to 100% contraction levels. The expected value graphs become as in Figure 1.

Even though we have worked with imprecise data, the decision analysis model is fairly robust, enabling us to evaluate the four alternatives. Based on Figure 1, we can draw three conclusions with a reasonable amount of confidence:

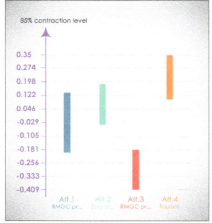

Figure 1. Scenario 1: evaluation of the four alternatives.

- *Alt.3* (RMGC project according to old provisions) is the least advantageous of the four, and can be discarded (at a contraction level of 85% there is no overlap with the others, and the values are negative and the lowest).
- *Alt.4* (Tourism) appears to be the optimal decision in this scenario.
- *Alt.1* (RMGC project after 2013 negotiations) and *Alt.2* (Zero alternative) overlap entirely, which means that in this scenario there is not enough data to differentiate between them, the consequences of each option being rather comparable. Figure 2 confirms that the difference between Alt.1 and Alt.2 is insignificant and that more detailed data is needed in order to better comparatively assess the two options.

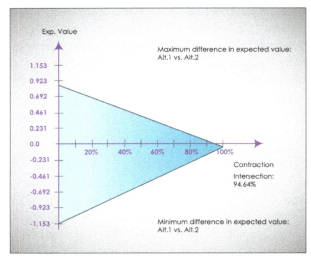

Figure 2. Scenario 1: comparison of alternatives 1 and 2.

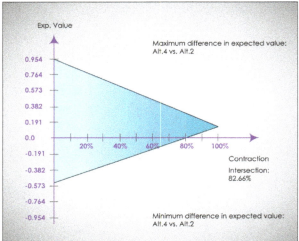

Figure 3. Scenario 1: comparison of alternatives 4 and 2.

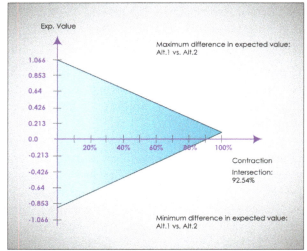

Figure 5. Scenario 3: comparison of alternatives 1 and 2.

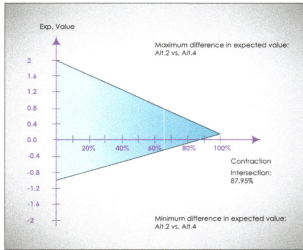

Figure 7. Scenario 8: comparison of alternatives 2 and 4.

Figure 3 compares Alt.2 with Alt.4 (and implicitly with Alt.1, due to the overlap between the two) and confirms the conclusion from Figure 1, namely that Alt.4, a tourist development project, would be the optimal solution.

Scenario 3. For this scenario, we checked the extent to which the credibility issues affect the evaluations of Alt.1 and Alt.3, in relation to the other alternatives. If the company and the Romanian government were to improve the transparency of their negotiations, steps and aims regarding the project and would initiate a permanent dialogue on the topic with citizens and civil society in the decision making process, credibility issues could be solved and make room for an open democratic discussion on the remaining four criteria. The expected value graphs for scenario 3 where we assigned a weight at most likely point 0 for the credibility criterion can be seen in Figure 4.

According to Figures 4 and 5, if we discard the credibility dimension and consider only economic, environment, social and cultural issues, the results remain mostly the same: Alt.3 can be dropped, Alt.4 is still the best, and Alt.1 and Alt.2 overlap, though the former becomes slightly better than the zero alternative. Compared with the first scenario, the only position that changes is that of Alt.1, the updated RMGC project, which becomes very slightly preferable to Alt.2.

Scenario 8. The legal impediments met by the RMGC project so far have blocked the implementation of the project, but have not yet led to a permanent dismissal of it by the Romanian authorities. Discussions and negotiations behind closed doors have taken place throughout the years, drawing mistrust and criticism from the opponents who feared that legislation could be bent to suit corporate and political interests. The lack of transparency and open public debate on parliamentary initiatives and governmental decisions has inflamed public opinion, making the credibility criterion more important and relevant than any other, especially since 2013. By making Roşia Montană a mono-industrial area and, as a consequence, blocking any other enterprise such as tourism from developing, local authorities are met with mistrust in choosing the best alternative for the area. Thus, the graphs in Figures 6–7 show the evaluation of the four alternatives when credibility has the highest weight, and all other criteria have smaller equal weights.

This is the only scenario in which the hierarchy changes to a larger extent. If credibility issues are the most important among all, the zero alternative becomes preferable, while tourism falls

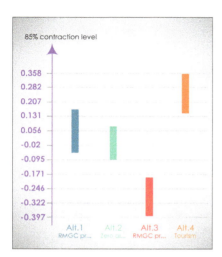

Figure 4. Scenario 3: evaluation of the four alternatives.

Figure 6. Scenario 8: evaluation of the four alternatives.

second and the RMGC project third. The results accurately describe the situation in which decision-makers found themselves, in particular in 2013 when it was confirmed that important data had been withheld from the public eye and a new mining bill was drafted without public consultation. Such actions diminish public trust in public authorities, thus creating the expectation that any development proposal promoted by local or national institutions cannot be trusted.

Scenario 9. Although we were not able to involve the decision makers-directly in this research phase, their contribution to the method design would be useful both for assessing the best alternative of development for Roşia Montană, and for creating a model for mining project proposals at large. Supporting this, the last scenario to be described in the present chapter aims to identify the main criteria for evaluation and relations thereof stipulated by parliamentary representatives as necessary for special public interest projects to be considered feasible. According to Art.3 from the 2013 draft bill for modifying and supplementing the Mining Law no. 85/2003 discussed by the Senate, special public interest projects would be the 'mining projects whose economic and social benefits derived directly or indirectly by the state and/or local administrative units are greater than the environmental negative effects; the benefits should be solidly argued and supported by the compulsoriness of environmental rehabilitation in the closure phase of the project'.[3] The main criteria of concern for special public interest projects would become: (a) economic and social and (b) environmental. Considering our decision tree for Roşia Montană, which can become a 'special public interest' project, we eliminate the cultural aspects, as well as credibility, and all sub-criteria from (a) and (b) remain the same.

Thus, in Figure 8, if we give equal weights to the economic and social aspects, on the one side, and to the environmental issues, on the other, the best solution for the development of the area is Alt.4, with Alt.1 and Alt.2 overlapping almost entirely, the zero alternative being very slightly better than the RMGC updated project.

The clearer differentiation of Alt.4 can be explained by the higher weights given in this case to the social aspects, as well as by disregarding the cultural aspects, which were not mentioned in the special public interest project definition. Cultural aspects weighed considerably more in the favour of the RMGC project in our previous scenarios, since this is one of the main areas in which they have invested throughout the years.

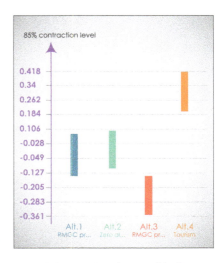

Figure 8. Scenario 9: evaluation of the four alternatives.

---

[3] See *Report of the Committee for Economy, Industry and Services*, No. XX/597/02.12. 2013, p. 5.

OTHER SCENARIOS ADVANCED IN THE PUBLIC DEBATES

If a different technology was used in the exploitation, one that would avoid the cyanide leaching process and the toxic tailings that raise the environmental concerns, it would be impossible to estimate weights within Alt.1, since Roşia Montană Gold Corporation is not willing to modify the technology. The entire business plan, feasibility and investment studies are built on the present technology. A separate alternative backed by a feasibility study of alternative exploitations of the deposits should be analysed by the Romanian state or by other investors. Alternatively, if Corna Valley was not used for the construction of the tailings management facility, the risk of toxic tailings permeating the underground waters would considerably diminish, according to the National Institute of Geology. In the multi-criteria tree, the difference would be visible by changing the possible outcomes for the subcriterion *Underground waters*, in case of the project approval. The interval [–1, 0] is changed with a most likely point 0. The change does not affect the final cardinal ranking of the alternatives.

If mining legislation is adopted so as to ease the approval of environmental permits needed for the implementation of the RMGC project, the risks and benefits of Alt.1 increase proportionally, as they can be replicated in other similar future projects. Also, taking into consideration the release of new licences for exploration by the National Agency for Mineral Resources, the precedent of the Roşia Montană project could lead to similar choices being employed by investors in the future. Similarly, if we consider the documentation provided by the National Institute of Research and Development in Tourism on Alt.4, we can see that their research and cost-benefit analysis aim at tourist development of not only the Roşia Montană area, but also of other areas in the Apuseni Mountains affected by mining closures after Romania's accession to the EU. A successful sustainable development through tourism could also be replicated.

RESEARCH LIMITATIONS

In relation to the uncertainty of the data and conflicting evaluations, the inherent problem that we faced was that multiple sources make conflicting arguments regarding the same issue. Due to the complexity of the issues and to the fact that most of the criteria in question are predictions, the only option for the analysis was to work with rather vague and gross evaluations, which resulted in a lower confidence in the differentiation between the four alternatives. Also, our limited resources did not allow us to organise workshops with the stakeholders involved or other means of obtaining a more precise and direct assessment of their position on the topic. This reveals both that our research was mostly limited to secondary data, and that a rigorous stakeholder analysis was not feasible. However, the current research represents a well-documented starting point for further, more refined decision analyses that would help to better differentiate between the alternatives.

A FEASIBLE ALTERNATIVE

Drawing on the sensitivity analysis, we can conclude that the alternative of implementing the project with the old provisions (Alt.3) from the 1999 licence can be dropped, because it is clearly the most disadvantageous of the four options. In addition, in most cases, the tourism alternative (Alt. 4) turns out to be the optimal one. However, we must take this result with caution because in certain cases the difference between the updated project with the provisions from the 2013 Agreement (Alt.1) and the zero alternative (Alt.2) is not significant, given that the data available for this latter option comes from imprecise and uncertain projections. These precautions are reflected in Scenario 8, where credibility issues are prioritised, and, as a consequence, the best alternative of those available becomes that of not doing anything (Alt.2). Given the current data on Alt.2, supplied more by RMGC than by the Romanian government, it is difficult to assess whether it is better to launch the project in its updated form (Alt.1) or to take no further action (Alt.2). In most cases, these two alternatives largely overlap, or the differentiations are rather insignificant. There is only one scenario where there is a clear hierarchy between the two options: if we value the credibility, legality and transparency of the process more, the situation shifts and Alt.2 becomes a wiser decision. This result can be translated in a valuable recommendation for the mining company and for the political decision-makers. If these stakeholders want the continuation of the project and its acceptance by civil society, the requirement would be to increase the transparency of the process and improve the credibility and legal aspects, entering an honest dialogue with the civil society. If these aspects cannot be met, the decision-makers need to pay attention to the alternatives available for a sustainable development in the area. The tourism alternative, which seems to be a potentially very attractive option, ultimately depends on political will and on how such a project would be implemented. In addition, Scenario 8 reflects the current situation, where action has been frozen as a result of the massive protests, which were to a great extent due to the lack of transparency, the legality problems and the credibility of the whole process.

Naturally, any decision model faces obstacles and limitations regarding firm conclusions, in particular when there are multiple sources that hold conflicting arguments regarding the same issue. This, taken together with the complexity of the issues and the fact that most of the criteria in question are predictions with a high level of uncertainty and controversy, as well as the lack of reliable, research-based projections and several other factors, including problems with transparency, complicate the analysis significantly. However, the more intuitive approaches utilised so far have been even more obscure and the current research constitutes a more refined decision analysis and a well-documented starting point for further analysis, which would also help better differentiate between Alt.1 and Alt.2, which at the moment are held as the most viable options and which, in our analysis, are hard to prioritise one over the other. From these results, there are some future obvious directions of inquiry and action:

- Research in cooperation with other EU member states on alternative technologies leading to environmentally safer mining methods for Roşia Montană and similar areas, supported by cost-benefit analyses and sustainability evaluations.
- Performing an even more elaborated analysis by expanding the multi-criteria tree with more detailed technical information, leading to a wider number of branches and sub-criteria, after gaining more input on: tourism development, local authority plans in case the project is rejected for good, public opinion preferences and perceived risks and needs.
- Introducing more alternatives for sustainable development in areas where state-funded mining has ceased.

ACKNOWLEDGEMENT

This research would not have been possible without the documentation made available via the civil society protests and journalistic investigations, which released the licence contracts and made way for a parliamentary public hearing involving the main stakeholders.

FURTHER READING

Betriea, G., Sadiqa, R., Morinb, K. and Tesfamariama, S. Selection of Remedial Alternatives for Mine Sites: A Multicriteria Decision Analysis Approach. *Journal of Environmental Management*. 119, pp. 36–46. 2013.

Erzurumlua, S. and Erzurumlub, Y. Sustainable Mining Development with Community Using Design Thinking and Multi-criteria Decision Analysis. *Resources Policy*. 46(1), pp. 6–14. 2015.

Esteves, A.M. Evaluating Community Investments in the Mining Sector Using Multi-criteria Decision Analysis to Integrate SIA with Business Planning, *Environmental Impact Assess Review*. 28, pp. 338–348. 2008.

Mihai, A., Marincea, A. and Ekenberg L. *Final Report of Median Research Centre, Bucharest, Romania to eGovlab, Department of Computer and Systems Sciences*, Stockholm University. 2015.

Straka, M., Bindzár, P. and Kaduková, A. Utilization of the Multicriteria Decision-making Methods for the Needs of Mining Industry. *Acta Montanistica Slovaca Ročník*. 19, pp. 199–206. 2014.

Decision Making in Urban Planning

An urban development project involves many stakeholders, including the municipality, builders, investors, organisations and citizens. Typically, all of these stakeholders have expectations and address issues and qualities that they would like to see realised in the project. Sometimes stakeholders' interests coincide, but often they are in conflict. In this chapter we look at how a municipality can organise planning, negotiation and decision making in a development project that includes many issues and stakeholders. We take the municipality of Upplands Väsby as an example to illustrate the challenges and a possible solution. The municipality has been one of the locations in which our research project has established collaboration to link theory and academic research to practical implementation.

The concept of sustainable urban development is widely embraced in contemporary Swedish planning. The objective is clearly expressed. Urban development projects should progress based on an analysis of their social, environmental and ecological impacts. The development plan eventually adopted should provide solutions that are sustainable from the perspective of all three dimensions.

As the concept of sustainability is often considered on a very abstract level, consensus can usually be achieved among stakeholders. Who would favour a development that is described as 'non-sustainable'? However, the issue of sustainable development becomes more complicated when we have to apply the concept in practice, in a specific development project. What is 'social sustainability'? To some stakeholders the core of the concept lies in urban space as an arena for social interaction. From this perspective issues concerning social and creative meeting-places, culture, and the quality of urban public spaces such as parks, squares, and streets are crucial. For others social sustainability equals social

This chapter is based on Cars, G. and Ekenberg, L. *Planning, Negotiation and Decision Making in Development Projects*. Manuscript.

integration; to them activities which combat segregation and social exclusion come to the fore. For yet others issues concerning public participation and dialogues with the general public are crucial. To them, inclusive planning processes and empowerment of citizens are stressed as the core of social sustainability.

In addition to the problem of identifying the focus and core of the three dimensions of sustainability (social, economic, and environmental) there is the problem of implementing sustainability in practice. In most urban planning projects there is an inherent conflict between the three dimensions of sustainability. Of course there are situations when all three dimensions can be satisfied, such as a creative builder applying innovative construction methods, having contacts with suppliers of local renewable building materials, and being knowledgeable about the demands and preferences of potential future residents. The innovative construction methods make the project economically feasible. The use of local and renewable materials meets the demands for environmental sustainability, and the knowledge about residents' preferences makes it possible to meet social dimensions of sustainability. Unfortunately this situation is not common. In a typical urban development project the three dimensions of sustainability are characterised by inherent conflict that cannot easily be resolved. There is no single planning alternative that can satisfy all dimensions of sustainability.

An example can illustrate this conflict. In a typical housing project advocates for environmental sustainability put forward proposals for the construction of zero-energy buildings. The technology for such construction is available. In parallel, interest groups focusing on social sustainability are advocating the construction of affordable housing. These two interests are conflicting in an irreconcilable way – there is no alternative that satisfies both interests. The decision-maker has to make a choice: to satisfy environmental demands or social demands, or to make a compromise and trade-off between them. Typically in urban planning decisions are taken based on decision-makers' ambitions to find a balance between conflicting interests.

The dilemma facing the decision-maker is that giving weight to and balancing conflicting interests is a complicated task. Urban development includes many stakeholders with varying interests. A typical project might include five to ten qualities that stakeholders consider important to prioritise. Many of these issues can be solved in different ways: often numerous options are available. For a human being it is way beyond the capacity of the brain to compare and systematically assess the value of all possible outcomes.

The dilemma facing the decision-maker is often solved by 'gut feeling' rather than a systematic comparison of alternatives; the decision-maker does not actually know what the best alternative is, but has an overall feeling that guides his or her decision making. It could, for example, be that the decision-maker gives priority to good outcomes on some of the issues of relative importance, or issues for which the outcome can easily be assessed. This means that there is a strong likelihood that the alternative providing the best outcome is not chosen. If all possible outcomes had been systematically assessed, an alternative providing more value could have been chosen, rather than the value provided by intuition or 'gut feeling'.

NEW CONDITIONS FOR URBAN PLANNING

During the last few decades our values and preferences regarding what is considered a good living environment have changed dramatically. Schematically, the dream of the 1960s and 1970s was for a nuclear family living in their own home, in a suburb, having access to the material things that were considered as symbols of a good life; a TV set, a car etc. Our preferences are very different compared with what they were some decades ago. Today 'urban quality' is a concept widely embraced. Not least in Upplands Väsby, it is recognised that residents have very different values and preferences than in the past. Significant efforts have been made to capture information about residents' values and their ideas on how to develop urban quality. Ultimately the ambition has been to gain information about qualities that would meet the residents' views of factors contributing to an attractive and lively urban environment. When the outcome of dialogues and other public meetings are summarised it is possible for the municipality to identify key ingredients that would improve the attractiveness of the municipality's social and living environment.

A strategy to improve the urban quality and thereby the social environment has been launched. An overarching objective in this strategy is to improve urban qualities, such as by creating social and creative meeting places, establishing various kinds of cultural venues and attractions, making busy streets walkable by giving priority to pedestrians and cyclists, and improving the quality of public spaces such as parks and squares.

Philosophies concerning housing construction are an important component in this transformation from suburban to urban. Previously, housing schemes often were of relatively low density, built in green areas and separated from their surroundings by traffic arteries. Different arenas of daily life such as workplaces, housing, services and leisure time activities were physically separated.

The new approach to urban development schemes is quite different. New housing estates are built in dense, multifunctional and city-like environments. Streets are not merely for traffic: equally important is their role as a social spaces where open and public ground floors with shops, cafés and cultural activities provide places for social interaction.

UPPLANDS VÄSBY – THE FOUR-LEAF CLOVER ESTATES

Upplands Väsby is a suburban municipality located some 25 kilometres north of Stockholm. It has a long industrial history, but the major expansion of population took place in the 1960s and 1970s when a large number of housing units were constructed to provide housing for people moving into the Stockholm region. Upplands Väsby became a dormitory suburb for people working elsewhere in the region, dominated by housing areas of different types, and locally based services.

Around 2010, a decision was taken by the municipal council to redevelop the area known as the Four-Leaf Clover Estate, an area of 22 hectares located adjacent to the present centre of the municipality. The area in question partly covers greenfield land and partly older buildings that have been demolished. The entire development site is owned by the municipality. The ambition of the municipality is to build a new modern city district, providing the urban qualities that have been recognised in dialogues with residents.

In early stages of planning the crucial question for successful development was addressed: How can the municipality ensure that the building companies actually recognise and adjust to these 'new' approaches to planning and construction, and do not continue 'business as usual'? What incentives are necessary to achieve new approaches and a new way of thinking about quality? Yet another concern was the realisation that urban quality is not achieved by one single measure. Rather, urban quality presupposes that a large number of issues are addressed and handled in an integrated fashion. Also it was realised that most of these qualities cannot be regarded as definitive in terms of whether they are present or not: there are no 'yes or no' answers. Rather these urban qualities must be measured on a scale ranging from low to high quality. Given these challenges it was decided to create a scoring system that would make it feasible to systematically evaluate and prioritise proposals put forward by different building companies.

The key issue was to create an effective incentive to get builders to adopt new approaches to construction. The price of land was identified as a key factor that could provide this incentive. When a municipality owns the land to be developed it is common practice to sell it to the builder before construction starts. The price is usually related to the construction planned for the site: typically the builder purchases land at a price based on the number of square metres of floor space planned in the project. In Upplands Väsby an average price would be 3500 SEK per square metre of floor space. To provide incentives for new philosophies in building it was decided that the price of land should be reduced for builders that met the demands for 'urban quality' as specified by the municipality.

HOW TO ASSESS QUALITY – THE SCORING SYSTEM

It was an explicit ambition of the municipality that the area should be developed into an exciting and dense urban fabric with a mix of activities: housing, workplaces, services, culture, and places for social meetings. The area was divided into a number of smaller plots to be assigned to different building companies.

In order to safeguard the urban qualities that the municipality wants to see realised in construction, a system was devised to give the building companies incentives to come up with new and creative ideas that would promote urban quality. Based on this insight the municipality invented a scoring system. The core of this system was that construction companies that responded and included the urban qualities identified as desirable by the municipality would pay a reduced price for the land they were to purchase from the municipality.

The municipality began developing the scoring system by identifying five 'qualities' that were considered to cover the core of the urban quality that was to be achieved. The qualities were:

- Urban design and architecture: Buildings should vary in design, height, ownership, and architectural expressions, with a mix of functions, e.g. housing, workplaces, services, etc.
- Collaboration: Consultations, dialogues and active participation with residents were addressed as important qualities. Collaboration and coordination with other building companies and other stakeholders were seen as a dimension of quality. Contributions encouraging public and professional debate were regarded as desirable.
- Innovation: Promoting new techniques and construction methods to meet demands for environmental sustainability, e.g. low energy consumption, were regarded as important. New approaches to urban gardening and multipurpose use of space were identified as desirable qualities.

- Parking: The ambition is to allow for accessibility by car, but at the same time reduce the negative impacts of car traffic on urban life. Thus underground parking is prioritised as a feature that, coupled with carpooling and incentives to cycle and use public transport, provides quality.
- Premises: Realisation that the quality of premises facing streets, squares, and green areas are important for urban life. Ground floors of buildings can promote and encourage street life. The flexible use of premises and collaboration between actors in adjacent premises were also stressed as qualities.

The municipality realised each of these five qualities comprised a number of specific issues. Proposals from builders would likely contain a large number of features that they wanted to include in their projects. Also it was assumed that the ambition to meet the municipality's values would vary among builders. Therefore it was decided to classify proposals into three groups based on the ambition demonstrated and the extent to which they met the qualities identified by the municipality. Thus a proposal meeting the basic demands of the municipality would be classified as a Bronze proposal. A proposal with somewhat higher ambition would be classified as Silver, and an ambitious proposal, meeting and surpassing the qualities identified by the municipality, would be classified as Gold. The idea was then to set the price for purchase of land based on the quality of the proposal; a proposal classified as Gold would enable the builder to purchase land to a lower price than a proposal classified as Silver, and so on. In order to classify proposals a number of sub-issues were identified for each of the five qualities decided. The quality of urban design and architecture can serve as an illustration. The following criteria were established for approving proposals:

Quality: *Urban design and architecture*

Bronze: Requirements for meeting the Bronze level:
- Variation in design, height, and ownership
- Architectural quality and expressions
- A clear divide between public and private space
- Entrances to buildings from the street
- Buildings should be placed along streets, not spread out

Silver: In addition to meeting the requirements for the Bronze level, proposals had to:
- Contribute to a dense and attractive environment in which many people work and live, with premises for social meetings

- Promote and create incentives for a flourishing street life, including shops, restaurants, culture, and services
- Provide good daylight qualities
- Provide a flexible urban fabric
- Visually and physically permeable quarters (blocks)
- Rainwater taken care of in attractive open receptacles

Gold: In order to be classified as Gold, proposals had to meet the standards of both Bronze and Silver requirements and in addition:
- Accentuate qualities of the place
- Provide a strong, unique identity
- Offer a life-cycle perspective on the needs of residents for both privacy and social interaction
- Complexity and richness of information
- Architecture of very high quality

In parallel to classifying qualities that meet the Bronze, Silver and Gold levels, it was realised the five qualities identified did not have the same importance. For example, it was realised that the quality 'Urban design and architecture' was more important than, for example, the qualities 'Collaboration' or 'Innovation'. Thus relative weights had to be assigned to each of the five qualities.

Having come this far, difficulties arose at the start of classification of the proposals. A return to the example above will serve as an illustration. Assume that one proposal meets all the criteria for being classified for Bronze and Silver levels. However, when it comes to Gold the proposal meets some of the criteria, but not all of them. If it is classified as Gold the reduction of the price for land will be substantial. What should be the accumulated assessment, Silver or Gold?

Another dilemma occurring was the following. Assume that there are two proposals – equal in every way except one. Proposal A meets most of requirements for the Gold level, while proposal B meets all of the requirements. Both proposals are classified as Gold. Should they have the same reduction of the price for purchasing land?

The examples above are illustrations of problems in implementing the Bronze, Silver and Gold proposal model in practice. Assessments based on the model can be regarded as arbitrary and unfair. And yet one more problem arose, relating to the capacity of the human brain. No human being is equipped to assess, weave together and systematise all the information and data that has been assembled during the systematic assessment of the five qualities in deciding on the classification as Bronze,

Silver or Gold. The insufficiency of brain capacity becomes even more obvious if – which is often the case in real life – proposals are being revised.

SCORING SYSTEM FOR SYSTEMATIC ASSESSMENT OF OUTCOME

In order to handle the shortcomings of the Bronze, Silver and Gold classification scheme, a model that would provide accurate and immediate answers to the assessment problems was invented. The starting-point for the model was the five qualities and the sub-issues to be assessed for each of these qualities, and specifically the relative weights assigned to the five qualities by the municipality. We refrained from using the Bronze, Silver, and Gold classification, but instead further developed and detailed the scoring system. The model for assessing the proposals is described below. Initially we looked at the relative weights given by the municipality to the five qualities. These are presented in Table 1.

Table 1. Municipal reduction of the purchase price, per square metre of floor space (SEK).

	Gold	Silver	Bronze	Unacceptable
1. Urban design	125	75	0	−1000
2. Collaboration	60	40	0	−1000
3. Innovation	60	40	0	−1000
4. Parking	500	300	0	−1000
5. Premises	60	40	0	−1000

The table shows the relative weight the municipality assigned to five qualities. Thus Parking is regarded as the most important quality, while Collaboration, Innovation and Premises are regarded as relatively less important.

The quality 'Urban design and architecture' can used as an illustration of the municipality's assessment. If a proposal does not meet the requirement for being classified as Bronze, the purchase price will increase by 1000 SEK for each square metre of floor space (which in reality means that the builder is excluded from construction). If a proposal meets the Bronze level it is accepted as an option for the construction phase, but it will not get any reduction of the price. If a proposal meets the Silver level it will get a reduction of 75 SEK and if it meets the Gold level it will get a reduction of 200 SEK (75+125) per square metre of floor space.

Table 2. Urban design and architectural qualities reducing the purchase price, per square metre of floor space (SEK).

Urban design and architecture (Prior Bronze level)	"Perfect"	"Average"
Scoring: 0=acceptable, −1=not acceptable		
Variation design	0	0
Architecture	0	0
Divide public/private	0	0
Entrances facing the street	0	0
Buildings facing the street	0	0
Total score	0	0
(Prior Silver level)		
Scoring: Max. 12.5 per issue, max. 75 in total		
Dense and attractive	12.5	10
Promoting street life	12.5	12.5
Daylight	12.5	12.5
Flexible structure	12.5	10
Permeable quarters	12.5	5
Rain water	12.5	10
Total score	75	60
(Prior Gold level)		
Scoring: Max. 25 per issue, max. 125 in total		
Unique quality	25	25
Unique identity	25	25
Life-cycle perspective	25	10
Complexity and information	25	15
Architecture and urban form	25	5
Total score	125	80
Urban design and architecture		
Total overall score	200	140

When assessing the outcomes for the five qualities, instead of classifying as Bronze, Silver, or Gold, we created a value for each and every specific issue that had been identified by the municipality. Without changing the relative weight between the five qualities or the Bronze, Silver, and Gold levels, we detailed the system in a way so that each and every specific issue was assigned a value. This makes the result more accurate and precise. The model also has the merit that any change made can be read off immediately both in terms of how it affects the quality of which it is a sub-set, as well as the outcome as a whole. This elaboration of the model is shown in Table 2 below. We have chosen to illustrate the model with two fictitious building companies, one named 'Perfect', the other 'Average'.

As shown in Table 2 the model is constructed in such a way that if issues identified in the subset of issues constituting quality in terms of 'Urban design and architecture' are modified, the impact of that change can instantly be observed. In Table 3 below all the five qualities are summed up. Once again we illustrate using the two fictitious builders, 'Perfect' and 'Average'. The model makes it possible to analyse any modification of an issue included in the model and instantly get a confirmation of how the change has impacted on the 'quality' under which the issue is a subset, as well as for the overall outcome of the proposal.

Table 3. Qualities reducing the purchase price, per square metre of floor space (SEK).

	"Perfect"	"Average"
Urban design and Architecture		
Reduction of price	200	140
Collaboration		
Reduction of price	100	40
Innovation		
Reduction of price	100	55
Parking		
Reduction of price	500	300
Premises		
Reduction of price	60	40
Total reduction of price	960	575

The total value of reduction of the purchase price for all the five qualities is presented in Table 3. This elaborated model has two advantages compared with everyday practice where 'gut feeling' plays a role, but also compared with the Bronze, Silver, and Gold proposal scheme. First it contains more nuance and detail which allows for more precise results. Once again the quality 'Urban design and architecture' is used as an example. Assume that a proposal is assessed and classified as Silver, but close to being rated Gold level. If one of the sub-issues constituting the quality is altered in a positive way one of two things will happen. Either it will still be considered as a Silver level proposal, but a very strong one. This means that the price reduction for purchase will not be impacted by the improvement of the proposal. If, on the other hand, the improvement of the proposal would have caused it to be assessed as Gold level, it would have meant the possibility of a substantially lower price for purchase. With the model we introduced this kind of anomaly could be avoided. As the model is more nuanced the impact of all modifications of proposals, including small amendments, can be systematically assessed and thus impact on the purchase price. The advantage of the model compared with everyday practice is that the model has the capacity that any human brain lacks: to analyse and assess the outcome of alternative proposals where numerous options for development are available.

WAYS TO DEVELOP THE UPPLANDS VÄSBY MODEL

The above model is obviously a very simplified MCDA model, for pragmatic reasons, but has nevertheless turned out to be highly useful for practical purposes for groups not used to these kinds of models, while still providing a good structuring tool for this kind of evaluation. An obvious extension to develop the above analysis further would be to include more advanced MCDA techniques along the lines described earlier in this book. The qualities detailed above are obviously the criteria involved, and the providers are the alternatives.

There are in particular three key issues involved in such procurement processes: (i) requiring unrealistic precision, (ii) dealing with qualitative values in an erroneous way, and (iii) managing value scales without relevant understanding. These create dilemmas when handling scales without understanding exactly what they mean, which becomes even more uncertain when we are handling more qualitative aspects of the criteria. The first two can be handled by using the full apparatus of software such as DecideIT (see *Chapters 11* and *12* for details of the Delta method underlying DecideIT). The third one requires some preprocessing. It is concerned with the importance of managing value scales measuring completely different things, rendering the weights meaningless if not adequately addressed.

Assume a hypothetical procurement, for simplicity. The principles can easily be generalised to the case described above. We have here only two criteria to take into account and we have to specify the weights. Assuming they would be:

Cost 50%
Quality 50%

we receive two bids from suppliers A and B. We create a score table as follows on a ten-point scale that we have defined in the specifications:

	Cost	Quality
A	6	4
B	4	6

and obtain:

$V(A) = 0.5 \cdot 6 + 0.5 \cdot 4 = 5$
$V(B) = 0.5 \cdot 4 + 0.5 \cdot 6 = 5$

Now instead assume that we realise that we want to modify this and that we want quality to be more important, yielding the following weights:

	Cost	Quality
A	25%	75%
B	25%	75%

We would then obtain the result:

$V(A) = 0.25 \cdot 6 + 0.75 \cdot 4 = 4.5$
$V(B) = 0.25 \cdot 4 + 0.75 \cdot 6 = 5.5$

We have already specified the weights in the tender documents for the legal requirements to be met, so we cannot change that. But we can instead redefine the scales by calculating scaling factors. Assume that we have the weights w_i originally provided. Let v be our new weights and calculate $z_i = w_i/v_i$ (z_i are thus scaling factors for v_i). The scaling factors in our example are 25/50=0.5 and 75/50=1.5. Multiply the values with these and recalculate the mean values and keep the former weights (the legal requirement is still fulfilled by this). Now we obtain:

	Cost	Quality
A	3	6
B	2	9

$V(A) = 0.5 \cdot 3 + 0.5 \cdot 6 = 4.5$
$V(B) = 0.5 \cdot 2 + 0.5 \cdot 9 = 5.5$

We simply adjusted the scale in order to obtain the desired result anyway, without changing the weights. The weights that we initially stated are preserved, but we shifted the scales so that they fully meet our new weights.

This leaves a scope for arbitrariness, which at first glance makes the process meaningless. Now, perhaps it can be argued that we cannot reset values in this way: we are now no longer using our specified scales. But this is precisely what is extremely difficult to assess, particularly when we are dealing with qualitative values. These types of problem can arise unnoticed when you simply use any kind of unreflective intuition.

In a real-life situation it is commonplace for proposals to be modified frequently during the planning process. Modifications might be based on insights gained within the organisation of the developer responsible for the proposal, or as a result of comments from the municipality or dialogues and input from other stakeholders, e.g. residents, investors, organisations, or landowners. This means that the municipality is frequently approached by builders presenting revised proposals. These revisions might include several sub-issues under the umbrella of various qualities. Often these modification of proposals are not 100 % positive or negative, seen from the perspective of the municipality. A revised proposal might, for example, improve the quality of 'Innovation', while it at the same time meaning a poorer outcome on the quality of 'Collaboration'. This is a typical situation when the human brain is unable to assess the overall impact of the proposal. The model can instantly identify how the modification of a single issue impacts on the overall outcome.

The conclusion from our collaboration is clear. The municipal ambition to build an attractive city initiated work to analyse which qualities are important to promote in such a development. A rather simple model can be very helpful in analysing and identifying which of the proposals presented creates the most value, given the preferences of the municipality. Parallel to the conclusion that the simple model developed in Upplands Väsby was very useful, it was clear that this model could be further developed to become an even more powerful tool in analysis, negotiations, and decision making in urban planning and development.

FURTHER READING

Cars, G. and Engström, C.-J. Planning in a New Reality – New Conditions, Demands and Discourses, in M.J. Lundström, C. Fredriksson and J. Witzell (Eds.), *Planning and Sustainable Development in Sweden*. Stockholm: Föreningen för Samhällsplanering. 2013.

Nelken, M. *Negotiation: Theory and Practice*. Chatswood: LexisNexis. 2007.

Raiffa, H. *Negotiation Analysis – The Science and Art of Collaborative Decision Making*. Boston, MA: The Belknap Press. 2007.

17

Actory: Visualising Reputational Power to Promote Deliberation

When technology for e-democracy is conceived and developed, equality within groups is usually taken for granted. However, inequality in online communication is just as common as in other social contexts. Instead of ignoring these inequalities we have developed a tool that can explicitly address the inequalities and provide users with tools to change the rules of the system in favour of certain behaviours. Inequalities are measured and made visible to users of the system, and they change dynamically as actions are taken by users. We base the system on democratic meeting techniques and use the concepts of gamification to enforce certain strategies. Participants' scores within the game are dynamically calculated and reflect their activity, others' reactions to that activity and their reactions to others' activities. The calculations and weighting mechanisms are open to inspection and change by the users, and hierarchical roles reflecting game levels may be attached to system rights belonging to individual users and user groups.

In a popular discourse on the internet and democracy, it is suggested that, due to the absence of the body, the internet is a place where people can come together without too much passion and develop a consensus on rational grounds, and where technology diminishes differences between people, enabling a more participatory democracy. This notion of the internet as a medium that makes people's interactions more rational still characterises contemporary attempts to use it as a tool to support democracy.

However, research concerning interaction in social media such as chat rooms and online games shows that these are far from neutral places where participants are treated equally, but instead inequalities are just as prominent as in other social contexts, and hierarchies and status due to gender, race, ethnicity and other grounds of discrimination are reproduced online. Communication technology may even reinforce differences between individuals

This chapter is based on Hansson, K., Karlström, P., Larsson, A. and Verhagen, H. Reputation, Inequality and Meeting Techniques: Visualising User Hierarchy. *Computational and Mathematical Organization Theory*. 40(2). pp. 155–175. 2013, and on Hansson, K. Reflexive Technology for Collaborative Environments. *International Journal of Public Information Systems*. pp. 11–28. (1)2012.

and groups in society rather than bringing diverse groups and perspectives together, as the digital literacy and social networks needed to participate fully in important forums are quite limited. Even from a more radical democratic perspective, where difference on a societal level is emphasised and the importance of separatist counter-publics is proposed, in-group equality is taken for granted. Technology designed to support equal representation and analysis of representation is lacking.

Therefore, instead of treating technology as something neutral, we treat it as cultural production where norms and social practices are expressed in the design of systems. As a starting point, we challenge the presumption that members of an interest group are equals. Instead of developing a system based on the idea of equality, we suggest a system based on inequality: a tool that takes differences between people into account and even reinforces it in certain situations. The question we focus on in this chapter is: How to build such a system, and how to visualise and communicate power structures in the system's design without emphasising or simplifying them.

It should be clarified that by diversity we mean not only heterogeneity but also inequality. In other words, there are adverse as well as positive effects of diversity, and an urgent question is how to strengthen the positive ones and alleviate the negative ones. One method used in many meeting techniques is to clarify the diversity by communicating power structures to all participants, bringing power relations and hierarchy out for inspection, reflection and discussion. However, just displaying power structures might make them stronger rather than alleviating them. Therefore, some care must be taken with the aim of designing a system promoting diversity yet demoting fossilization of inequalities, and we have tried to find dynamic ways of representing participants' status and hierarchy in the system.

To find guidelines for the design of such a system, we have grounded our designs in social theory and democratic meeting techniques, among others. In the following section we look closely at democratic meeting techniques, social theory and game design for guidance on how to solve our problems. Thereafter we will elaborate on how to implement this in the design, followed by a formalisation of the political and theoretical positions into a mathematical model, as well as a preliminary evaluation and discussion of the system.

The resulting system is called 'Actory', the name indicating the use of actions and reactions of participants as a measurement, as it is activity that influences users' relative hierarchy and status.

METHODS FOR DEMOCRATIC MEETING PROCESSES

We have used Robert A. Dahl's norms for democracy for developing the tool as it is a useful way of defining participation on different levels, from states and institutions to smaller interest groups. Five criteria should be fulfilled to create the ideal democratic situation:

1. Participants should be equal members
2. Participants should set the agenda together
3. Participants should participate fully in the discussion
4. All the participants should have the same status when decisions are taken
5. Everyone should have an understanding of the discussion

These criteria are of course ideals that can never be fulfilled, but they can be used to analyse the situation from a democratic perspective in order to find methods to improve the level of democracy in the actual process. These meeting techniques are not a fixed set of methods but a way of maintaining a reflexive process.

Methods for democratic meeting processes as developed in critical pedagogy and in feminist-oriented movements can be seen as an elaboration of established meeting techniques (e.g. setting an agenda, having rules for turn-taking and speaking, and having procedures for voting). While these traditional techniques assume that all participants are relatively equal, the elaborated techniques emphasise that people do not participate equally, that they have different capacities to participate, and that they are treated differently depending on interacting power structures.

One method used to increase awareness of the power structures at hand is to observe the conditions for dialogue in the situation: who gets the most space to talk and the most attention from others, who is always ignored, and so on. As different communication forms produce different conditions for communication that support some people more than others, the importance of diverse forms of communication that take peoples' different capabilities and experiences into account is also emphasised. An informal discussion can be seen as a complex value system where participants control the stage by, for example, encouraging or ignoring some people and engaging in heated argumentation with others.

SOCIAL MEDIA AND DISCURSIVE DEMOCRACY

There are several examples of digitally mediated self-organised systems that contain functionality similar to those used in democratic meeting processes, such as wikis. In these contexts peers can develop a common discourse around shared interests, and in the long run these discourses can influence democratic decision making.

Self-organised systems such as social media can be understood as autonomous systems that go beyond the centralised power of the nation state, and where the network is the organisational principle. In this so-called open source production, decision making takes place in the collaborative, decentralised network of peers. Communication forms associated with social media are examples of where technology supports a discursive kind of democracy through a mix of different discussion forms, motivating and voting systems and possibilities to extend communication in different ways (linking, liking, blogging, digging and tweeting). They create value systems based on reputation to validate content rather than using the legitimacy of conventional institutions. In auction services such as eBay, where customers validate the trustworthiness of the seller, quality is measured by aggregating input from the crowd of users.

Despite the importance of the particular algorithms and calculations that are used when the micro feedback of the crowd is aggregated, the algorithms involved are never completely visible or open to changes by users. Furthermore, most reputation systems are modelled on economic interactions where the evaluation of reputation is used to decide whether to sell/buy to/from another agent or not. In this case, we want to reflect communicative interaction rather than economic interaction, interaction between one agent and many other agents simultaneously, and an evaluation that is social rather than economic.

Most games contain an economy of some sort where the challenge is to accumulate resources, where the users often gain levels and earn 'scores' by doing different activities. One can view the use of reputation in social media as an economic system for social capital or as a strategy game. Some social media tools use this game aspect in order to motivate the use of the system and to foster certain behaviours; for example LinkedIn encourages users to add information to the system in order to gain 'profile completeness', which means submitting different kinds of information about themselves and adding a certain number of contacts. Social networking websites use an economic challenge to make people explore and use all parts of the system, by giving active users extra attention and sometimes rewards for their participation. However, the functionality of this system is only partly revealed and thus is far from transparent.

FROM DEMOCRATIC METHODS TO SYSTEM DESIGN

Our ambition is to support democratic processes, outside governments and large organisations, in collaborative decentralised interest-based networks. In order to create such a system that supports more autonomous decentralised movements, we have instrumentalised some of the ideas and practices from democratic meeting processes and social media discussed in the previous section. Our ambition here is to create:

- *A discursive platform* that supports the development of common questions, rather than decision making. The idea is that anyone should be able to add an activity and act on it without the need for formal confirmation.
- *Ubiquitous voting* that takes place everywhere and is ongoing.
- *Measuring activity*: Reputation in the system is measured based on activity, and everyone's status in the system should be taken into account when judging action.
- *Visualised reputation*: The informal hierarchy expressed as reputation should be visualised.
- *Gamification*: in order to motivate and encourage participation gaining score should be challenging.

In the following sections we elaborate on each of these points describing how these norms and practices are expressed in the system design.

DISCURSIVE PLATFORM

Our intention is not to develop a formal voting system but a platform that supports development of common discourses – like the development of a political agenda or a collaborative cultural production. Therefore we build on the principles of a wiki, a platform that suits discursive processes. A wiki gives the user an opportunity to develop information in collaboration with other users in a simple way, the opportunity for anyone to raise a question and create a space for the discussion around it is technically unlimited.

In a more informal grouping, the subjective experience is important and it is the individual who decides what is relevant for her to discuss and how it relates to the overall theme. Therefore we have added the feature that the user who creates a post also controls this micro-forum and decides if she wants to invite others to the writing process or just as commenters. In order to make the information structure simple to use and to facilitate the development of a common discourse, we use association as a way of structuring instead of categorising. A requirement to link a post to an earlier post forces the user to refer to at least one source within the system and this contributes to an emphasis on the development of a common discussion.

VOTING

In a collaborative, decentralised network of peers, there are constant negotiations about what to do and cooperation is not steered by a centralised formal voting process. Democratic meeting methods acknowledge that the arrangements for voting are important for participation and outcome and therefore seek to vary forms of discussion and voting. Our proposed system emphasises different kinds of activities and gives scores not only for direct voting but for all kinds of attention: linking, commenting, clicking a like/dislike button, and rating. These different possibilities for expressing meaning as a numeric value can be unrestricted or restricted in time and quantity. In the scoring process, both users and their actions are given scores, creating a hierarchy not only between users but also between posts.

A 'like' option that is easy to click on is commonplace in social media as a way of providing users with a quick and easy method for expressing their opinions. This is often combined with a rating system that demands slightly more reflection. Some blogs provide users with a set of tools to evaluate and disseminate information widely. Our idea is to reconnect the value of this kind of informal voting directly to the user and also to create an understanding of the valuation process. The valuation is bi-directional; the reference is a way to legitimise one's own statement and also a way to legitimise other people who use the same reference. When linking to someone's post, it adds score both to the user and the post. The amount of score can also depend on the *actory index* of the user, which is the user's percentage of the total amount of score in the system multiplied by the total number of users.

ACTIVITY

Visualising a communication structure may make the represented structure more permanent. An important question then is how to make structures visible without entrenching hierarchies. Another question is how status should be estimated. A situation where everyone rates one another in a constantly on-going voting process is not only time consuming, it can also be difficult to get people to want to participate. Our solution to these two questions is to focus less on actors and more on actions. Following a critical and feminist pedagogic perspective, we assume participants will give more attention to people with high status and to people in their network. Reputation most often refers to an opinion that an agent has of another agent's intentions and norms. We emphasise that this opinion is influenced by socially structuring factors: people who have a high status may get more attention and their actions may be valued more highly by other users. Beginners and other people can compensate for their low status by being more active. The system may thus work in an emancipatory way. By visualising reputation as a way of formalising informal social processes, we will be able to use the system for understanding structural mechanisms empirically in unequal settings.

STATUS

If we assume that groups are always structured and therefore that the power distribution within the group is more or less unequal, transparency of the structures can clarify user strategies and system rules in an empowering way. We start with the premise that users receive recognition through the way they use the tool, and that others' reactions also depend on the status they attribute to the user due to structuring factors such as gender, class and ethnicity.

The system consists of three different parts: Activity, About and State. Activity is where new activities are suggested and debated within a group and are partly displayed on the public website as a news feature. About is where the result of the collaborative work is manifested outwards and where the overall topic that functions as the starting point for the work is expressed. State is where the individual score is visualised and roles and score levels are set (Figure 1). Of these three parts, State is of particular relevance here. Participants' State is measured in two ways: through the

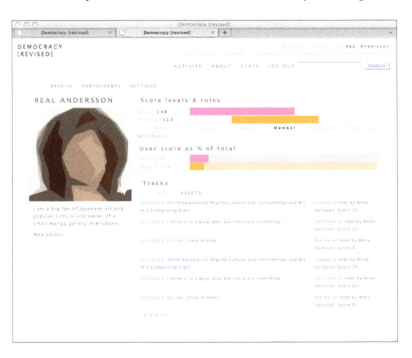

Figure 1. Web-based prototype built in Drupal, visualising user's state.

activities users initiate and by the reactions from others to these activities. Users' scores thus depend on the score for the activity the individual creates in the system (Acts) and the score others give the individual actions in the system (Reacts). Depending on the purpose of the system, the setting of the score can be changed, emphasising either Acts or Reacts.

GAMIFICATION

In order to motivate and encourage participation, the system has to be challenging and rewarding. One can see the system as a strategic game, where increasing one's influence is a goal in itself. Most games contain an economy of some sort where the challenge is to accumulate resources. Users often gain levels and 'score' by conducting different activities. The game aspect of the system can create an incentive to participate, even when the participant does not have an enlightened understanding of the 'game'. A certain hierarchy can be used as a means to develop a certain type of behaviour and communicate the functionality of the interface but also to create stability and to motivate people with high status (which we assume is due to knowledge and experience) to continue to participate. Users' score levels can have a direct function, giving a user who has gained a high score greater influence over the formulation of the collective goal. System roles could also be set dynamically, giving the user more and more influence over the system, instead of being set by an administrator.

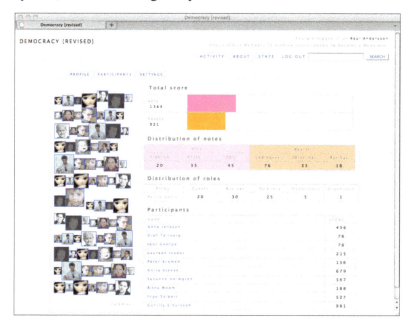

Figure 2. Web-based prototype built in Drupal, visualising distribution of total score and roles of users.

SUMMARY OF DESIGN PRINCIPLES

The system can be summarised in five design principles as follows:

1. A discussion forum, like a wiki, that supports open-source cultural production. Users have the right to edit their own posts and to delegate this right. Associations between posts structure the information.
2. Informal voting is done constantly and in different fashions: linking, commenting, liking/disliking, and rating.
3. The scores that are generated by users' activities depend on each user's total score level. A user's total score depends on their own activity and the score that others give that user's activity. The percentage of scores for users and posts is dynamic and depends on the total distribution of points among users and posts.
4. Transparency and visualisation clarify user strategies, system rules, roles and rights.
5. Hierarchy can be used as a way of communicating the system and motivating participation.

The system can be described as a wiki combined with an evaluation system that tracks all the activities of the users including the reactions of other users in relation to a specific action. Any comment, like/dislike or link action creates a score. Each new score affects other users' scores in all parts of the system, as each user's Actory index is calculated in relation to the total amount of score in the system. Furthermore, how many points are given (by making comments, links, like/dislike, grades) depends on who reacted. As the user's Actory index is constantly changing, and as some old posts might be updated with new links and comments, the order of the archive is dynamic as each post depends on changes in the total system.

IMPLEMENTATION

THE SCORING SYSTEM

Part of how the distribution of scores between users when they post or comment operates is illustrated in Figure 3. A distinguishing mark of the proposed system is that scoring is multi-directional. For example, when commenting on a post the commenting user receives a score, as this user demonstrates activity, as does the user responsible for the post and the post itself because these entities are subject to attention. Another example is that when writing a new post and linking to another post, both posts' creators receive a score.

We now outline how scores are calculated in the event of an action. Let an action x be initiated by user u_i. We now use two pre-defined mappings relative to the current system, the default score function $s(x)$ and the status impact function $t(x)$. See Figure 6 columns 'Score' and 'Status impact' for an example of s and t, respectively. The default score function simply represents the minimum score that an action generates, while the status impact function yields a multiplicative factor. We then define the status impact function for action x and user u_i, $t_i(x, j)$ as

$$t_i(x, j) = \begin{cases} t(x) \text{ if } i \neq j \\ 0 \text{ if } i = j \end{cases}$$

In words, the status impact function for user u_i equals zero if x was initiated by u_i, otherwise it equals $t(x)$. The score r awarded to user u_i for the action x initiated by any user u_j is obtained from the following equation:

$$r(x, j) = s(x)\left[1 + t_i(x, j) \cdot a_j\right]$$

where a_j is the Actory index for user u_j. This is defined in the next section.

In Figure 3, user B comments upon a post by user A. B receives a score of $r(x, j) = 20$ for the comment, as $r(x, j) = s(x)$. User A and the post that is commented on both receive scores for the comments from B. A receives a score of $r(x,j) = 20 \cdot (1+2 \cdot 1.5) = 80$. In Figure 4, user C creates a post that links to a post by user A. This generates a score for the post plus scores for user C and also for user A and for the post that gets linked to. As user C has a low Actory index, though, the generated score is rather low.

THE ACTORY INDEX

The intention is not only to visualise the user's relative status in the system but also to use this information to enhance hierarchy. We devised an *Actory index* that is used to generate scores which are dependent on users' statuses within the system. For any instance of the system we have a finite set of users $U = \{u_1, u_2,..., u_N\}$, where each user u_i is associated with a score level s_i, i.e. the amount of score they have achieved from actions or reactions. The Actory index a_i for a user u_i is defined as u_i's percentage of the total score in the system multiplied by the number of users, such that

$$a_i = N \frac{s_i}{\displaystyle\sum_{u_j \in U} s_j}$$

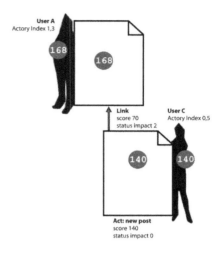

Figure 3. The distribution of score between users and activities when a user creates a post.

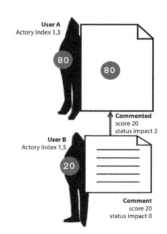

Figure 4. The distribution of score between users and activities when a user comments on a post.

In this manner the Actory index has an upper bound of N, the number of users. This enables a visualisation of greater inequalities between users in systems with many users than in systems having just a few users.

This suggested logic was implemented and tested in a spreadsheet using a scenario with three fictional users involved in a dialogue that consisted of 28 activities. Figure 5 illustrates the implementation of the scoring system in our Drupal prototype. The table *track linkage* stores the linked and the linking activity. The user who created the linked activity receives a linked score in the *user_scores* table. The user who is linking the activity receives a new post score in the *user_scores* table. The *set_score* table stores variables that can be set and changed by the user/organiser.

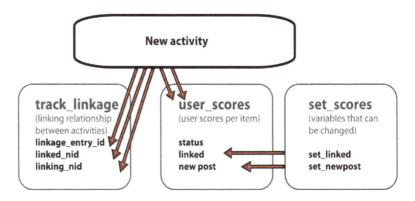

Figure 5. The scoring system in Drupal when creating an activity.

DESIGNING THE RULES OF THE SOCIAL GAME

Informal voting is ubiquitous and is performed in different ways: linking, commenting, liking/disliking and rating. We have chosen to use these features for the sake of simplicity. They are common in social media and are simple to understand and use for most users. The score given for each feature depends on the social context and what kind of discussion one would like to promote. Different behaviours may then be stimulated and rewarded by redefining the score and the use of the Actory index. What emphasis is put on each feature thus creates the informal rules of the collaboration. The rules can be set and changed by the organiser but can also be set by the users. What each user can do depends on how the system is configured from the start. Permission to change the score and the importance of status impact can be open to the administrator only, to a few users depending on their status in the system, or to all users.

Rights		Variables		Roles				
		Score	Status impact	Guest	Novice	Member	Moderator	Organizer
Acts	new post	140	x0	x0	x0	x0	x0	x0
	edit	10	x0	x0	x0	x0	x0	x0
	comment	20	x0	x0	x0	x0	x0	x0
	like	10	x0	x0	x0	x0	x0	x0
	dislike	0	x0	0	x0	x0	x0	x0
	rate	20	0	x0	x0	x0	x0	x0
	Edit public pages	10	x0	x0	x0	x0	x0	x0
	Setting Values	0	x0	x0	x0	x0	x0	x0
	Score needed			0	100	200	500	
Reacts	comment	20	x2	x0	x0	x0	x0	x0
	liked	10	x3	x0	x0	x0	x0	x0
	disliked	-10	x2	x0	x0	x0	x0	x0
	linked	70	x2	x0	x0	x0	x0	x0
	rated 1	-15	x2	x0	x0	x0	x0	x0
	rated 2	-10	x2	x0	x0	x0	x0	x0
	rated 3	10	x2	x0	x0	x0	x0	x0
	rated 4	30	x2	x0	x0	x0	x0	x0
	rated 5	45	x2	x0	x0	x0	x0	x0
	Score needed			0	0	200	500	
	Total score needed			0	100	400	1000	Invitation

Figure 6. Template 'Initiative': *Thresholds, amount* and *total score* of user *activity* related to *roles* and *rights*. Variables changeable by users are in red. Grey areas show what rights are connected to which role.

We exemplify our system with two templates reflecting different goals with respect to the type of activity aimed for in the discussions. In Figures 6 and 7, the values that are coloured in red may be changed by users with the status 'organiser', and the grey areas indicate different permissions due to user status. In the template 'Initiative' in Figure 6, the value of adding a new post is set relatively high in order to promote new initiatives. Features such as like/dislike provide an easy way of expressing an opinion that does not demand much in terms of critical thinking.

In the example in Figure 6, those actions are therefore not associated with high scores relative to other actions. For instance, to rate something is a more cognitively demanding action than simply to like or dislike it, which justifies its higher minimum value in the suggested template. The rating is also conducted in relation to the history of the collaborative work, thus votes from users with higher status are given a greater reward. In this way, the status of users that have worked for a long time on the topic is emphasised, making it more difficult for new users to change the rules for discussion as well as the overall topic.

Rights		Variables		Roles				
		Score	Status impact	Guest	Novice	Member	Moderator	Organizer
Acts	new post	0	x0	x0	x0	x0	x2	x0
	edit	0	x0	x0	x0	x0	x0	x0
	comment	20	x0	x0	x3	x5	x5	x0
	like	20	x0	x0	x1	x0	x0	x0
	dislike	0	x0	x0	x1	x0	x0	x0
	rate	40	0	x0	x0	x0	x0	x0
	Edit public pages	10	x0	x0	x0	x0	x0	x0
	Setting Values	0	x0	x0	x0	x0	x0	x0
	Score needed			0	100	400	570	
Reacts	comment	40	x0	x0	x0	x0	x0	x0
	liked	10	x0	x0	x0	x0	x0	x0
	disliked	-10	x0	x0	x0	x0	x0	x0
	linked	100	x3	x0	x0	x0	x0	x0
	rated 1	-15	x3	x0	x0	x0	x0	x0
	rated 2	-10	x3	x0	x0	x0	x0	x0
	rated 3	10	x3	x0	x0	x0	x0	x0
	rated 4	30	x3	x0	x0	x0	x0	x0
	rated 5	45	x3	x0	x0	x0	x0	x0
	Score needed			0	0	200	530	
	Total score needed			0	100	600	1100	Invitation

Figure 7. Template 'Debate': thresholds, amount and total score of user activity related to roles and rights.

The score given can thus have an informative and symbolic function. If attached to roles, it creates a 'game' where users attain levels and receive extended rights by earning scores within the system. In the example concerning setting roles and rights in Figure 6, the 'Guest' has the right to read and comment on others' posts and like them but cannot create posts or rate others' posts. To become a 'Novice' the user has to obtain a score of 100. As a 'Member' the user has rights to do everything except edit public pages. To be allowed to do this, the user has to achieve the level of 'Moderator' which demands a sustained contribution to the topic. To become an 'Organiser' with the rights to set the values and thus be able to co-create the rules for the game, the user has to be invited by an organiser.

In the template 'Debate' in Figure 7, the ambition is to reward debate and to give attention to other users. Therefore a new post does not give the active user a score. Instead the user who created the post that is linked to is rewarded. The user can receive score by commenting, liking/disliking, and rating but her activity foremost gives score to others. Users' statuses are emphasised and the score given depends on who reacts. For example, if a user with an Actory index of 1.8 (which is 180% of average) creates a post, the linked post and its user receives $100 (1 + (3 \cdot 1.8)) = 640$. But if the active user's Actory index is 0.2 the linked post and its user receives $100 (1 + (3 \cdot 0.2)) = 160$.

In order to proceed from the level of 'Guest' to 'Groupie' the user not only has to gain score but also perform certain actions: at least three comments, one like, and one dislike. As a guest, the user is not allowed to create posts or rate other posts and thus can only comment on others' posts and like/dislike. These rules follow the norm for common netiquette in online discussion lists, where new users are supposed to lurk for a while and give attention to the on-going discussion before positioning themselves. To be able to participate in the rating the user has to have submitted at least five comments. In this template, it is only the 'Boss' who has the right to edit the public part of the groupware, where the objectives of the group are listed and the collective work is abstracted.

PRELIMINARY EVALUATION

The focus of the study reported here has been to implement a system model and a graphical interface that represent and encourage discursive political practice in explicit ways. The system design is a partial answer to the question of how to account for diversity in groupware. In order to analyse the effect of the tool on group dynamics it should be part of a longitudinal study by, for example, performing repeated experiments with various settings of rules and parameters. Experiments will test the mathematical models empirically and investigate whether various settings would stimulate different kinds of behaviour. The other side of the coin is of course participants' attitudes towards the system – how participants understand the scoring system and the interface. Development of Actory takes place in an iterative manner, and the first usability studies focused primarily on the latter – how participants understand the system. Two studies were performed. The first study had a small group of participants who conducted scenario-based tasks, and the second study lasted for three months for a group with the goal of developing a project.

In the first study, a small representative group of participants was selected among artists, art teachers and art students at the Royal Institute of Fine Arts in Stockholm. The reason for choosing participants from the art world was that hierarchies are always present in art communities but are also highly implicit and difficult to navigate, especially when participating in collaborative projects. The group was recruited using an open call to participate and consisted of two women and four men aged between 25 and 50 years. They were all from different European countries except for one artist who was from Columbia. They shared an interest in communication technologies; half of them claimed that they had very good computer skills, four of them were used to publishing information on the Web, and one had moderated several e-mail lists.

The usability tests took 20–30 minutes each. During the tests, the participants explored the tool using simple scenarios, after which they were interviewed about their impressions of the tool and its possible uses for them. The tool contained fictional profiles and a fictional on-going conversation about organising an art exhibition. The informants were asked to play one of the profiles when acting out the scenarios.

Two types of results stand out: navigational issues and issues relating to our model of status and hierarchy. Our foremost interest lies in the latter, but the former is always an issue in novel prototypes. The informants had reported difficulties with navigating within Actory; as it was still a prototype it was not yet very user friendly and required a lot of information to be understandable. The tool was perceived as not very intuitive and too textual. The informants also felt that it was difficult to get an overview and to understand the goal of the website of which the tool was part. This is a problem shared with other blog-like interfaces; new users jump into the middle of the conversation and have to reconstruct the narrative by exploring former posts. One of the main reasons for the confusion was the fictional profiles and conversations:

'Looks like I have logged into someone else's account'.

The informants' impressions of the tool were clearly marked by their previous experiences of social media. One of the informants described the tool as 'a mix between a forum and Facebook'. Another informant compared it to a social forum she used that was a place for people in the local art world to publish news about different art events, and she suggested that the tool could have a similar functionality.

Regarding participants' attitudes towards the system's views on group hierarchy etc. they had difficulties understanding the meaning and the functionality of the 'status' indicator. One of the participants thought it was related to dating services as she connected the word 'status' with civil status. Half of the informants did understand the functionality and the concepts on the status page. However, surprisingly, there was only one informant who actually questioned the basic idea behind the tool:

> Maybe the score method is simplistic. It is too simple for a big [thing]. Social relations are not that, as a simple score. It seems like a game. When you sit down around a table and talk about a project, everything is not a game.

The reason that the lack of questioning surprised us is that we had expected more concerns regarding privacy, control, suppression, etc. to be raised. The lack of problematising the idea with the tool may be explained by various forms of participant bias: the situation; that the informants wanted to show that they were capable of understanding the tool; and also that they wanted to please the researchers. The informants were probably also there because of their interest in communication technology. Maybe the reactions would have been much more negative if they were a more representative group of artists and art students at the school. Previous research has shown that social media such as Facebook were seen as something rather negative among art students at the Royal Institute of Art, as a too rational way of handling social relations. Even though most art students use Facebook, they do not like it.

In a follow-up study, twelve people used the tool over three months, generating around 30 posts and ten times as many comments and likes/dislikes. The tool was used by a group of artists and researchers to develop a common research project and as a complement to meetings in real life to prepare meetings and to have a place for feedback on sketches.

One important insight from both studies was that navigation easily becomes a problem due to the organic structure that is a result of basing the system on discursive practice. Just as in an ordinary blog, the user mostly enters in the middle of a conversation and it takes a while to understand the context. But unlike an ordinary blog, Actory consists of many parallel 'blogs' that mix into each other. If the user does not constantly follow the flow of information it is easy to get lost. A more traditional navigation may therefore be necessary, for example a collaborative menu, as in a wiki.

In the prototype, the scoring system could not be changed by the users but was open for inspection. However, the users were engaged in the discussion and had no interest in the scoring system itself (i.e. how scores were set, etc.). Still, the scoring system as such worked as intended. It triggered some people to contribute more to the discussion. The emphasis on reactions to each other's posts also meant that the group as a whole developed a higher sensibility for the roles in the discussion even when they met in real-life settings. The tool and the discussions about the meeting situation triggered by the tool helped foster a certain behaviour and culture in the group.

DISCUSSION

In this chapter we have challenged the norm in the area of e-participation that all the participants in an interest group are equal. Instead, we have created a tool that assumes the opposite: that everyone is different and that differences create meaning. To find forms for this, we have combined democratic meeting techniques with a scoring system from social media and designed a web-based groupware that functions as a strategic game. Our ambition has been to clarify informal norms and structures by formalising them and to make it possible to debate and influence them, as when using democratic meeting techniques. The focus has been on the discursive democratic processes that take place in collaborative group discussions online.

To answer our first research question – *How should a system based on diversity be conceived?* – we have proposed a system that measures users' own activities and the reactions towards these activities. We have assumed that users will react differently to other participants based on the status position they attribute to the actor, and thus the resulting system visualises these informal structures by counting reactive activity. In this way we avoid a situation where participants judge the status of other participants directly and where status attached to a certain participant is emphasised. Instead, participants' statuses in the system change dynamically and depend both on users' own actions and others' reactions, as well as on the changing scores of all users and posts in the system. This is the answer to our second research question: *Is it possible to visualise and communicate power structures in the system's design without emphasising or simplifying them?* We have created a system that recognises and expects hierarchies without linking them to any designated identity position. This fits well with the idea of status and power as being created in relation to others and not assigned to a fixed category.

We also go one step further. Instead of avoiding hierarchy, we emphasise it in order to create a strategic game and to explore hierarchy as a way of enhancing participation. One might ask how the emphasis on the game can create a social culture that promotes collaboration around a common goal. Here the use of game elements in social media has influenced us. In social media, games are sometimes used as a means to inform the user of how to use the platform. Strategy is another important part of the game, understanding the relation of whom you support and vice versa and how the sum of your actions rather than a single move influences your score.

Preliminary studies with our prototype 'Actory' have confirmed that such a system may foster certain behaviours, but have also shown difficulties for users in navigating a non-hierarchical system.

It will be interesting to see other game aspects in the design that can be emphasised for different purposes. In our tool, most game aspects have to do with exploration. Creating a map over the terrain makes it easier to navigate, but in order to maintain a challenge one should not make it too easy for the players. There is therefore a point in not revealing all the possibilities and rules in detail but letting the details be revealed when the user has used the system for a while. Locked doors is another game concept that motivates, meaning that knowing there is a higher level is enough, you do not have to declare exactly what the benefits of reaching that level are or how to do it.

Our ambition has been to create a dynamic voting system that reflects the complex systems of meaning in social groups. One of the shortcomings of the system in its current state is, not surprisingly, that it is complex and therefore difficult to explain. To reveal all the rules and give out a lot of information leads to problems with information overload. Just because all the rules are revealed does not mean that users can embrace them all. The usability tests clearly showed the limitations of users' ability to make sense of too much information. Here, the use of gaming challenges like locked doors can create motivation to participate even for those who fail to understand the overall meaning of the 'game rules'. The rules of communication may instead be presented at a more moderate pace, and understanding can be created through practice rather than by reading a detailed manual.

In this version of the system we have not taken history into account. Therefore the status of a post does not change with the passage of time. But if a post becomes old, its relevance usually diminishes if no other users link or like it for a period of time. The ambition to make the system modifiable by users can also be developed further. As a way of supporting diversity we have devised abilities to express opinions in a variety of fashions. To start with, we have used the most commonly used symbols for discussion and voting online, such as 'comment', 'like/dislike' and 'rate'. These different modes of expression are fixed in this version of the system, but a less static and more modifiable system could easily be developed in a future version.

Further empirical research on the platform in use will investigate how users interact with each other and the system, and further incorporation of the algorithms and Actory index into e-participation platforms will resolve some of the usability issues in navigating the system.

CONCLUSION

We have proposed a groupware that takes diversity and power into account, influenced by democratic meeting methods and social media practices. Instead of treating technology as a neutral means to an end, we regard it as cultural production and use it as a way of expressing and changing norms and social practices. The resulting system is a prototype of a collaborative platform with a game functionality where participants' status is measured and transformed through a dynamic voting process. The participants' status as users depends on their own activity and the reactions of others to these activities: links. likes/dislikes, rating and commenting. Importance is given to users' activity as well as their status position. We assume that users will react based on the actual activity and the status they attribute to the actor. The status position we assume depends on the level of closeness as well as on intersected factors such as gender, class, age and ethnicity. By measuring participants' activity in relation to each other's actions instead of only their rating of each other, we visualise the presence of structuring factors rather than the actual structure. Participants advance in the system by gathering scores and can be given different possibilities to influence the rules based on their score. By looking at the collaborative work in the groupware as a strategic game and using hierarchy as a way to motivate participation, we open up the possibility to communicate complex processes through practical action.

The system will be developed further towards two different uses:

1. A collaborative tool for interest-based networks. This tool can serve as a way to draw attention to individual initiative by visualising how status is created. By using the score as a way to dynamically create roles and provide rights, as in a strategic game, informal roles in the group are visualised and formalised and thus become easier to understand and influence.
2. A research tool for empirically analysing the significance of status, role, transparency and motivation in group processes. The system can be set up differently for different experimental purposes and groups.

FURTHER READING

Dahl, R.A. *Democracy and its Critics*. New Haven, CT: Yale University Press. 1989.

Garcin, F., Faltings, B. and Jurca, R. Aggregating reputation feedback. M. Paolucci (Ed.), *Proceedings of the First International Conference on Reputation: Theory and Technology* – ICORE 09, Gargonza, Italy. 2009.

Klemp, N.J. and Forcehimes, A.T. From town-halls to wikis: exploring Wikipedia's implications for deliberative democracy. *Journal of Public Deliberation* 6(2): Article 4. 2010.

Lourenço, R.P. and Costa, J.P. e-Participation: a discursive approach. D. Ríos Insua and S. French (Eds.), *E-democracy: A Group Decision and Negotiation Perspective*, pp. 163–184. Dordrecht: Springer. 2010.

18

Njaru:
Developing Tools for Deliberation
in Multiple Public Spheres

Despite the democratic ambition expressed in goals such as collaborative government or open government, the obstacles to a more participatory and open way of organising government are many. Among other things there are still huge technical and institutional barriers, and a more collaborative government also brings some obvious problems regarding deliberative democracy. There is also a general lack of knowledge about who, in terms of gender, nationality and social grouping, actually participates online and in what way. Currently available tool support systems have no means of identifying the users and the interests they represent in any way that makes the information production more transparent, and there are no strategies to address the issue. There is also a lack of structural support for deliberative processes integrating decision support systems with discussion tools.

In this chapter we present the development of a strategy and a tool that address these problems, departing from a case study of the information structures in an urban development project.

REPRESENTATIVENESS AND DELIBERATION IN A PARTICIPATORY GOVERNMENT

Concepts such as *transformational government* and *open government* are promising a fundamental institutional transformation where a more collaborative government is supported by social media applications and reformed regulations. These transformations are about making the government more informed by including the public in the sourcing of data. It is also about efficiency, distributing some of the data production and management to a diversity of private and public sector actors. This transformation also concerns deliberative aspects of social media, and a means to develop knowledge in a citizen-to-government

This chapter is based on Hansson, K. and Ekenberg, L. Deliberation, Representation and Motivation in Participatory Tools for the Public Sector. *Proceedings of the European Conference on Information Systems (ECIS)* 2014. Tel Aviv, Israel. 2014.

dialogue. 'Open' means that transparency and information sharing on different levels (within government, between government and the public and in the public sphere) is the default mode in government operation in order to promote understanding and accountability. It should also support innovations by being interoperable and open for reuse, both by various government agencies and the private sector.

As the use of participatory and social media has become widespread in society and enabled a more collaborative information production, there are new potentials for transformative developments in areas such as government, work life, science, and emergency response. In civic life, a more participatory, crowd-based regime is believed to boost innovation and strengthen democracy through projects like crowdsourced policymaking and participatory budgeting. In organisations, open-design practices and wiki technologies are used to enhance collective intelligence within and between agencies, and to develop government information. In science, data is collected and developed by the public. During emergencies, crowds have been engaged in data sourcing as well as performing physical activities.

What all these contexts have in common is that they encompass components for deliberative discussions, in one way or another, and thus support a collaborative government where political problems and solutions are developed more directly with various groups of people. Not very surprisingly, new online platforms for participation have not solved many old problems regarding democracy. Equal rights and transparency are not enough; we need means to develop a more participatory deliberative conversation to develop a consensus on how to solve common problems. This means that there is a need to have an enlightened understanding of the problem, there should be a broad deliberation from agenda setting to discussion and voting, and those affected by an issue should participate or at least be acknowledged.

Digital divide and differentiation makes more obvious the problem with lack of representativeness and means for developing broad deliberative processes. Social media in particular reproduces phenomena from other social contexts, such as discrimination due to gender or race. Agonistic conflicts between groups and public spheres dominated by strong interests make consensus impossible. Moreover, discussions in social forums are often problematical from an egalitarian perspective and are lacking means for enabling a deliberative process where different views are considered. Slightly more structural tools exist, with a potential to provide better structural and analytical support, but they are very seldom integrated with popular discussion forums. Instead, many platforms incorporate peer-communication and discussions as a way of reaching consensus, but then the discussions are seldom combined with any reasonable means to enable a deliberative process, making the discussions unstructured and unfocused. On the other hand, a highly driven analytical framework might result in a strongly reduced participation and exclusion, as not everyone can handle it. There is a need for methodologies and tool support that support community and consensus processes while also acknowledging agonistic conflicts and supporting a diversity of interest communities. The lack of representativeness in the development of data in online settings because of digital differentiation and dominant discourses, as well as lack of structured easy-to-use discussion forums, needs to be better addressed. In this research project we have therefore investigated informal and formal communication practices in planning processes to develop a methodology and tool support to visualise discursive processes as well as structural support for more informed deliberative processes.

RESEARCH METHODS AND DATA

A participatory design methodology for accomplishing different levels of information must acknowledge the need for support of interaction on multiple levels, supporting a broad citizen-to-citizen discussion in various forums and formats in more informal groups, supporting data gathering through surveys, focus groups, town meetings and crowd sourcing, providing tools for aggregating and analysing data as well as making the data easily accessible and promoting interoperability. Informed by these ideas, we have grounded the participatory design process in two very different cases of urban planning. In the municipality of Upplands Väsby, the officials reached out to the residents and invited them to participate in a vision process for how the municipality could develop in the future. In Husby, the residents were presented with a finished plan that would significantly change their living conditions.

The data for the case studies that informs the design process consisted of a media content analysis, participant observations, semi-structured interviews with officials and residents, art exhibitions, and seminars with stakeholders, residents and experts. These together represented a broad spectrum of perspectives in terms of age, educational background and occupation. The results of the interviews and the resulting design ideas were discussed with the participants, which further informed the study. It turned out that there is a plurality of communicative spheres more or less connected with the spheres officials were using. Consequently we created a community software that could be used on different interaction levels by the public administration, while addressing the community as a whole when surveying attitudes and opinions from focus groups or by other local groups of citizens.

To base the design in perceived needs, the design concept for the software was developed involving municipality officials, the IT-department of the municipality and the people responsible for citizen dialogues. The design and testing was conducted in an iterative manner, starting with a cognitive walkthrough with a small group of potential users using a low-fi prototype, before developing a large scale platform. In the following section we suggest a strategy for supporting existing democratic structures and present the development of a tool that departs from this strategy.

SUPPORT FOR DIFFERENT LEVELS OF COMMUNICATION

Using a participatory methodology, we addressed different information levels while supporting the communication. Hence, we developed a tool for supporting a plurality of forums, citizen feedback and interaction in dialogues and surveys, means to aggregate and analyse data as well as sharing and reuse of information. But we also needed a support tool for communication between these levels; making discussions on the conceptualisation level more informed by direct access to available data on the calculation level; enabling data produced at the conceptualisation level to be aggregated on the elicitation level and published at the calculation level to inform the debate on the conceptualisation.

The result is the design concept, summarised in Figure 1 as a wiki-like tool, where issues can be suggested, developed and voted on, and where the representativeness of the participation can be described. The basic functionality of the tool resembles many other publishing and discussion systems but includes and further develops important missing features. To start a discussion around an *Issue*, the initiator of the group sends an invitation to other participants to form a group. The initiator of an Issue is the one who decides when to close it, and how to use the result. This person has the role of the expert and moderator of discussion. Just as in a wiki all changes of the Issue are stored in *History*. The initiator can restrict the right of other users to develop the Issue, but by default others can *Comment*, *Edit*, and add additional *Documents*. Unlike most publishing and discussion systems, the participant can also structure the discussion by integrating *Options* (and Sub-options) in the text, which can be given a *Rating*, and *Pro/Con* arguments. *Statistics* shows outcomes of ratings in relation to user groups, and in *Followers*, the users' individual contributions to the issue are measured.

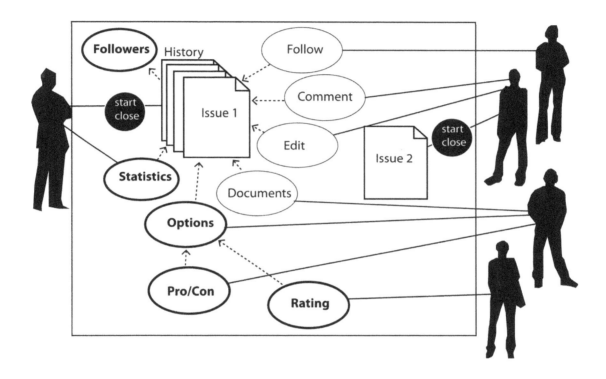

Figure 1. The basic features of the design concept.

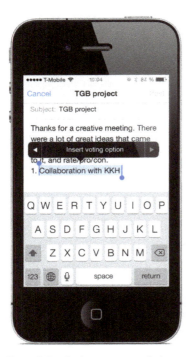

Figure 2: Text in the post can easily be converted to a voting option.

Figure 3: Text tagged as voting option can be 'voted' on, and the user can add pros and cons arguments.

Figure 4: Voting options in post with nested pros and cons arguments.

Figure 5: Users are categorised and their total activity and popularity is summarised as a score.

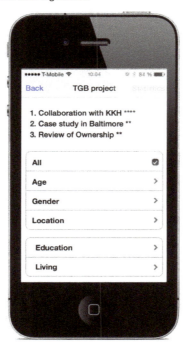

Figure 6: Users can see if differences in user categorising affect voting.

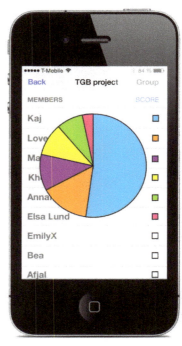

Figure 7: Each issue has a user group. The score reflects each user's actions and other users reacted on these.

The page and the related discussion may also have a time limit. A user can provide a deadline for participants to submit opinions on the matter. In this way an asynchronous but still relatively time intensive discussion can be created. This can be compared to an auction where the bidding (the argument) runs for a limited time, and the seller (the author) uses the information obtained when making a decision.

To create an easy-to-use deliberation tool integrating means for structured debate without sacrificing usability, we started out with a conventional interface on a mobile device, looking much like an ordinary e-mail or discussion forum. But, in addition to ordinary text formatting features like bold and lists, the text can also be formatted as voting options (Figure 2). Text tagged as voting option can be 'voted' on, and the user can add pros and cons arguments, arguments that also can be nested (Figures 3 and 4). The editing can continue during 'voting', and the user can changes their votes during the process.

To create means to analyse the debate from a representative point of view users are categorised (or categorise themselves), according to criteria such as age, gender and location (Figure 5). New criteria can easily be added depending on context. The result of the voting on alternatives can then be analysed from different perspectives, and it is thus possible to see if differences in user categorising affect voting (Figure 6).

However, from a deliberative democratic perspective, the discussions leading up to opinions are just as important to understand in terms of representation as the final opinions and it is important to understand who participated and who did not as well as who got more feedback on their actions than others. This is measured in the user score, which measures both users' activity and how much following activity this activity creates (Figure 7). The statistics and scoring make it possible to analyse the opinions developed in various forums from a representativeness perspective. They also create a starting point for an increased awareness of how opinions are dominated and structured, which, in turn, provide information on how structures can be altered, for instance by changing the way discussions are organised, when one group's perspective is never expressed in the discussions.

The tool is connected to the communication levels in different ways. (1) It can be used on a discursive level to organise the public and develop discussions. (2) It can be used on an interaction level in communication between residents and the municipalities, for example, as a tool for making surveys in large groups, or as a meeting place for focus group discussions on a certain subject.

(3) The tool contains means to collect data on user actions and demography and to visualise it, which is useful on an investigation level to analyse representativeness. Finally, (4) on an open data level, the tool can make it easier to access relevant data, but will also keep information at a desired level of secrecy.

Thus, to address the lack of methodologies and tool support for community and consensus processes, also recognising possible conflicts while supporting a diversity of communities, we have developed a methodology and software exemplifying how these questions can be handled in practice. The methodology thus points out ways of handling information on different levels and the tool supports communication between these levels; making the deliberative process on the discursive level more informed by structural support and by available data from the open data level. Parts of the data are also metadata on interaction structures and participation, showing how the data is socially produced. Making the tool accessible for anyone by default, supporting individual agency rather than an institutional perspective, enables a diversity of communities.

DISCUSSION

There is a general shift in the area of e-government from a focus on services and efficiency towards an emphasis on deliberative and innovative aspects, not the least for a more participatory democracy. However, as is discussed in this chapter, there are several obstacles involved and a main, albeit not very surprising, result of our work is that it is highly important to understand who, and whose interests, are represented in the various deliberative discussions, as well as developing supporting methods and tools that can be used to obtain as complex and varied information about the issue at hand as possible.

The design presented here can be used to maintain reflexions regarding democratic issues on an everyday basis, monitoring democratic processes on different levels and contexts, such as, for example, in the context of the local soccer club involving its members in stipulating the organisation's budget. It can also be the municipal officials that are interested in identifying groups not represented by the general opinion, to find other means to contact these groups, or ways to visualise their absence in the decision processes. It can also be used to support a diversity of public spheres, making it easier to participate in several parallel discourses, with groups of people who may not know each other but who share a common interest.

The suggested methodology points out ways of handling information developed on different levels, supporting individual agency and enabling a diversity of communities, but also provides a tool for democratic reflexion from a micro perspective, helping the individual to analyse how the information is developed and by whom.

Needless to say, despite our enthusiasm, it is still far from clear whether such a tool in actual fact will substantially contribute to delimit the abovementioned issues regarding deliberation and representation and it is definitely too premature to draw any firm conclusions regarding the use of it. All transparent systems are vulnerable and many discussions need to take place without any recording or monitoring. Nevertheless, such tools have a capacity to structure the arguments, for example, when summarising and archiving meeting notes, and function as a library for information around issues. It can furthermore provide a visualisation of the individuals' influence on the collective opinions. But a system of whatever kind, however successful it might be with respect to the various features included, can never be useful in isolation. It must be put in a context of a broad participatory methodology, from an active civil sector, to the citizen-government dialogue, to internal communication and innovation, and in such a context, it has a potential for being an important instrument for public decision processes.

CONCLUSION

In this design research we show how a general participatory methodology on different levels of governance can be supported by a groupware that integrates tools for analysing representativeness and discourse formation, with structured discussion tools.

Based in case studies of urban planning processes in the Swedish municipalities of Husby and Upplands Väsby, we have designed a wiki-type participatory tool providing the users with integrated and easy to use means for structuring and analysing the discussion.

Unlike the dominant research field, which usually has a government perspective, this community software takes the individual actor as a starting point, whether this actor is a certain official, someone from an organisation or just any resident. The interface and all the available tools are the same, independent of whether it is a resident or a municipal official that is the user.

In practice, this means that the actors within different organisations are highlighted as owners of specific questions. It also means that a municipality survey can have competition from other actors using the same survey instrument. The tool thus questions the traditional dichotomy between the state and the citizens in liberal democracy that seems to be a norm in much e-government research.

The tool also makes it possible to weight the information according to whom it represents, and is thus able to understand better the relevance of the information, for example if it is a general opinion or a strong group's special interest.

The limitation in this design research is that the tool has not been tested on any larger scale or for a longer amount of time. The tool has foremost been useful for communicating the more abstract participatory methodology to different stakeholders and participants in the research project. In practice the methodology demands major institutional and cultural changes. The design process is an exploration of what such a change could look like in practice.

FURTHER READING

Dahl, R.A. *Democracy and its Critics*. New Haven, CT: Yale University Press. 1989.

Garcin, F., Faltings, B. and Jurca, R. Aggregating Reputation Feedback, in M. Paolucci (Ed.), *Proceedings of the First International Conference on Reputation: Theory and Technology – ICORE 09*, Gargonza, Italy. 2009.

Klemp, N.J. and Forcehimes, A.T. From Town-halls to Wikis: Exploring Wikipedia's Implications for Deliberative Democracy. *Journal of Public Deliberation*. 6(2): Article 4. 2010.

Lourenço, R.P. and Costa, J.P. e-Participation: A Discursive Approach, in D. Ríos Insua and S. French (Eds.), *E-democracy: A Group Decision and Negotiation Perspective*, pp. 163–184. Dordrecht: Springer. 2010.

19

Evaluation of an Online Learning Environment

This chapter is based on Kivunike, F., Ekenberg, L., Danielson, M. and Tusubira, F.F. Towards a Structured Approach for Evaluating the ICT Contribution to Development, *The International Journal on Advances in ICT for Emerging Regions.* 7(1). pp. 1–15. 2014.

The evaluation and selection of initiatives in ICT for development (ICT4D) is a complex decision problem that would benefit from the application of MCDA techniques. Besides facilitating multidimensional and multi-stakeholder assessments MCDA provides a means for handling uncertainty arising from incomplete and vague information. This is a key requirement for the evaluation of the contribution of ICT to development, which relies on stakeholders' value judgements, perceptions and beliefs about how ICT has affected people's lives. In addition MCDA techniques offer a structured process for evaluation of development outcomes as an alternative to the predominantly descriptive, and often difficult to report, ICT4D evaluation approaches. They further relax the requirement of quantitative measures that call for data that is in some cases not accessible, and may be more taxing for the stakeholders.

As a structured decision making process the MCDA methodology typically consists of three stages: (1) information gathering or problem structuring – involves the definition of the decision problem to be addressed as well as the criteria and alternatives where necessary, (2) modelling stakeholder preferences – the structured decision problem, that is, criteria and alternatives are modelled using a decision support tool; and (3) evaluation and comparison of alternatives. While the application of MCDA techniques to decision making situations in the context of developing countries is appropriate, it is challenged by cultural, organisational, and infrastructural barriers, among other factors. Examples of such barriers include low literacy levels, lack of reliable electricity supply, and uneven access to ICT infrastructure, as well as resistance from elites resulting from leaders being afraid of losing their political position. This calls for adoption of the MCDA approach and process in a way that takes into account the contextual limitations in the developing country context, and the specific ICT4D evaluation exercise. This section illustrates how an MCDA technique can be applied for the evaluation of an ICT4D initiative. It specifically applies the technique using a subsection of the proposed criteria for the evaluation of the impact of an online learning environment on students' access to learning.

EVALUATING THE IMPACT OF E-LEARNING ENVIRONMENTS ON STUDENTS

The Makerere University E-Learning Environment (MUELE) is one of several initiatives aimed at leveraging faculty effectiveness and improving access to learning at Makerere University. MUELE is a learning management system (LMS) based on Moodle which has been in existence since 2009 and boasts a steady growth of users over the years. Active courses increased from 253 in 2011 to 456 in 2013, while the users increased to 45,000 in 2013 from 20,000 in 2011. Despite this progress, and even after lecturers were trained in online course authoring and delivery, the use of MUELE is mostly as a repository of course information. This has been attributed to attitudes towards the adoption of e-learning, concerns from lecturers regarding the increase in workload resulting from large student numbers, and increased course preparation time. Consequently this illustrative study seeks to establish whether MUELE has improved students' access to learning. More specifically we sought to establish whether MUELE contributed to improved (access to) learning; and to assess how the initiative performed on the different output and outcome indicators, highlighting the most significant outcomes. The criteria consist of the output and outcome indicators relevant for the evaluation of the impact of MUELE on access to learning. This is a subsection of the criteria suggested in *Chapter 8*, specifically aimed at evaluating improved access to formal and/or non-formal education. The criteria also include the contextual factors known to have an effect on the use of ICT to support learning.

The proposed criteria consisted of two decision models; the outputs and outcomes decision models. Using the output model (see Figure 1) we sought to establish the perception of students on whether MUELE had improved their access to learning. Using the outcomes model we sought to measure the actual improvement in student learning. The contextual factors had an influence on both models, either facilitating or restricting the improved access to learning. Preference modelling and elicitation considered two aspects: (1) evaluating the relative importance of criteria (eliciting

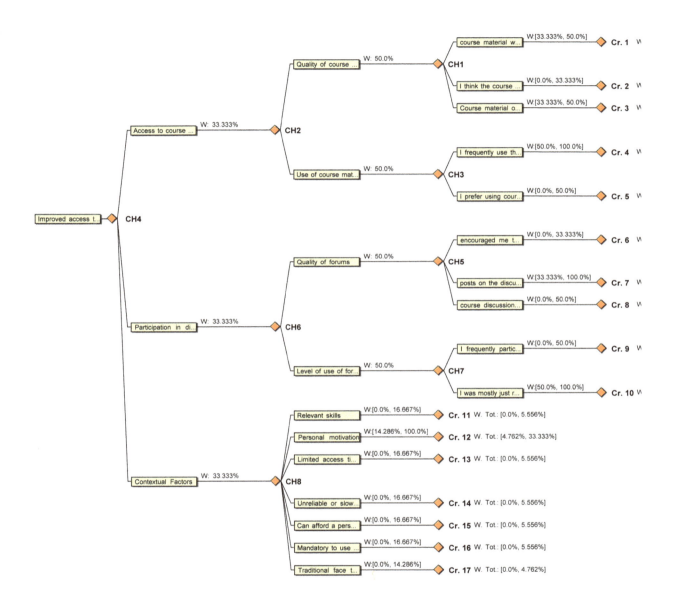

Figure 1. Output evaluation model.

weights); and (2) evaluating the initiative performance against criteria (eliciting scores).

Weight Elicitation: This is expressed through the assignment of a weight which reflects the importance of one dimension (criteria) relative to the others, and can be achieved through various methods. Ideally weight elicitation should be performed for each of the levels of the decision tree hierarchy. This study applied the rank-order approach in which criteria were ranked in order of importance from most to least important including equal ranks, as well as the assigning of weights. Rank-ordering was performed for the outcome model and the bottom-level criteria of the output model (output indicators). Equal weights were assumed for the other levels of the hierarchy, i.e. outputs and output indicator categories. The weights were developed through consultation with experts in the field – lecturers and MUELE administrators – who assessed the relative importance of the criteria.

Eliciting Scores: This involved evaluating perceptions of how MUELE had performed on various criteria. Responses were elicited from students who had used MUELE for at least a year or more. Verbal-numerical scales which have been applied in various domains as well as binary (yes/no) scales were used for the elicitation. The verbal-numerical scale is a combination of verbal expressions (e.g. unlikely, strongly agree etc.) and the corresponding numerical intervals (see Table 1). Since elicitation involved vague and imprecise value judgements of how e-learning had improved learning, it was appropriate to adopt a verbal-numerical scale. While the verbal responses enabled stakeholders to state their preferences in a vague manner, the corresponding numerical ranges were applied for representation and analysis in the decision analysis tool. Studies have established that people assess in terms of words or numbers in varied ways; however the use of a combined verbal-numerical scale is a more effective and simplified elicitation approach.

Since multiple responses were elicited from the students and experts, aggregation was required for the elicited information. The aggregation approach was dependent on the nature of response scales; for example, the simple weighted sum approach was applied for the aggregation of the students' responses obtained from the verbal-numerical scale. This involved assuming equal weights for each stakeholder and calculating the expected value. The simple weighted sum approach has been used in the aggregation of imprecise values because it has proven to be the most effective

Table 1. Example of a verbal-numerical scale.

Verbal Statement	Interval range
Virtually certain	[100–99]%
Very likely	[98–90]%
Likely	[89–66]%
Neutral	[65–33]%
Unlikely	[32–10]%
Very unlikely	[9.0–1.0]%
Exceptionally unlikely	[0.9–0.0]%

aggregation approach. Since the ranking and binary (yes/no) scales are ordinal, the mode was applied as the preferred measure of central tendency to obtain the aggregate value(s) for the analysis.

RESULTS: ANALYSIS AND EVALUATION

In this study the DecideIT decision support tool was used to analyse and evaluate the decision problem. DecideIT is based on multi-attribute value theory and supports both precise and imprecise information. DecideIT supports various data formats: imprecise data in terms of interval values, comparative statements or weights and even precise values. The rank-ordered values depicting the relative importance of criteria were modelled as comparative statements, while the student perceptions obtained through the verbal-numerical and binary (yes/no) scales were modelled as intervals and precise values respectively. Evaluation was performed for each of the models (outputs and outcomes) and the results are discussed below.

RESPONDENT DEMOGRAPHICS

Eight experts, four male and four female, were consulted on the ranking of importance of indicators used to evaluate the impact of an e-learning environment on improved student learning. Seven were lecturers, while one of them was an administrator in charge of MUELE. Twenty students, seventeen male and three female, participated in the evaluation of the impact of MUELE on improved access to learning. With the exception of two students in their second year and three who had completed their studies, the majority (15) were in their final year of study, and had used MUELE for an overall period of two to four years. Most of the participants (10) used it two or three days a week, seven used it almost every day, while two rarely used it and one used it once a week. Finally, while fourteen of the student participants were aged 16 to 25 years, the remaining six were aged 26 to 35. Clearly the sample is not sufficiently representative of the student population that uses MUELE, however it was sufficient to illustrate the structured evaluation process.

Value Profiling: provides an assessment of how outputs (evaluated in terms of output indicators) have performed in meeting the overall objective. It assesses the contribution or relevance of the outputs to the overall objective. In this case the quality and level of use of course material are the most significant contributors to improvements in accessing learning materials, while participation in online discussions is average. Finally, satisfaction with the quality

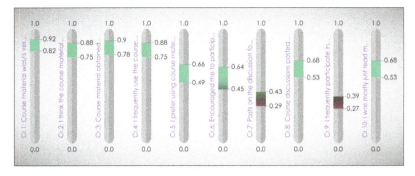

Figure 2. Performance of individual outputs on improved access to learning.

of discussion forum posts is the least contributor to improved access to learning (Figure 2). Evidently MUELE is mostly used as a repository of course materials, as previously established.

Tornado Graphs: These facilitate the identification of the critical issues that have the highest impact on the expected value (Figure 3). The least contributing (outputs) indicators as per the value profiling analysis above, i.e. participation in the discussion forums (Cr.7, Cr.9, Cr.10, Cr.8), were the most critical aspects affecting the expected value measure. On the other hand, the high contributors, i.e. the quality and level of use of course material, had the least impact on the expected value. Such information may challenge decision-makers to develop strategies for the improvement of the current initiative or streamline the development of future similar initiatives. For example, establishing that participation in discussion forums is a critical aspect in realising improved learning through MUELE would challenge the lecturers to engage the students actively in this activity, or to investigate further why this is an important aspect.

Expected Value Graph: The expected value interval of the outputs measures student performance in terms of the extent to which access to MUELE has improved access to learning (Figure 4). This implies that, based on the outputs, it is perceived that MUELE had a fairly high potential for improving access to learning with very limited possibility or chances of failure. This serves as confirmation of the ICT potential to improve access to learning in this particular context.

OUTCOME MODEL EVALUATION

Expected Value Graph: This depicts an expected value interval and the focal point of all interval statements (the 100% contraction value) at 0.73 (Figure 5). This implies that the different outcomes

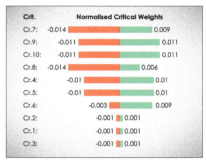

Figure 3. Critical outputs in the realisation of student learning.

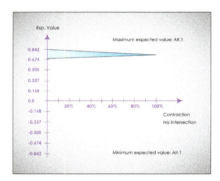

Figure 4. Expected value of the outputs' contribution to improved access to learning.

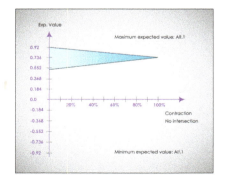

Figure 5. Expected value graph evaluating the outcomes' contribution to improved access to learning.

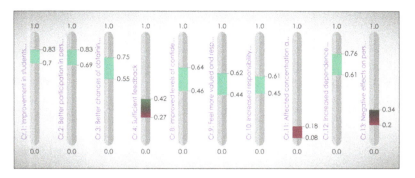

Figure 6. Performance of individual outcomes in terms of outcome indicators.

derived from MUELE effectively contributed to improved access to student learning.

Value Profiling: The outcomes to which MUELE most significantly contributed were improvements in student learning, facilitation of student participation in personal learning, and a better chance of obtaining employment (Figure 6). There was an average effect on the psychological aspects, i.e. improved levels of confidence and whether people felt more valued or respected. There was however a low chance that MUELE had a significant negative impact such as affecting concentration or self-discipline, as well as personal health. On the other hand, there was a high chance that access to MUELE increased student dependence on computers.

Tornado Graphs: The contextual factors, i.e. relevant skills, limited access to computers, unreliable or slow internet connection, ability to afford a personal computer, as well as the mandatory requirement to use MUELE, were the most critical aspects affecting the realisation of improved access to student learning (Figure 7). The difference in factors affecting the realisation of outputs and outcomes is essential for mid-term evaluation; helping implementers address the identified gaps and ensure the success of the initiative.

CONCLUSION

As is seen from the results above, the aim in such an analysis is not necessarily to obtain an aggregated value explaining the overall performance of an initiative. The focus is on facilitating a structured approach to explaining various aspects, such as how an initiative performs on different outcomes or the most critical factors affecting the realisation of the overall objective. It is important to note that while the findings in this illustrative example may not be representative of the status of e-learning at

Crit.	Normalised Critical Weights		
Cr.14:	-0.025		0.031
Cr.16:	-0.025		0.031
Cr.17:	-0.025		0.031
Cr.18:	-0.025		0.031
Cr.19:	-0.025		0.031
Cr.15:	-0.017		0.031
Cr.12:	-0.023		0.024
Cr.6:	-0.016		0.029
Cr.4:	-0.034		0.002
Cr.11:	-0.016		0.016
Cr.3:	0.0		0.029
Cr.7:	0.0		0.029
Cr.9:	-0.023		0.006
Cr.8:	-0.014		0.013
Cr.13:	-0.023		0.004
Cr.10:	0.0		0.024
Cr.20:	-0.017		0.0
Cr.2:	-0.002		0.001
Cr.5:	-0.002		0.001
Cr.1:	-0.002		0.0

Figure 7. Critical outputs in the realisation of student learning.

Makerere University, they are a good illustration of the evaluation process. For example, the realisation that contextual factors are an essential aspect in meeting the initiative goal will shift the focus from just providing the e-learning environment to addressing the most critical contextual factors. Furthermore, the low performance of discussion forums will probably encourage further investigation into the pedagogical requirements that would integrate forums into the students' learning process.

The MCDA tool provides a rich, detailed and structured assessment of the different factors which warrants further investigation into its use as an ICT4D evaluation approach, indicating that such a structured approach can facilitate a sufficient assessment of the performance of the development initiative as well as the most critical factors influencing the attainment of the development goals. The model does not, however, explicitly address any unintended benefits or negative consequences that are prevalent in any development initiative.

FURTHER READING

Kivunike, F., Ekenberg, L., Danielson, M. and Tusubira, F. Towards an ICT4D Evaluation Model Based on the Capability Approach. *International Journal on Advances in ICT for Emerging Regions.* 7(1), pp. 1–15. 2014.

Kivunike, F., Ekenberg, L., Danielson, M. and Tusubira, F. Criteria for the Evaluation of the ICT Contribution to Social and Economic Development. Sixth Annual SIG GlobDev Pre-ICIS Workshop, Milan, Italy. 2013.

Talantsev, A., Larsson, A., Kivunike, F. and Sundgren, D. Quantitative Scenario-Based Assessment of Contextual Factors for ICT4D Projects: Design and Implementation in a Web Based Tool, in Á. Rocha, A.M. Correia, F.B. Tan and K.A. Stroetmann (Eds.), *New Perspectives in Information Systems and Technologies* 1(275), pp. 477–490. Cham: Springer. 2014.

A Low Carbon Society by 2050: The Stockholm-Mälar Region Case

There is general concern in many parts of the world, including Europe, about the importance of limiting the emissions of greenhouse gases in order to combat the constant increase in global temperature occurring as a result of climate change. In the EU the decision to aim for low carbon (or zero net carbon) emissions to the atmosphere has already been taken, with the aim of avoiding the projected global increase of 2 degrees Celsius by 2050. After the UN Climate Change Conference in Paris in December 2015 we could even talk about an ambition to limit temperature increase to 1.5 degrees.

Sweden has adopted this as a strategic goal. Such aims also have consequences at lower administrative levels: regional (within a nation), county (in Sweden, 'län') and municipality/city. Non-governmental stakeholders at such levels, for example industrial or civil society organisations or ordinary citizens, are involved in these strategic discussions. In this chapter the researchers for the Swedish contribution to the EU's COMPLEX project report on the ongoing analysis of multi-layered and multi-actor realities in the efforts in the Stockholm-Mälar Region to find ways of moving towards a low carbon society by 2050. Here the positions of various actors, the formal and informal forms of reasoning, planning and acting – and the outlines of strategies for the long-term future – are at the heart of the process and thus of central interest for our analysis of the decision making positions and structural approaches.

The issues of importance relate to climate change, low carbon society, regional policy, and climate change policies. It pertains to an actor space including the region, counties and municipalities, but also the basis for individual decision making. It deals with multi-level, multi-actor and multi-stakeholder issues with regard

This chapter is based on Svedin U. and Liljenström H. including exerpts from Gren I-M. using parts of her EU COMPLEX project report *Cost-effective Land Use Dynamics towards a Low Carbon Economy in the Stockholm-Mälar Region.*

to public policy, industrial strategies, civil society developments, and societal transformations.

From several angles the already existing EU goal of reaching a net zero carbon future by 2050 is high on the political agenda in many parts of Europe. This holds true not least for the Swedish government, where this goal has already been confirmed and consolidated as a national goal. The major reason for the strong need to achieve this goal is the challenge of climate change – and within this frame to stay within the maximum increase of 2 degrees Celsius for the entire planet. For this to happen the phasing out of carbon emissions (and other greenhouse gas (GHG) emissions as well) is essential. But as it is the carbon dioxide emissions that are most significant this is the sector where the key strategic restrictions have to be applied. In a discussion frame of the 'planetary boundaries' we are facing, we find that, of the nine suggested boundaries, climate change is high on the list and that globally we have probably already passed what could be considered an acceptable position. The need now is to enforce countermeasures stringently at all administrative and political levels from the global to the local. This holds true for Sweden and its sub-regions and localities.

NET CARBON EMISSIONS

If such a global goal of major reduction of net carbon emissions to the atmosphere is to be achieved at a global level it is necessary for relevant contributions to be provided at all underlying scales – and in many cases these must be more drastic both in terms of tempo and/or volume. Thus such a goal has implications for Swedish regions like the Stockholm-Mälar Region (our chosen test area) in the mid-to-south-east of Sweden. (In the EU regional classification this is regions SE 11 and parts of SE 12 including the capital city of Sweden, Stockholm (see Figure 1).

In this region (SE 11 and parts of SE 12) both the largest urban area of Sweden (the national capital with a population of 1.5 million) and its connected suburban area are found – as well as a much broader area of very rapidly increasing population in the region at large, including both medium-sized and smaller cities and agricultural and forestry areas. Figure 2 shows the Stockholm-Mälar Region.

Given the EU policy background and the Swedish national goals for low net carbon emissions, the design of policies in this region is of high relevance for the future. They include strategically defined goals and the process by which policies could be developed regarding paths towards a low carbon net emission society by 2050 – of relevance for the features of this region, given its historical background and contemporary situation.

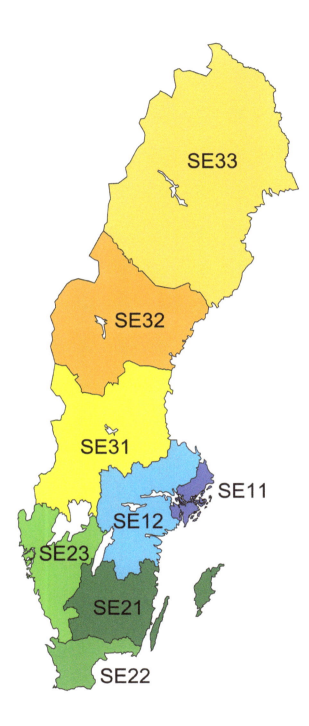

Figure 1. Map of Sweden with EU regional classifications. Source: Swedish Environmental Protection Agency.

Figure 2. Overview of the Stockholm-Mälar Region (source: Swedish Environmental Protection Agency).

A LOW CARBON SOCIETY

For the Swedish part of the EU research project COMPLEX, (run by research groups at the Swedish University of Agricultural Sciences and at Stockholm University, and activities by and at the Sigtuna Foundation) these challenges are of direct relevance. The project deals with structures to support the relevant decision making for low carbon modelling, suggested framings of the societal transformations, and connected processes that might be considered necessary. The following presentation focuses on the Swedish part of the project and how the possibilities for transformation may emerge, including how innovative responses might be formulated, but also how resistance to change and connected possible reversals could be envisioned and hopefully overcome.

The selected test region has a central place in the history of Sweden. Without going into detail of more than a millennium of development – and an even longer history stretching back beyond Viking times – it can be stated that this is a thriving European region. It benefits from a combination of central (during the last millennium, royal) governmental functions for the country; nodes of trade networks; central academic institutions (at university level from 1477 in Uppsala, and later in many other places in the region, with world-leading institutions today in Stockholm); central church offices for over a millennium; and vibrant mining (mostly iron), manufacturing, forestry, agricultural, and economic sectors.

In short, for over a millennium this has been – and still is today – a region that embraces both long traditions and very advanced technologies and industrial endeavours within a global network. It is also a region balancing the national capital of Sweden, with its highly urban features, with medium-sized and smaller urban nodes as well as rural areas with highly developed agricultural and forestry activities. It embraces new functions and capacities, from new types of consultancies to a vibrant tourism sector. It is definitely a region with a very high orientation to innovation, in many cases of global high-tech significance in telecommunications, medical/pharmaceutical specialities and in other areas of cutting-edge technologies.

Thus in connection with its modern societal features and cultural value frame it is a part of the world where experimentation in many of the aspects needed for the transition to low-carbon transformation are already present – or are potentially possible. The region not only has the means to face the challenges of the future for itself, but is also a focus of strong interest for wider European – and global – actors, at a moment when many parts of the world are seeking to combat the challenges of climate change within less than a generation.

THE STOCKHOLM-MÄLAR REGION

The greater Stockholm-Mälar Region is home to some three million people – approximately one-third of Sweden's total population – and its population is rapidly expanding. Politically, it consists of the five Swedish counties (län) of Stockholm, Uppsala, Örebro, Västmanland and Södermanland. In the context of Europe's recognised regions, other counties (län) such as Östergötland are included with the SE 11 and SE 12 regional areas. The region has certain characteristics:

- A great variety of geographic and social features
- A long historical evolution in a socio-economic-cultural frame
- A layered governance structure
- An innovative cultural style and many globally highly-ranked academic institutions

In the rest of this chapter we will examine more aspects of the possible transition to a low carbon society in this region. We will draw out the significant features and look at the lead sectors in which we can imagine key innovations that might be of particular importance for the transition. We are engaged in exploring how the professional planning groups are currently discussing these matters both with regard to the multi-layered system of formal governance, as well as in the activities of industry and civil society. As a result we are very interested in the current thinking with regard to these issues in the formal public sphere and also in society at large, as they form an important basis for policy formation in the wider democratic system.

EXPLORATION OF MINDSETS ABOUT THE KEY ISSUES – AN INITIATIVE DEALING WITH ORDERS OF MAGNITUDE

In order to understand the possibilities for transitions – and ideas to promote them – it is important to have a general understanding of key factors. So let us start with the Swedish energy situation. Current energy provision in Sweden is characterised by traditional fossil fuels supplemented by a strong hydropower component which, together with a contribution from nuclear power, provides a robust electricity profile. In addition there is rapid expansion (although from an initially low level) of wind and solar energy sources, and the bioenergy sector is also expanding quickly – including its use in the public transport sector, for the bus system. There is also very rapid development in energy-saving measures, such as in the construction sector (in building design etc.).

The main focus areas of the total energy system being addressed are the transport sector and consumer spending (both on goods produced within Sweden and imported). The entire food system is under increasing scrutiny. And a proposal to change over the entire road transport vehicle fleet from fossil fuels by 2030 has recently been addressed in a major government investigation (statlig utredning) led by Professor Thomas Johansson. The implementation of this investigation is being vigorously debated in the political domain, with a distinct orientation towards innovation.

There is a clear need for collaboration between different strata of society. There is also a call for a collaborative understanding of – and progress towards – the changes that such transformations may entail. The process has to provide an understanding of how our society could develop, not only in terms of instrumental features in technology and economy but more deeply in terms of what society, that is, 'we' – and coming generations – might aspire to in our living space. Following this line of thought, a number of connected issues arise:

- Capacities for change in general in the Swedish system
- Political structures and challenges to the governance system
- Partial sectorial change capabilities

With regard to overall capacities for change, the existing situation looks advantageous. There is a strong tradition of technical innovation and a climate of entrepreneurship at the individual and small scale level, as well as in major industrial endeavours, in the energy, infrastructure, food, construction and real estate sectors. This tradition can be harnessed if the visions for a low carbon society could be accepted as a framework for elaborations about the future in the coming decades. Image creation is in multiple hands.

The political culture of Sweden – not least in our case region – would suit a process with such aims if driven with force and enthusiasm, focusing not only the problems and costs of the transition but on the possibilities and competitive advantage for Sweden. In an organisational political perspective, however, there is a need for further development of the interplay between levels of organisation – in which regional and national priorities could be connected in new and constructive ways with efforts to encourage plurality and local action. This is directly connected to the power of municipalities to take decisive action in the direction of non-fossil fuel pathways – both for their internal use, and also in collaboration with higher levels of organisation. New approaches will also be needed to explore modes of interplay between the capital city, medium-sized cities, urban areas of other kinds, and rural interests and possibilities.

All these avenues have to be explored in an active societal debate in which the overriding goals for society are elaborated upon in parallel and integrated with a number of more specific and practical solutions. This will require a society encouraging experimentation, plurality, and visionary approaches. It also depends on the capacity to allocate resources for large-scale investments to support the needs arising from climate change – but also matching other 'grand challenges' emerging in the world. In this way regional approaches will be of great importance in connecting the local and the global.

THE SWEDISH PART OF THE EU COMPLEX PROJECT

Facing these challenges, and especially seeing opportunities for a regional approach in a country like Sweden, with its technical and economic capacities and its long-term commitment to democratically led change, the Swedish part of the EU COMPLEX project has as overriding objectives:

- providing processes, understanding and instruments for support of the transition to a low carbon society by 2050 with particular application to the Stockholm-Mälar Region
- analysing strategic societal choices and their consequences
- designing various tools for analysis of economic and social development
- probing the impact of policy instruments, and connected processes with the aim of scientifically supporting decision making functions at various levels
- exploring connected emerging land-use patterns

In the model-oriented part of this work to be further developed and finalised, the objectives will include:

- The models are intended to aid stakeholders in their decision making, linking policies at the (sub-national) regional level to those at the levels of households and municipalities, as well as connecting to national and even supra-national levels.
- With regard to models, the project has explored gaming sessions with stakeholders in order to investigate the relationship between such actors and their understanding and use of various types of models.
- The dynamics of environmental and economic factors and their connected land-use change require analysis and models that can capture the inherent complexity. Also issues at the level of individuals in terms of cognitive conditions are being

examined in the current research. This may, for example, relate to decisions by individuals as to their 'best' option choice in daily transport solutions.

THE DECISION MAKING PROCESS – SOME REFLECTIONS ABOUT CONDITIONS

It needs to be stated that:

- Understanding and action should be approached through a systems-thinking perspective.
- Policy creation and research have a mutual symbiotic relationship.
- When dealing with energy outlooks related to climate change it is important to ask the following types of questions: Energy outlooks for whom? What kind of energy outlook? For what purpose?
- With regard to the diversity of land use, the four Fs need to be considered: food, fibre, fuel and feed – not forgetting that land use in an urban context also has other functional characteristics (buildings, roads, airports, harbours, industrial areas and other infrastructure).
- Within a biosphere perspective, biodiversity also has to be considered, involving considerations about the service functions of various elements of the ecosystem.
- In a natural resource perspective, the connection to emerging 'green economy' considerations is needed, e.g. how connections to 'circular economy' and other sequence-oriented perspectives will increasingly have to be considered.

Which mechanisms of governance should be developed to create innovative conditions that will lead us seamlessly towards a low carbon society? Do we need new steering mechanisms to pave the way for such a transition? And which interactions might need to be fostered between knowledge, values and actions? Based upon whose responsibility or societal mandate?

The transition towards a low carbon society has already started in our case region. This is seen in diversification and the development of technologies including solar and wind power, and their decreasing costs. It is also seen in the emerging bio-based fuel solutions and their institutionally-enforced adoption, and in the growing interest in electric cars. Governance mechanisms will need to be developed and adjusted to secure an energy transformation, which is not yet imminent. Many changes may require more general consideration, for instance, with regard to the tension between micro and macro, and between public policy implementation versus market mechanisms.

FURTHER READING

Rockström, J., Steffen, W., Noone, K., Persson, Å., Chapin, F.S., Lambin, E.F. *et al.* A Safe Operating Space for Humanity. *Nature.* 461, pp. 472–475. 2009.

Svedin, U. Challenges for Planetary Stewardship at the Entry of the Period of the Anthropocene, in W. Leal Filho *et al.* (Eds.), S*ustainable Development, Knowledge Society and Smart Future Manufacturing Technologies.* World Sustainability Series. Cham: Springer. 2015.

Svedin, U. Urban Development and the Environmental Challenges – Green Systems. Considerations for the EU, in W. Leal Filho *et al.* (Eds.), *Sustainable Development, Knowledge Society and Smart Future Manufacturing Technologies.* World Sustainability Series. Cham: Springer. 2015.

Epilogue

Public participation plays different parts in different democracy models and the role of a public decision support system (PDSS) naturally differs depending on its character, e.g. how it enables a broader participation as well as providing new communication channels for more public opinion formation and decision making. In a so-called strong democracy model, where the public should participate in all stages of the decision making process, a PDSS would take the role of an interactive tool to facilitate public discussion, such as in a policy-making model where the public is supposed to be invited to discuss the importance of certain criteria and have opportunities to study the effects of various stated preferences. In the more common 'thin' model, the public is normally only consulted in the policy creation and monitoring stages, while a PDSS has a different character (depending on the domain under consideration). In both cases, a significant problem is that most tools are also seldom combined with any reasonable means of enabling a deliberative democratic process in which relevant facts from multiple points of view are taken into consideration, making them as deceptive as more common types of debates.

Public participatory decision making is thus balancing on the borders of inclusion, structure, precision and accuracy, while trying to incorporate citizens' input in various processes in more or less structured formats. To simply enable more participation will not yield enhanced democracy and there is definitely a need for more elaborated elicitation and decision analytical tools.

Many general process models, decision making methods, and accompanying tools for participation involving web-based platforms that support public decision making processes in an informative and participatory manner, have been suggested in the past. These typically, and more or less successfully, collect and present debates and information perceived to be of relevance for an issue at hand but generally do not provide structuring tools for the actual decision process or decision evaluation.

Instead, the various specialised support tools for formalised decision making require, to a large extent, idealised and unrealistic assumptions. They also tend to use over-simplified aggregation mechanisms, particularly in multi-stakeholder situations, where there normally is a lot of uncertainty involved in the elicitation of the stakeholders' preferences, a huge amount of methodological issues involved, and the current state-of-the-art does not provide a ready solution. Except for the actual participation in the various processes, a central element is the actual elicitation of information and the relaxation of precise judgements of importance in order to reduce the gap between the various theoretical models and their practical relevance.

Earlier methods have failed to provide reasonable decision processes for citizen participation that more systematically promote inclusion and transparency as well as providing useful tools for qualified decision analysis. These should at least include:

- realistic but efficient elicitation processes, and a utilisation of a broad spectrum of modalities to enable as broad participation as possible;
- procedures for handling all relevant quantitative, qualitative and structural information in decision situations; and
- reasonable and interactive decision rules that utilise the above information in a consistent framework that is computationally meaningful.

Besides providing a more realistic representation that is less demanding for users, another advantage with methods based on more approximate judgements is that the decision support process can become more interactive, and in turn lead to improved decision quality, as well as being especially suitable for group decision making processes since each individual's importance judgements can be fully represented by a union of all the group's members judgements.

One solution is to interpret various statements as regions of significance where the elicitation procedures can be divided into extraction (extracting information through user input), representation (capturing the information in a formal structure) and interpretation (assigning meaning to the captured information).

Even with adequate tool packages, an approach to democratic decision making processes must entail the different views of citizens being acknowledged as input, which calls for models encompassing different points of view, different perspectives, multiple objectives and multiple stakeholders, using different methods. We included artistic performances, while investigating whether art can form a basis for constructive dialogues and expressions of preferences, formulations and solutions.

The solution to the issues with democracy therefore lies not only in studying various computational machineries and web phenomena, but also in actually addressing the issues by developing new tools, methods and working cultures for interpreting the citizen interaction and discourse. This should then include everything from more basic forms of web-based technologies in questionnaires explicitly designed so that preference statements can be exploited for decision evaluation and aggregation in a meaningful way (both conceptually and computationally), to more elaborate forms such as innovative theatre performance formats.

We can conclude by stating that a decision theory without applications is meaningless, that public decision making is in a highly doubtful state and that there are significant difficulties involved. To use such a theory in a participatory setting, we must take into account the complex issues of how governance arrangements and the formal planning process can be structured to effectively accommodate inputs from various citizens in a decision framework, including usable and transparent decision methods equipped for handling citizens and multiple categories of other decision-makers.

Assuming that the participatory aspects can be covered, the input must be handled and an adequate process model should carry a decision through from agenda setting and problem awareness to feasible courses of action via formulation of objectives, alternative generation, consequence assessments, and trade-off clarifications.

There are still significant problems involved, however. As we have seen, various elicitation methods use a variety of questioning procedures to elicit weights, but such methods are relatively infrequently used and most do not offer adequate support for realistic decision making. In most decision situations involving various stakeholders conflicts arise, and modules for systematic negotiations and tools for analysing trade-off effects will be key features. But the potential benefits of structured negotiation processes are often severely underutilised in real-life settings.

In the models we have developed, we utilise decision structuring and evaluation procedures as extensions to earlier decision analytic methods, and tools combined with elicitation models that make use of the information the decision-maker is able to supply, to provide means for aggregating imprecise weight statements from different stakeholders.

The objective of such a model is of course to enable the use of a process model for public decision making, specifically aimed at the inclusion of many stakeholders and possibly also many decision-makers, and also integrating assessments made from a vast number of methods, utilising different ontological and epistemological positions, while creating tools that constructively combine mixed qualitative and quantitative methods.

This has called for extensions of generic theories of decision making such as probability based multi-criteria decision analysis, and an execution of the decision steps appropriately.

We hope that initiatives of the type described here could be a major step in the use of well-informed decision analysis for evaluation of critical societal issues, and provide applicable and computationally meaningful public decision mechanisms, involving multiple-criteria, points of view, scenario analyses, uncertain appraisals of the decision parameters involved, and visual formats for presentation of the relevant information. Hopefully, this will have a significant impact of the applicability of decision theory in participatory democracy and on modernising the field of decision, policy and societal risk analysis.

Publications

Anya, O., Carletti, L., Coughlan, T., Hansson, K. and Liu, S.B. The Morphing Organization: Rethinking Groupwork Systems in the Era of Crowdwork, *Proceedings of Group14 ACM International Conference on Supporting Groupwork, Sanibel Island, FL*. 2014. http://dx.doi.org/10.1145/2660398.2660428

Barkhuus, L., Rossitto, C., Ekenberg, L., Forsberg, R. and Sauter, W. Interactive Performances as a Means of Social Participation and Democratic Dialogue, *International Reports of Socio-informatics, Proceedings of COOP 2014 Workshop on Cooperative Technologies in Democratic Processes*. 2014. http://dx.doi.org/10.1145/2639189.2641213

Bohman, S. Information Technology in eParticipation Research: A Word Frequency Analysis, in E. Tambouris, A. Macintosh and F. Bannister (Eds.), *Electronic Participation, Lecture Notes in Computer Science*, pp. 78–89. Berlin and Heidelberg: Springer. 2014. http://dx.doi.org/10.1007/978-3-662-44914-1_7

Bohman, S., Hansson, H. and Mobini, P. Online Participation in Higher Education Decision Making. *JeDEM – eJournal of eDemocracy and Open Government*. 6(3), pp. 267–285. 2014.

Borking, K., Davies, G., Danielson, M., Ekenberg, L., Idefeldt, J. and Larsson, A. *Transcending Business Intelligence*. Stockholm: Sine Metu. 2011.

Cars, G. and Ekenberg, L. Planning, Negotiation and Decision Making in Development Projects. Manuscript.

Caster, O. and Ekenberg, L., Combining Second-Order Belief Distributions with Qualitative Statements Decision Analysis, in Ermoliev Y., Marti K., Makowski M. (Eds.), *Managing Safety of Heterogeneous Systems: Decisions under Uncertainties and Risks*, pp. 67–87. Berlin and Heidelberg: Springer. 2012. http://dx.doi.org/10.1007/978-3-642-22884-1_4

Caster, O., Norén, N., Ekenberg, L. and Edwards, R. Quantitative Benefit-Risk Assessment using only Qualitative Information on Utilities, *Medical Decision Making*. 32(6), pp. E1–E15. 2012. http://dx.doi.org/10.1177/0272989x12451338

Cunningham, P., Cunningham, M. and Ekenberg, L. Assessment of Potential ICT-Related Collaboration and Innovation Capacity in East Africa. *Proceedings of IEEE GHTC*. 2015. http://dx.doi.org/10.1109/ghtc.2015.7343961

Cunningham, P., Cunningham, M. and Ekenberg, L. Factors Impacting on the Current Level of Open Innovation and ICT Entrepreneurship in Africa. *The Electronic Journal of Information Systems in Developing Countries*. 73(1), pp. 1–23. 2016.

Cunningham, P., Cunningham, M. and, Ekenberg, L. Baseline Analysis of Three Innovation Ecosystems in East Africa, *Proceedings of ICTer2014*. 2014. http://dx.doi.org/10.1109/icter.2014.7083895

Cunningham, P., Cunningham, M. and, Ekenberg, L. Stakeholder Roles and Potential Models to Support Collaborative Open Innovation in East Africa, *IFIP WG9.4, 13th International Conference on Social Implications of Computers in Developing Countries*. 2015.

Danielson, M. and Ekenberg, L. A Risk-Based Decision Analytic Approach to Assessing Multi-Stakeholder Policy Problems, in A. Amendola, T. Ermolieva, J. Linnerooth-Bayer and R. Mechler (Eds.), *Integrated Catastrophe Risk Modelling: Supporting Policy Processes*, pp. 231–248. Springer. 2013. http://dx.doi.org/10.1007/978-94-007-2226-2_14

Danielson, M. and Ekenberg, L. Automated Decision Making for Autonomous Agents, *International Journal of Intelligent Mechatronics and Robotics*. 3(3), pp. 22–28. 2013. http://dx.doi.org/10.4018/ijimr.2013070102

Danielson, M. and Ekenberg, L. Development of Software for Decision Analysis, *Proceedings of The 12th IEEE International Conference on Intelligent Software Methodologies Tools and Techniques.* 2013. http://dx.doi.org/10.1109/somet.2013.6645661

Danielson, M. and Ekenberg, L. Rank Ordering Methods for Multi-Criteria Decisions, in P. Zaraté, G. Camilleri, D. Kamissoko and F. Amblard (Eds.), *Group Decision and Negotiation. A Process-Oriented View*, pp. 128–135. Cham: Springer. 2014. http://dx.doi.org/10.1007/978-3-319-07179-4_14

Danielson, M. and Ekenberg, L. Software Development of Linear Programming Algorithms for Decision Analysis Applications, *Journal of Communication and Computer.* 8(9), pp. 793–806. 2011.

Danielson, M. and Ekenberg, L. The CAR Method for using Preference Strength in Multi-Criteria Decision Making. *Group Decision and Negotiation.* 25(4), pp. 775–797. 2016. http://dx.doi.org/10.1007/s10726-015-9460-8

Danielson, M. and Ekenberg, L. Using Surrogate Weights for Handling Preference Strength, in B. Kaminski, G.E. Kersten and T. Szapiro (Eds.), *Multi-Criteria Decisions, Outlooks and Insights on Group Decision and Negotiation*, pp. 107–118. Cham: Springer. 2015. http://dx.doi.org/10.1007/978-3-319-19515-5_9

Danielson, M., Ekenberg, L. and He, Y. Augmenting Ordinal Methods of Attribute Weight Approximation, *Decision Analysis.* 11(1), pp. 21–26. 2014. http://dx.doi.org/10.1287/deca.2013.0289

Danielson, M., Ekenberg, L. and Larsson, A. Generalised Risk Constraints in Decision Trees with Second-Order Probabilities, *Proceedings of 1st International Conference on Risk Management, Assessment and Mitigation.* Athens: WSEAS Press, 2012.

Danielson, M., Ekenberg, L. and Sygel, K. Robust Psychiatric Decision Making using Surrogate Numbers, *Proceedings of SOMET 2015*, Cham: Springer. 2015. http://dx.doi.org/10.1007/978-3-319-22689-7_44

Danielson, M., Ekenberg, L., Fasth, T. and Larsson, A. POLA – Software Package for Multi Criteria Decision Analysis for the Swedish Municipalities. 2015.

Danielson, M., Ekenberg, L., Idefeldt, J. and Larsson, A. DecideIT – Software Package for Decision Analysis. 2004–2016.

Danielson, M., Ekenberg, L., Larsson, A. and Riabacke, M. Weighting Under Ambiguous Preferences and Imprecise Differences in a Cardinal Rank Ordering Process, *International Journal of Computational Intelligence Systems.* 7(1), pp. 105–112. 2014. http://dx.doi.org/10.1080/18756891.2014.853954

Ekenberg, L. A Participatory Model for Public Decision Analysis, *Proceedings of 13th Group Decision and Negotiation – GDN 2013*, pp. 3–7. 2013.

Ekenberg, L. Citizens' Communication, in R. Forsberg and L. Milles (Eds.), *Women in Science*. Stockholm: Styx, 2013.

Ekenberg, L. Communal decisions, in K. Hansson (Ed.), *Performing the Common*, Berlin: Revolver Publishing. 2015.

Ekenberg, L. Decision Analysis in Sweden. *Decision Analysis Today.* 33(1). 2014.

Ekenberg, L., Hernwall, P. and Tollmar, K. Enabling New Democratic Processes in Schools: FlashPolls – Student Participation and Contextual Polling, *International Reports of Socio-informatics, Proceedings of COOP 2014 Workshop on Cooperative Technologies in Democratic Processes.* 2014.

Ekenberg, L. Public Participatory Decision Making, in *Intelligent Software Methodologies, Tools and Techniques*, in H. Fujita and A. Selamat (Eds.), CCIS 513, pp. 3–12. Cham: Springer. 2015.

Ekenberg, L., Danielson, M., Larsson, A. and Sundgren, D. Second-Order Risk Constraints in Decision Analysis, *Axioms* 3, pp. 31–45. 2014. http://dx.doi.org/10.3390/axioms3010031

Ekenberg, L., Forsberg, R. and Sauter, W. Antigone's Diary – A Mobile Urban Drama, a Challenge to Performance Studies and a Model for Democratic Decision Making, *Contemporary Theatre Review.* 25(4). 2015. http://dx.doi.org/10.1080/10486801.2015.1078325

Ernst, M. and Sauter, W. Antigone's Diary – Young Audiences as Co-creators of GPS-guided Radio Drama, *Nordic Theatre Studies.* 27(1), pp. 32–41. 2015.

Fasth, T. and Larsson, A. Portfolio Decision Analysis in Vague Domains, *Proceedings of the 2012 IEEE IEEM*, pp. 61–65. 2012.

Fasth, T. and Larsson, A. Sensitivity Analysis in Portfolio Interval Decision Analysis. Proceedings of the Twenty-Sixth International Florida Artificial Intelligence Research Society Conference, pp. 609–614. 2013.

Fasth, T., Kalinina, M. and Larsson, A. Admissibility Concepts for Group Portfolio Decision Analysis Introduction and Problem Description. *Proceedings of 13th Group Decision and Negotiation – GDN 2013*, pp. 445–448. 2013.

Fasth, T., Larsson, A. and Ekenberg, L. Online Scalable Preference Elicitation Using Bipolar Cardinal Ranking, Manuscript.

Fasth, T., Larsson, A., Ekenberg, L. and Gilbert, Å. A Review of External Post-Clearance Inspection in Mine Action, *The Geneva International Centre for Humanitarian Demining.* 2012.

Hansson, K. A Microdemocratic Perspective on Crowdwork. *Group14 ACM International Conference on Supporting Groupwork*. 4. 2014.

Hansson, K. Accommodating Differences: Power, Belonging, and Representation Online. PhD dissertation, Stockholm University, 2015.

Hansson, K. and Bannister F. The Non-Government and Voluntary Sector, ICT and Democracy – Introduction to the Special Issue. *The International Journal of Public Information Systems*. 2015(1), pp. 1–4. 2015.

Hansson, K. and Ekenberg, L. Deliberation, Representation and Motivation in Participatory Tools for the Public Sector. *Proceedings of the European Conference on Information Systems 2014, Tel Aviv, Israel*. 2014.

Hansson, K. and Ekenberg, L. Embodiment and Gameplay in Networked Publics, *International Journal of Public Administration in the Digital Age*. Forthcoming.

Hansson, K. and Ekenberg, L. Embodiment and Gameplay: A Framework for Exploring Inequalities in Collaborative Information Production, Examining the Essence of the Crowds: Motivations, Roles and Identities, Workshop at ECSCW 2015.

Hansson, K. and Ekenberg, L. Learning from Information Crises: Exploring Aggregated Trustworthiness in Big Data Production, *ECSCW 2015: Conflict IT: Technologies and Collaborative Practices in Conflict Areas*. 2015.

Hansson, K. and Ekenberg, L. Managing Deliberation: Tools for Structuring Discussions and Analyzing Representation, *Transforming Government: People, Process and Policy*. 10(2), pp. 256–272. 2016. http://dx.doi.org/10.1108/tg-03-2015-0011

Hansson, K. and Ekenberg, L. Multiple Perspectives, Representation and Motivation in Collaborative Tools Online, paper presented at the *CSCW2014 workshop Structures for Knowledge Co-creation between Organisations and the Public (COP2014)*. 2014.

Hansson, K. and Gustafsson Fürst, J. Methodology for Sustainable E-Participation: Redistribution, Representation and Recognition, in L. Anido Rifón and L. Álvarez Sabucedo (Eds.), *Proceedings of MeTTeG 2013, 7th International Conference on Methodologies, Technologies and Tools Enabling E-Government, October 2013, Vigo, Spain*, 2013.

Hansson, K. Art as Participatory Methodology. *Tidskrift för Genusvetenskap [Journal for Gender Studies]* (1), pp. 25–47. 2013.

Hansson, K. Controlling Singularity: The Role of Online Communication for Young Visual Artists' Identity Management. *First Monday* 20(5). 2015. http://dx.doi.org/10.5210/fm.v20i5.5626

Hansson, K. Mediating Authenticity: Performing the Artist in Digital Media. Great Expectations: Arts and the Future, *The European Sociological Association's Research Network on the Sociology of the Arts (RN02) Mid-Term Conference*, Guildford, UK: University of Surrey, pp. 1–22. 2010.

Hansson, K. Reflexive Technology for Collaborative Environments. *International Journal of Public Information Systems*. 2012(1), pp. 11–28. 2012.

Hansson, K. The Design Process as a Way to Increase Participation in a Research Project about the Art World. Situating Ubiquity. Media Art, Technology and Cultural Theory, Stockholm. 2011.

Hansson, K. The Desires of the Crowd: Scenario for a Future Social System. *Leonardo Electronic Almanac*. 20(1), pp. 182–191. 2014.

Hansson, K., Cars, G., Danielson, M., Ekenberg, L. and Larsson, A. Diversity and Public Decision Making, *Proceedings of ICDOG 2012: International Conference on e-Democracy and Open Government*. 2012.

Hansson, K., Cars, G., Ekenberg, L. and Danielson, M. The Importance of Recognition for Equal Representation in Participatory Processes, *Footprint – Delft Architecture Theory Journal*. 13. 2013.

Hansson, K., Ekenberg, L. and Belkacem, K. Open Government and Democracy: A Research Review, *Social Science Computer Review*. 33(5), pp. 540–555. 2015. http://dx.doi.org/10.1177/0894439314560847

Hansson, K., Ekenberg, L. and Danielson, M. An e-Participatory Map over Process Methods in Urban Planning, *Proceedings of CeDEM 2013: Conference for E-Democracy and Open Government*, pp. 119–132. 2013.

Hansson, K., Ekenberg, L., Gustafsson Fürst, J. and Liljenberg, T. Performing Structure: Fine Art as a Prototype for Participation, *Proceedings of the 17th International Symposium on Electronic Art ISEA*. 2011.

Hansson, K., Ekenberg, L., Gustafsson Fürst, J., Danielson, M., Liljenberg, T. and Larsson, A. Prototyping for Participatory Democracy: Fine Arts as Means for the Study of Multi-modal Communication in Public Decision Making, *Proceedings of the Interactive Media Arts Conference IMAC* 2011.

Hansson, K., Karlström, P., Larsson, A. and Verhagen, H. Actory : A Tool for Visualizing Reputation as a Means to Formalize Informal Social Behavior. *Proceedings of the Second International Conference on Reputation: Society, Economy, Trust ICORE 2011, Montpellier*. 2011.

Hansson, K., Karlström, P., Larsson, A. and Verhagen, H. Reputation, Inequality and Meeting Techniques: Visualising User Hierarchy, *Computational and Mathematical Organization Theory*. 20(2), pp. 155–175. 2013. http://dx.doi.org/10.1007/s10588-013-9165-y

Hansson, K., Larsson, A., Danielson, M. and Ekenberg, L. Coping with Complex Environmental and Societal Risk, *Management Decisions: An Integrated Multi-Criteria Framework, Sustainability*. 3(9), pp. 1357–1380. 2011. http://dx.doi.org/10.3390/su3091357

Hansson, K., Verhagen, H., Karlström, P. and Larsson, A. Formalizing Informal Social Behavior – Developing a Visual Tool to Support Collaborative Discussions. *Proceedings of CCSocialComp, Seventh International Conference on Collaborative Computing, Orlando*. 2011. http://dx.doi.org/10.4108/icst.collaboratecom.2011.247149

Hansson, K.E., Danielson, M., Ekenberg, L. and Buurman, J. Handling Multiple Criteria in Flood Risk Management, in A. Amendola, T. Ermolieva, J. Linnerooth-Bayer and R. Mechler (Eds.), *Integrated Catastrophe Risk Modelling: Supporting Policy Processes*. Cham: Springer. 2013.

Kivunike, F., Ekenberg, L., Danielson, M. and Tusubira, F. Developing Criteria for the Evaluation of the ICT Contribution to Social and Economic Development, *Proceedings of 6th Annual GlobDev Pre-ICIS Workshop: ICT in Global Development*. 2013.

Kivunike, F., Ekenberg, L., Danielson, M. and Tusubira, F. Perceptions of the Role of ICT on Quality of Life in Rural Communities in Uganda, *Information Technology for Development*. 17(1), pp. 61–80. 2011. http://dx.doi.org/10.1080/02681102.2010.511698

Kivunike, F., Ekenberg, L., Danielson, M. and Tusubira, F. Towards a Structured Approach for Evaluating the ICT Contribution to Development, *The International Journal on Advances in ICT for Emerging Regions*. 7(1), pp. 1–15. 2014. http://dx.doi.org/10.4038/icter.v7i1.7152

Kivunike, F., Ekenberg, L., Danielson, M. and Tusubira, F. Using a Structured Approach to Evaluate ICT4D: Healthcare Delivery in Uganda, *The Electronic Journal of Information Systems in Developing Countries* 66(8), pp. 1–16. 2015.

Kivunike, F., Ekenberg, L., Danielson, M. and Tusubira, F. Validating a Structured ICT for Development Evaluations Approach, in e-Infrastructure and e-Services for Developing Countries, Eds. A. Nungu *et al.*, LNICST 147, pp. 251–260, Springer. 2015. http://dx.doi.org/10.1007/978-3-319-16886-9_26

Larsson, A., Firth, D. and Ekenberg, L. Screening and Decision Analysis in City Traffic Planning, Proceedings of the 2011 IEEE Forum on Integrated and Sustainable Transportation Systems. 2011. http://dx.doi.org/10.1109/fists.2011.5973608

Larsson, A., Kuznetsova, A., Caster, O. and Ekenberg, L. Implementing Second-Order Decision Analysis: Concepts, *Algorithms and Tool, Advances in Decision Sciences 2014*. 2014. http://dx.doi.org/10.1155/2014/519512

Larsson, A., Riabacke, M., Danielson, M. and Ekenberg, L. Cardinal and Rank Ordering of Criteria – Addressing Prescription within Weight Elicitation, *International Journal of Information Technology and Decision Making* 14(6), pp. 1299–1330. 2014. http://dx.doi.org/10.1142/s021962201450059x

Linnerooth-Bayer, J., Ekenberg, L. and Vari, A. Catastrophe Models and Policy Processes. Managing Flood Risk in the Hungarian Tisza River Basin: An Introduction, in *Integrated Catastrophe Risk Modelling: Supporting Policy Processes*, Eds. A. Amendola, T. Ermolieva, J. Linnerooth-Bayer, and R. Mechler, Springer. 2013.

Mihai, A., Marincea, A. and Ekenberg, L. An MCDM Analysis of the Roşia Montană Gold Mining Project, *Sustainability* 2015(7), pp. 7261–7288. 2015. http://dx.doi.org/10.3390/su7067261

Riabacke, M., Danielson, M. and Ekenberg, L. State-of-the-Art, in *Prescriptive Weight Elicitation, Advances in Decision Sciences 2012*, Chapter ID 276584. 2012. http://dx.doi.org/10.1155/2012/276584

Riabacke, M., Danielson, M., Ekenberg, L. and Larsson, A. Employing Cardinal Rank Ordering of Criteria in Multi-Criteria Decision Analysis, in *Proceedings of the 10th International FLINS Conference on Uncertainty Modeling in Knowledge Engineering and Decision Making, World Scientific Proceedings Series on Computer Engineering and Information Science*, 7. 2012. http://dx.doi.org/10.1142/9789814417747_0013

Svedin, U. and Liljenström, H. Paths to a Low Carbon Society by 2050 – the Stockholm-Mälar Region Case. Including excerpts from Gren, I-M., Marbuah, G. and Tafesse, W. Cost-effective Land Use Dynamics Towards a Low Carbon Economy in the Stockholm-Mälar Region. *The EU COMPLEX Project*. 2015.

Sygel, K., Danielson, M., Ekenberg, L. and Fors, U. Handling Imprecise Information in Emergency Psychiatric Care, *Proceedings of ICSSE: IEEE International Conference on System Science and Engineering* 2015.

Thompson, M. and Beck, Bruce M. *Coping with Change: Urban Resilience, Sustainability, Adaptability and Path Dependence*. UK Government Future of Cities: Working Paper – Foresight, Government Office for Science, 2015.

Wärnhjelm, M., Ekenberg, L., Fasth, T. and Larsson, A. En hållbar handelspolicy: Handelsutveckling i staden, Swedish Association of Local Authorities and Regions, Swedish Transport Administration. 2015.